D1739516

THE
FREEDOM OF
INFORMATION ACT
AND POLITICAL ASSASSINATIONS
VOLUME 1

The Legal Proceedings of Harold Weisberg
v. General Services Administration,
Civil Action 2052 - 73

together with the
January 22 and 27 Warren Commission Transcripts

David R. Wrone, Editor

FOUNDATION PRESS, INC.
UNIVERSITY OF WISCONSIN
STEVENS POINT
STEVENS POINT, WI 54481

CONTENTS

INTRODUCTION

The Freedom of Information Act has played a vital role in securing access to the evidentiary base of recent controversial events, particularly political assassinations. As the information released by FOIA suits and the vast amount of material generated by the suits enters into the mainstream of American scholarship, the practical implication of freedom as a dynamic component in maintaining the integrity of our basic institutions is clearly demonstrated.

The Freedom of Information Act and Political Assassinations is a series bringing together court-tested documents containing evidence essential for scholarly investigation of the continuing controversy surrounding political assassinations. The series demonstrates the operation of the Freedom of Information Act lawsuits by presenting the court record of proceedings and the numerous documents released by the actions.

Volume 1 gathers documents concerned with the Warren Commission's investigation of President John F. Kennedy's assassination. The Legal Proceedings of Harold Weisberg v. General Services Administration, Civil Action 2052-73, together with the January 22 and 27 Warren Commission Transcripts is the record of a suit brought to examine an executive session transcript of the Warren Commission classified Top Secret. In the course of the proceedings the secrecy question, a plague on public discussion of the investigation for a decade, is resolved. The suit also generated the January 22 and 27 executive session transcripts, documents indispensable for an understanding of the inner workings of the Warren Commission and important for an understanding of the legal proceedings.

In the tumultuous days following the November 22, 1963, assassination of President John F. Kennedy, his successor, Lyndon B. Johnson, appointed a special President's commission to investigate the tragedy and report its findings. Seven men of national stature composed the commission: the chairman, Chief Justice of the Supreme Court Earl Warren, Congressmen Hale Boggs and Gerald R. Ford, Senators Richard Russell and John Sherman Cooper, New York banker John J. McCloy, and retired Director of the Central Intelligence Agency Allen Dulles.

The Commission enlisted J. Lee Rankin, a former Solicitor General of the United States, as its chief counsel, gathered a small staff of attorneys and clerks, and then spent nine months at their task, utilizing the several investigative bodies of the federal government, especially the Federal Bureau of Investigation. On September 24, 1964, it submitted an 888 page Report, followed several days later by a massive 26 volume appendix of Hearings and Exhibits—ten thousand pages of documentation. The 300 cubic feet of Commission records were deposited in the National Archives. [1]

The Warren Commission concluded that Lee Harvey Oswald, a ne'er-do-well worker in the Texas School Book Depository in Dallas, alone and unaided, shot and killed President Kennedy, wounded the Governor of Texas, J. B. Connally, who was riding in the limousine with Kennedy, and wounded James T. Tague, a citizen standing several score yards away. Oswald, while in flight, also killed a police officer. Soon after Oswald's arrest, he was killed by Jack Ruby, the owner of a sleazy night club. No trace of a conspiracy could be discovered.

Although the general public remained unconvinced of the validity of the official findings, the major institutions found little difficulty in accepting them and vigorously defended the conclusions against the growing number of critics and their published works. The critics argued the Warren Report and its 26 volumes of supplementary material were insufficient to support the conclusions based on them.

Errors, falsifications, and diversionary matter riddled the Report. Rather than a thorough examination of the evidentiary base, it was largely a psychological study of Oswald with an extensive treatment of his possible motives. In its limited efforts at examining the evidence, it was severely faulted. For example, the Report contained evidence that placed several rifles in the Book Depository, but it presented a discussion on only the one attributed to Oswald. [2]

The 26 volumes lacked the documentary evidence claimed by the Warren Commission and fared even worse than the Report in the eyes of the critics. The volumes, a chronological and subject matter wilderness without parallel in federal publications, were not indexed.[3] Vast quantities of trivia such as the dental records of Jack Ruby's mother and sundry speeches of right-wing theoreticians stuffed many volumes. The weighty tomes did not provide the essential evidence in the assassination. For example, they did not have the key documentary evidence which would connect the bullet fragments and tracings found interior to the body of President Kennedy with the bullet and bullet fragments found exterior to the body and which were linked to the alleged murder weapon found in the Book Depository.[4]

Thus the Commission did not link Oswald to the murder. At the same time documents scattered in various volumes showing a conflict with the time of the police officer's murder and the known activities of Oswald effectively excluded Oswald from committing the murder. [5]

When the dissenters turned to the records lodged by the Warren Commission in the National Archives, they encountered Top Secret classifications on many of the records. Much of the material was restricted and was sealed for 75 years; from public forums leading governmental officials affirmed this status. The Top Secret classification, one of several security classifications, meant that the restricted material was so sensitive that its release might damage relations between nations and endanger national security. While periodic reviews of the Warren Commission records resulted in declassification and downgrading of many files, some remained under Top Secret classification.

In researching those records in the public domain, critics found evidence which greatly diminished any remaining confidence in the validity of the official conclusions. For example, Charles Givens, an individual used by the Warren Commission to place Oswald on the sixth floor of the Book Depository near the purported assassin's lair about the time of the assassination has also executed an affidavit actually placing Oswald on the first floor. [6]

Neither the published nor the unpublished records of the Warren Commission provided a satisfactory picture of the assassination and the course of events during the transition within the executive branch. The body of critical evidence mustered by the dissenters, including an impressive array of evidence found external to the official probe, pointed to a coverup by the federal government and the framing of Lee Harvey Oswald. Despite the punch of some of the critical arguments, the defenders of the official conclusions remained adamant in their belief in the integrity of the official investigation and scoffed at the naysayers. The sealed records, the public was continually told, contained the clinching evidence and would, when released in the next century, remove the last shred of lingering doubt.

In 1972 critic Harold Weisberg, who had written four books and had done exhaustive research in the available documentary evidence, sought to examine the transcript of the January 27, 1964, executive session of the Warren Commission. The federal archivists in the National Archives invoked the Top Secret classification of the transcript and denied Weisberg's request.

Weisberg's research had led him to believe an improper classification had been imposed on the January 27, 1964, transcript. The transcript, purportedly verbatim, constituted an entire chapter in Warren Commission member Gerald Ford's book, <u>Portrait of the Assassin.</u> [7] After a fruitless pursuit of administrative remedies for changing the status of the transcript, Weisberg's attorney, James Hiram Lesar, filed suit in the United States Court of Appeals for the District of Columbia under the provisions of the Freedom of Information Act, 5 U.S.C. 552, for access to the January 27, 1964, executive session transcript.

The defendant in the suit is the United States General Services Administration under which the National Archives operates and is represented by attorneys from the Department of Justice. The suit, assigned the docket number of Civil Action 2052-73 with Judge Gerhard Gesell presiding, was waged entirely through the filing of legal documents with the court.

C. A. 2052-73 and the documents generated by it touch upon the careers of many of the highest officials in American government. In this respect, the case is highly unusual. Three presidents of the United States are vitally connected with it. The document being contested relates to the investigation of the murder of President Kennedy. The integrity, if not the legitimacy, of the administration of President Lyndon B. Johnson is at issue through the functioning of his commission to investigate the tragedy which elevated him to the presidency. Future President Gerald R. Ford's act of publishing a government document classified Top Secret is central.

Chief Justice Earl Warren chaired the January 27 executive session, implicating the integrity of the court. A former Solicitor General of the United States, J. Lee Rankin, filed a key affidavit for the defense which failed to stand up to facts presented in rebuttal by the plaintiff. The Archivist of the United States, James B. Rhoads, became a principal person in the proceedings, swearing the document was properly classified Top Secret. Richard Russell, the powerful senator from Georgia, charged that a Warren Commission record he had made had been falsified.

The activities of intelligence and investigative agencies—the principal subject discussed in the classified transcript—are deeply enmeshed in the case. The question of the duties of the staff of the Warren Commission, comprised of many esteemed lawyers, professors of law, and several future federal judges, is paramount for a complete picture of the case.

Perhaps the most unusual aspect of the case came after Judge Gesell denied Weisberg access to the transcript. Within days Archivist Rhoads declassified and released the transcript. The record established in C. A. 2052-73, Weisberg and Lesar believe, paved the way for access to a second executive session transcript—the January 22, 1964—without recourse to a legal suit.[8] The two transcripts are intimately related in subject matter.

The Freedom of Information Act proved to be an invaluable tool in securing essential information on the investigation of President Kennedy's murder. Controversial facts were presented in federal court where informed persons, including those responsible for classifying the contested document, discussed them. The proceedings demonstrated that the Warren Commission records in the National Archives did not require a Top Secret classification for reasons of national security. The Top Secret classification was an artifice.

C. A. 2052-73 is notable, also, for the area of law concerned with security classification. This case apparently marks the first time the federal government was defeated in its attempt to invoke national defense as a means of restricting public access to information.

These proceedings clearly illustrate one of the main purposes for the development of the Freedom of Information Act. When Congress wrote the Act, it intended that the possible embarrassment of public officials should not be a reason for denying the public information. Without the fiction of secrecy placed upon the documentary record of the Warren Commission, it would have been politically impossible to have maintained the conclusions of the Warren Report and to have them sustained by the media and other institutions.

The significance of the Freedom of Information Act for the functioning of a democratic society, however, must be found ultimately in the documents obtained under it. In political terms access to knowledge is central to a government based on consent of the governed; to the degree that knowledge is available the health of a constitutional democracy is maintained. The integrity of institutions rests on the principal of free access to information, because the insight necessary for action rests upon it. One of the most deadening mechanisms of control over the conduct of everyday life comes neither from the callous imposition of brute force nor from the ruthless exercise of censorship but from the quiet denial of knowledge.

The denial of the essential facts of the investigation into the assassination of President John F. Kennedy wielded a pernicious influence over the lives of a generation. In an era of nuclear armament every major system—save one—devised by the nation through the centuries failed to maintain the principles upon which they had been formed and had functioned. Only the federal court system enabled a citizen to cut through the crepuscular world of bureaucratic secrecy and official coverup.

In historical terms the documents obtained through these legal proceedings show us that despite our being told for ten years by officials, Warren Commission members and staff, the communication systems, and others that the official conclusions were sound and that there was no coverup, the truth was the reverse. The investigation hid the truth.

The commission members sat in fear of the FBI and the intelligence agencies. They were appalled at what their investigation was discovering, but they did not know what to do. The January 22 transcript records their disbelief in Oswald as the assassin and their shock that the FBI wanted them to conclude the investigation without the agency having run out all kinds of leads. "Oh, terrible," said one member. The commissioners were stunned by what they had discovered concerning Oswald's background and the activities of the FBI. The reality of an intelligence coverup faced them squarely.

In the transcript the following exchange occurs. Although the poor transcription of the stenotape did not identify "A:", apparently it refers to J. Lee Rankin whose name was misspelled as Rawkin when identified:

> A: They [the FBI] would like to have us fold up and quit.
> Boggs: This closes the case, you see. Don't you see? . . .
> Rankin: They found the man. There is nothing more to do. The Commission supports their conclusions, and we can go on home and that is the end of it.

Dependant upon the various investigative agencies, the Warren Commission was powerless to proceed against intimidation without a serious confrontation involving extraordinary public controversy, reorganization of the approach to the assassination investigation, and, perhaps, even more dire actions. The President's Commission chose to acquiesce and spent the remaining months attempting to reconcile the bitter reality with a public report that had to be made.

From fear flowed the coverup activities, the attempt to hide the facts, the chaos found in the 26 volumes, and all the obfuscating tactics which marked the following years. In fact the coverup began with the January 22 transcript itself when the members agreed amongst themselves not to leave even a record of the scheduling of the session, let alone a transcript of it. Commission member Dulles moved: "I think this record ought to be destroyed."

If it had not been for the scholarship of Harold Weisberg and the legal expertise of James Lesar, the record might have suffered such a fate. Weisberg discovered a copy of the stenotape; Lesar forced it into transcription and the public domain.

The chilling impact of fear partially accounts, too, for Gerald Ford's act in publishing the January 27 executive session transcript. Ford gave the transcript unindicated editing which changed its meaning and with it the historical record presented in the book.[9] Ford's version of the Top Secret transcript would have been the only record available to the public for 75 years.

The legal proceedings are reproduced with very little editing, it being largely orthographical and duly noted in an emendation section. To assist the reader, numbers were editorially assigned to each set of documents. Thus, the

Complaint is printed, "1. Complaint". With each exhibit a brief editorial description of the document is added. Thus, Exhibit A of "1. Complaint" is followed by the editorial, "Letter of Harold Weisberg to Dr. James B. Rhoads".

Related documents generated during the course of the proceedings but not part of the court record are included in a separate section. These have been provided through the kindness of Attorney James Lesar and Harold Weisberg. Two executive session transcripts of the Warren Commission, January 27 and January 22, are reproduced in the order of their release from classification.

LITERATURE ON C. A. 2052-73

Harold Weisberg gives a critic's perspective of C. A. 2052-73 and an analysis of the documents it generated in Whitewash IV, 1-165, as well as extended commentary in Post Mortem, see the index under Freedom of Information law. For an analysis of the January 27, 1964, transcript and a photographic reproduction of it, see Whitewash IV, 36-212; for an analysis of the January 22, 1964, transcript and a photographic reproduction of it, see Post Mortem, 475-487. James Lesar provides a legal analysis in Whitewash IV, 166-215. For a lengthy historical essay, see David R. Wrone, "The Gratuitous Mystery," Madison Capital Times, December 1, 2, 3, 4, 1975. The case was central in the abruptly cancelled hearing before the Government Information and Individual Rights Subcommittee of the Committee on Government Operations chaired by Congresswoman Bella Abzug during the Ninety-Fourth Congress, Second Session. The Committee Print is entitled: National Archives-Security Classification Problem Involving Warren Commission Files and Other Records. The case figures strongly in Howard Roffman, "Freedom of Information: Judicial Review of Executive Security Classifications," University of Florida Law Review (1976) volume XXVIII, 551-568.

FOOTNOTES

[1] [U. S. Warren Commission], Report of the President's Commission on the Assassination of President John F. Kennedy (Washington: Government Printing Office, 1964); [U. S. Warren Commission], Investigation of the Assassination of President John F. Kennedy: Hearings Before the President's Commission on the Assassination of President Kennedy (Washington: Government Printing Office, 1964) 26 volumes.

[2] David R. Wrone, The Assassination of John Fitzgerald Kennedy. An Annotated Bibliography (Madison: State Historical Society of Wisconsin, 1973); Harold Weisberg, Whitewash—the Report on the Warren Report (Hyattstown, Maryland: Harold Weisberg, 1965); Warren Report, 601.

[3] [Howard] Willens to [J. Lee] Rankin, Memorandum, February 28, 1964. National Archives.

[4] Howard Roffman, Presumed Guilty. Lee Harvey Oswald in the Assassination of President Kennedy (Cranbury, New Jersey: Farleigh Dickinson University Press, 1975).

[5] Harold Weisberg, Post Mortem. JFK Assassination Cover-Up Smashed (Frederick, Maryland: Harold Weisberg, 1975), 493.

[6] Sylvia Meagher, "The Curious Testimony of Mr. Givens," The Texas Observer, August 13, 1971, 11-12.

[7] Gerald R. Ford and John R. Stiles, Portrait of the Assassin (New York: Simon & Schuster, 1965).

[8] "January 22, 1964" file. James Lesar Archive.

[9] Harold Weisberg, Whitewash IV. JFK Assassination Transcript with legal analysis by Jim Lesar (Frederick, Maryland: Harold Weisberg, 1974), provides a line by line comparison of the Ford version with the original.

1.
COMPLAINT

1. Plaintiff brings this action under the Freedom of Information Act, 5 U.S.C. 552.

2. Plaintiff is HAROLD WEISBERG, an author residing at Route 8, Frederick, Maryland.

3. Defendant is the UNITED STATES GENERAL SERVICES ADMINISTRATION, located at F Street, between 18th & 19th Streets, N. W., Washington, D. C.

4. The document which Plaintiff seeks is a transcript of the January 27, 1964, executive session of the Warren Commission. This transcript is in the possession of the United States Archives and Records Service, a division of the General Services Administration.

5. In 1968 Plaintiff several times requested access to the January 27, 1964, transcript. In his letter of May 4, 1968, to Dr. James B. Rhoads, Archivist of the United States, Plaintiff renewed his request for disclosure of the January 27 transcript. (See Exhibit A) This request was denied by Dr. Rhoads in his letter of May 20, 1968. (See Exhibit B)

6. In a letter to Plaintiff dated June 21, 1971, the then Acting Archivist, Mr. Herbert E. Angel, stated that the January 27, 1964, transcript was being withheld from research under the provisions of 5 U.S.C. 552 (b) (1) and (b) (7). (See Exhibit C)

Filed: November 13, 1973.

7. 5 U.S.C. 552 (b) (1) exempts from disclosure matters that are:

> "specifically required by Executive order
> to be kept secret in the interest of the national
> defense or foreign policy"

5 U.S.C. 552 (b) (7) exempts from disclosure matters that are:

> "investigatory files compiled for law en-
> forcement purposes except to the extent avail-
> able by law to a party other than an agency"

8. Plaintiff has requested that he be provided with a copy of the executive order requiring that the January 27 transcript be kept secret in the interest of the national defense or foreign policy. No such order has been provided him.

9. Representative Gerald R. Ford's book, Portrait of the Assassin, contains many purportedly verbatim quotes from the January 27, 1964, transcript. Notwithstanding the fact that the National Archives has declared that the January 27 transcript is classified pursuant to executive order, Representative Ford testified before the Senate Rules Committee on November 5, 1973, that he did not use classified material in his book. In the New York Times of November 6, 1973, reporter Marjorie Hunter gave the following account of Mr. Ford's testimony on this point:

> Mr. Ford also defended himself against
> criticism that he had profited from his service
> on the Warren Commission that investigated
> the assassination of President Kennedy by
> writing a book and contributing to a magazine
> article.
>
> He admitted receiving $10,000 for the
> book, "Portrait of an Assassin," and $5,000
> for the magazine article, but said the material
> was not classified and that he merely tried to
> make readable the information that later ap-
> peared in the commission's report. (Emphasis
> added)

10. Plaintiff avers that the January 27, 1964 transcript is improperly classified.

11. Plaintiff further asserts that, regardless of whether or not the January 27 transcript is properly classified, Representative Ford has been given what in effect is an exclusive literary copyright on government information not made available to other persons. Plaintiff believes this to be contrary to the intent of the Freedom of Information Act.

12. On January 6, 1972, Plaintiff appealed the decision to deny him access to the January 27, 1964, transcript. On February 8, 1972, Mr. Richard Q. Vawter, Director of Information of the General Services Administration, responded by stating that this and other transcripts of Warren Commission executive sessions:

> . . . are now under further review by the Office of the General Counsel to determine whether recent developments in the state of the law are such as to require release of portions of the documents previously withheld. We are therefore treating your letter as a request to reconsider our decision regarding the transcripts rather than as an appeal therefrom. You will be notified shortly of our decision, and may then appeal any portion of that decision which denies you access to these transcripts. (See Exhibit D)

In a letter dated March 6, 1972, Mr. Vawter repeated this statement. To the best of his recollection, Plaintiff believes that there has been no further response from the Director of Information in the year and eight months since the March 6, 1972, letter.

13. Having exhausted his administrative remedies, Plaintiff now brings this complaint under the Freedom of Information Act. Plaintiff alleges that under the terms of the Freedom of Information Act the records he seeks must be made available to him. Plaintiff notes that the Freedom of Information Act provides that the District Court shall determine the matter de novo, and that the burden is on the defendant to justify its refusal to disclose the requested documents.

WHEREFORE, Plaintiff prays this honorable Court for the following relief: that Defendant be ordered to produce and make available for copying the transcript of the January 27, 1964, executive session of the Warren Commission, and such other relief as this Court may deem just and equitable.

/s/ _____
JAMES HIRAM LESAR
1231 4th St., S. W.
Washington, D. C. 20024
Telephone: 484-6023
Attorney for Weisberg

DATED: November 13, 1973

EXHIBIT A.

Letter of Harold Weisberg to Dr. James B. Rhoads.

May 4, 1968

Dr. James B. Rhoads
Archivist of the United States
Washington, D. C.

Dear Dr. Rhoads:

This is to tell you that I know enough about the transcript of the executive session of the Warren Commission of January 27, 1964, to express the opinion that it cannot in its entirety be denied me for the reason specified. I herewith renew my request for it. If there is any part of it that you withhold, I think, because of the knowledge I have, it is only fair to ask you to itemize the subjects discussed.

It is obvious that what was provided me that purports to be a verbatim transcript of the executive session of September 18, 1964, is not that and was not prepared by the until-then official reporter. After the first paragraph it is in the form of minutes. I respectfully renew my request for the stenographic transcript of this executive session.

Because of the misarrangement of these transcripts as supplied to me, in no order whatsoever, I would appreciate a list of all the sessions on which these that are denied are also indicated.

Sincerely,

/s/

Harold Weisberg

P. S. As additional executive-session transcripts are declassified, I would like to receive them. As similar materials are to be released, I should like to be informed of it.

In the past, I have been informed that you keep a list of what is sought that is denied, such as the spectrographic analysis, and that those interested will, when the decision is reached, be notified. If you intend additional departures from this policy, I would like to know.

HW

EXHIBIT B.

Letter of James B. Rhoads to Harold Weisberg.

GENERAL SERVICES ADMINISTRATION
National Archives and Records Service
Washington, D. C. 20408

May 20, 1968

IN REPLY REFER TO: N

Mr. Harold Weisberg
Coq d'Or Press
Route 8
Frederick, Maryland 21701

Dear Mr. Weisberg:

This is in reply to your letter of May 4, 1968, concerning records of the Warren Commission.

We believe that the transcript of the executive session of the Commission of January 27, 1964, is correctly withheld from research under the terms of existing law (5 U.S.C. 552).

No verbatim transcript of the executive session of September 18, 1964, is known to be among the records of the Commission.

It is our impression that the copies of the transcripts of executive sessions were in order when they were mailed to you and that copies of the charge cards which indicate the transcripts that are withheld from research were included. The transcripts or minutes for the following sessions are available for research, except certain pages in some of the transcripts which are withheld and are indicated within each transcript concerned: December 5 and 16, 1963; January 21, February 24, March 16, April 30, and June 4, 1964; and September 18, 1964 (minutes only). The transcripts for the following sessions are withheld from research: December 6, 1963; and January 27, May 19, and June 23, 1964.

You will be notified if any additional transcripts of executive sessions or specific records you have previously requested become available for research. We have not undertaken and cannot undertake to notify researchers of the availability of all material relating to particular subjects in which they may be interested, and we have made no departures from this policy. You have been notified orally of the availability of the transcript of the conference relating to a psychiatric evaluation of Lee Harvey Oswald held on July 9, 1964.

The transcripts of testimony before the Commission are available except certain pages which contain material deleted by the Commission in its published Hearings.

Sincerely,

/s/

James B. Rhoads
Archivist of the United States

EXHIBIT C.

Letter of Herbert E. Angel to Harold Weisberg.

GENERAL SERVICES ADMINISTRATION
National Archives and Records Service
Washington, D. C. 20408

June 21, 1971

Mr. Harold Weisberg
Coq d'Or Press
Route 8
Frederick, Maryland 21701

Dear Mr. Weisberg:

This is in reply to your letter of May 20, 1971.

The following transcripts of proceedings of executive sessions of the Warren Commission and parts of these transcripts are withheld from research under the provisions of the "Freedom of Information Act" (5 U.S.C. 552) which are cited for each item:

Transcripts

       1. December 6, 1963 5 U.S.C. 552, subsection (b) (6).
       2. January 27, 1964 5 U.S.C. 552, subsections (b) (1) and (b) (7).
       3. May 19, 1964   5 U.S.C. 552, subsections (b) (1) and (b) (6).
       4. June 23, 1964   5 U.S.C. 552, subsections (b) (1) and (b) (7).

Parts of Transcripts

    1. Dec. 5, 1963, pages 43-68   5 U.S.C., subsection (b) (6).
    2. Dec. 16, 1963, pages 23-32 5 U.S.C., subsection (b) (6).
    3. Jan. 21, 1964, pages 63-73 5 U.S.C., subsection (b) (1) and (b) (7).

As we have previously informed you, the transcripts withheld from research
have not been made available to any researcher since they have been in our
custody.

No additional material has been made available for research since the completion of the 1970 review, of which we informed you in our letter of February 5, 1971.

Sincerely,

/s/

HERBERT E. ANGEL
Acting Archivist
of the United States

EXHIBIT D.

Letter of Richard Q. Vawter to Harold Weisberg.

UNITED STATES OF AMERICA
GENERAL SERVICES ADMINISTRATION
WASHINGTON, D. C. 20405

Feb. 8, 1972

Mr. Harold Weisberg
Coq d'Or Press
Route 8
Frederick, Maryland 21701

Dear Mr. Weisberg:

This is in reply to your two letters dated January 6, 1972.

A review by the National Archives of its correspondence with you beginning
July 24, 1971, failed to reveal a written request from you on that date for
copies of pages in Commission Document 1408 or after that date until the

request in your letter of December 17, 1971. A check of service orders prepared around July 24, 1971, however, disclosed that copies of pages 10, 11, and 26-28 in CD 1408 were mailed to you with copies of other records on August 10, 1971, presumably as a result of a telephone call from you. The examination of the service orders also disclosed that a copy of a strip of paper received with the WDSU film was mailed to you with copies of other records on July 15, 1971, as a result of a telephone call from you on July 13, 1971. Enclosed are new copies of the pages in CD 1408 and the strip of paper received with the WDSU film.

The only specific records mentioned in your letters that have been denied to you under the terms of 5 U.S.C. 552, subsection (b), are the transcripts of Warren Commission executive sessions. These transcripts were reviewed by our Office of General Counsel before they were denied to you by Acting Archivist Herbert E. Angel in his letter to you of June 21, 1971. These transcripts are now under further review by the Office of the General Counsel to determine whether recent developments in the state of the law are such as to require release of portions of the documents previously withheld. We are therefore treating your letter as a request to reconsider our decision regarding the transcripts rather than as an appeal therefrom. You will be notified shortly of our decision, and may then appeal any portion of that decision which denies you access to these transcripts.

Since 1966 the National Archives has corresponded with you concerning a great many individual documents among the records of the Warren Commission. This correspondence now comprises two thick files. Records that could be furnished to you under procedures established by proper authority for the Commission's records were made available to you. Only records withheld under those procedures were denied to you. Some of the records that were originally denied to you in this correspondence were made available for research by the 1970 review. Lists of the material made available by that review were sent to you early in 1971.

Under these circumstances I think it is your responsibility to determine the individual documents other than the transcripts concerning which you wish to appeal and to prepare your own appeal. If you will submit a numerical list clearly identifying these documents, you will be given a specific response concerning each document.

During the more than five years that the National Archives has tried to be of service to you, its staff has often gone beyond normal limits in responding to your requests, and you have at times expressed your appreciation for the work done for you. In fairness to other researchers, however, the National Archives staff cannot perform an unlimited amount of work for you or carry on a constant correspondence with you.

I believe you have a copy of the letter agreement of October 29, 1966, concerning the clothing of President Kennedy and the X-rays and photographs relating to the autopsy of President Kennedy. Access to those materials is based on the terms of the agreement. I have been informed by the Archivist that if you will select a pathologist or any other qualified person and secure the approval of his application to examine the materials by the Kennedy family representative, Mr. Burke Marshall, the National Archives will be pleased to show the materials to him.

Sincerely,

/s/

Richard Q. Vawter
Director of Information

Enclosures

2.
PLAINTIFF'S INTERROGATORIES

Under Rule 33 of the Federal Rules of Civil Procedure, Plaintiff addresses the following interrogatories to the Defendant:

1.   Is there any Executive Order which specifically requires the transcript of the January 27, 1964, Warren Commission Executive Session to be kept secret in the interest of the national defense or foreign policy?

2.   What is the number of any Executive Order cited in response to Plaintiff's interrogatory No. 1?

3.   On what date was any Executive Order cited in response to Plaintiff's interrogatory No. 1 published in the Federal Register?

4.   Has any Attorney General of the United States ever made a determination that it is not in the national interest to disclose the transcript of any Warren Commission Executive Session or the report of any interview or scientific test made by or for the Federal Bureau of Investigation during its investigation into the assassination of President John F. Kennedy?

5.   If the answer to Plaintiff's interrogatory No. 4 is yes, when and by whom was this determination made?

6.   Is the January 27 transcript being withheld from research on the grounds that it is part of an investigatory file compiled for law enforcement purposes?

7.   If the answer to Plaintiff's interrogatory No. 6 is yes, what is the specific law enforcement purpose for which the January 27 transcript is being withheld?

8.   Have any court proceedings been initiated relevant to any law enforcement purpose cited in response to Plaintiff's interrogatory No. 7?

Filed: November 29, 1973.

9.   If the answer to Plaintiff's interrogatory No. 8 is yes, what are the titles of these court cases and in what courts were they initiated?

10.   Are any future court proceedings contemplated with respect to any law enforcement purpose cited in response to Plaintiff's interrogatory No. 7?

11.   With respect to any court proceedings cited in response to Plaintiff's interrogatories No. 8 and No. 10, what harm or prejudice would the government suffer if the January 27 transcript were to be disclosed to Plaintiff Weisberg?

12.   Has the disclosure of parts of the January 27 transcript by Representative Gerald Ford harmed the government in any of the court proceedings cited in response to Plaintiff's interrogatory No. 8?

13.   Has the disclosure of parts of the January 27 transcript by Representative Gerald Ford prejudiced any future court proceedings cited in response to Plaintiff's interrogatory No. 10?

14.   If Representative Gerald Ford's disclosure of parts of the January 27 transcript has harmed the government in any law enforcement proceeding cited in response to Plaintiff's interrogatories No. 8 or No. 10, what is the nature of that harm?

15.   Has the Department of Justice or the General Services Administration recommended that any action be taken against Representative Gerald Ford for publicly disclosing parts of the January 27, 1964, transcript stated by the General Services Administration to be classified?

16.   Has the Department of Justice or the General Services Administration communicated to the Senate Rules Committee or any other congressional committee the fact that Representative Gerald Ford publicly disclosed parts of the purportedly classified January 27 transcript?

17.   Has the Department of Justice or the General Services Administration recommended that any action be taken against Representative Gerald Ford for testifying that he did not reveal any classified information in his book Portrait of the Assassin?

18.   Was the January 27 transcript ever given to any law enforcement officer of the State of Texas, including:

     a) Dallas County District Attorney Henry Wade?

     b) Texas Attorney General Waggoner Carr?

     c) Special Assistant to the Texas Attorney General Leon Jaworski?

19.   Was the January 27 transcript ever given to any court or law enforcement agency in the State of Texas?

20. Was the January 27 transcript ever given to any federal agency, including, but not limited to, the following:

    a) The Central Intelligence Agency?
    b) The Federal Bureau of Investigation?
    c) The Office of Naval Intelligence?
    d) The Defense Intelligence Agency?
    e) The National Security Agency?

21. To what "recent developments in the state of the law" was Mr. Richard Q. Vawter, Director of Information, General Services Administration, referring in his February 8, 1972, letter (See Complaint, Exhibit D) to Mr. Harold Weisberg?

Please note that under Rule 33 of the Federal Rules of Civil Procedure you are required to serve upon the undersigned, within 30 days after service of this notice, your answers in writing and under oath to the above interrogatories.

DATED: November 29, 1973   /s/ _____

                                JAMES HIRAM LESAR
                                Attorney for Plaintiff
                                1231 Fourth Street, S.W.
                                Washington, D.C. 20024

CERTIFICATE OF SERVICE.

I hereby certify that I have this 29th day of November, 1973, served copies of the foregoing interrogatories upon the attorneys for the Defendant, the General Services Administration, by mailing them to the Attorney General for the United States, Mr. Robert Bork, U. S. Department of Justice, Washington, D. C., and Mr. Michael Ryan, Assistant United States Attorney for the District of Columbia, Civil Division, United States Courthouse, 3rd and Constitution, N. W., Washington, D. C. 20001.

                                /s/ _____
                                JAMES HIRAM LESAR

3.
DEFENDANT'S MOTION FOR EXTENSION OF TIME WITHIN WHICH TO ANSWER OR OTHERWISE PLEAD WITH RESPECT TO THE COMPLAINT AND TO RESPOND TO INTERROGATORIES

Defendant, by its attorney, the United States Attorney for the District of Columbia, respectfully moves the Court pursuant to Rule 6 (b) (1), Federal Rules of Civil Procedure, for an extension of time to and including February 13, 1974, within which to answer or otherwise plead with respect to the complaint, and within which to respond to plaintiff's interrogatories.

In support of this motion, defendant submits herewith a memorandum of points and authorities.

/s/ _____
EARL J. SILBERT
United States Attorney

/s/ _____
ARNOLD T. AIKENS
Assistant United States Attorney

/s/ _____
MICHAEL J. RYAN
Assistant United States Attorney

Filed: January 14, 1974.

14

MEMORANDUM OF POINTS AND AUTHORITIES IN SUPPORT OF DEFENDANT'S MOTION FOR EXTENSION OF TIME WITHIN WHICH TO ANSWER OR OTHERWISE PLEAD WITH RESPECT TO THE COMPLAINT AND TO RESPOND TO INTERROGATORIES. JANUARY 14, 1974.

Rule 6 (b) (1), Federal Rules of Civil Procedure.

Defendant's response to the complaint is currently due on January 14, 1974. While it is anticipated that defendant will submit a motion to dismiss or, in the alternative, for summary judgment, the agency involved has experienced delay in the preparation and transmittal of materials necessary for the preparation of such a motion. To date, counsel for defendant has not received those materials, and will need the requested extension to receive the materials and properly prepare a motion in this case.

In addition, defendant's response to plaintiff interrogatories is currently due on January 14, 1974. Those interrogatories, mailed on November 29, 1973, were originally due on January 2, 1974. Rules 33 and 6, Federal Rules of Civil Procedure. Although counsel for defendant tried unsuccessfully to contact plaintiff's counsel on January 2, 1974, on January 3, 1974, counsel orally stipulated that responses to plaintiff's interrogatories might be due on the answer date of January 14, 1974. Plaintiff's interrogatories require research and the drafting of responses within the agency, and inasmuch as that process is also incomplete, and counsel for defendant has not yet received those responses, a like extension of time is requested.

For the foregoing reasons, defendant respectfully requests that its time to respond to the complaint and to plaintiff's interrogatories be extended to and including February 13, 1974.

/s/ _____
EARL J. SILBERT
United States Attorney

/s/ _____
ARNOLD T. AIKENS
Assistant United States Attorney

/s/ _____
MICHAEL J. RYAN
Assistant United States Attorney

ORDER.

Upon consideration of Defendant's Motion for Extension of Time Within Which to Answer or Otherwise Plead with Respect to the Complaint and to Respond to Interrogatories and the entire record herein, it is by the Court this ____ day of _____, 1974.

ORDERED that Defendant's time to answer or otherwise plead with respect to the complaint and to respond to plaintiff's interrogatories be and it hereby is extended to and including February 13, 1974.

_____
UNITED STATES DISTRICT JUDGE

CERTIFICATE OF SERVICE.

I HEREBY CERTIFY that service of the foregoing Defendant's Motion for Extension of Time, etc., supporting Memorandum of Points and Authorities and proposed Order has been made upon plaintiff by mailing a copy thereof to his attorney, James H. Lesar, Esq., 1231 Fourth Street, S. W., Washington, D. C. 20024, on this 14th day of January, 1974.

/s/ _____
MICHAEL J. RYAN
Assistant United States Attorney
U. S. Courthouse
Room 3421
426-7375

4.
ORDER

Upon consideration of Defendant's Motion for Extension of Time Within Which to Answer or Otherwise Plead with Respect to the Complaint and to Respond to Interrogatories and the entire record herein, it is by the Court this 16 day of January, 1974,

ORDERED that Defendant's time to answer or otherwise plead with respect to the complaint and to respond to plaintiff's interrogatories be and it hereby is extended to and including February 13, 1974. No further extension will be granted.

/s/ _____
GERHARD GESELL
UNITED STATES DISTRICT JUDGE

Filed: January 16, 1974.

5.
DEFENDANT'S MOTION TO DISMISS OR, IN THE ALTERNATIVE, FOR SUMMARY JUDGMENT

Defendant, by its attorney, the United States Attorney for the District of Columbia, respectfully moves the Court to dismiss the instant action for lack of jurisdiction over the subject matter and for failure to state a claim upon which relief can be granted. Rule 12 (b) (1) and (6), Federal Rules of Civil Procedure.

In the alternative, defendant respectfully moves the Court for summary judgment in defendant's favor on the ground that there is no genuine issue as to any material fact and defendant is entitled to judgment as a matter of law. Rule 56, Federal Rules of Civil Procedure.

In support of its motion, defendant submits herewith a statement of material facts as to which there is no genuine issue, a memorandum of points and authorities, and the affidavit of James B. Rhoads, Archivist of the United States, National Archives and Records Service, General Services Administration (Government Exhibit 1). Also incorporated herein, made a part hereof by reference and filed simultaneously with this motion, are Dr. Rhoad's answers to plaintiff's interrogatories.

/s/_____
EARL J. SILBERT
United States Attorney

_____
Filed: February 13, 1974.

18

/s/ _____
ARNOLD T. AIKENS
Assistant United States Attorney

/s/ _____
MICHAEL J. RYAN
Assistant United States Attorney

CERTIFICATE OF SERVICE.

I HEREBY CERTIFY that service of the foregoing has been made upon plaintiff by mailing a copy thereof to his attorney, James H. Lesar, Esquire, 1231 Fourth Street, S. W., Washington, D. C. 20024 on this 13th day of February, 1974.

/s/ _____
MICHAEL J. RYAN
Assistant United States Attorney
U. S. Courthouse
Room 3421
Washington, D. C. 20001
Telephone: 426-7375

MEMORANDUM OF POINTS AND AUTHORITIES IN SUPPORT OF DEFENDANT'S MOTION TO DISMISS OR, IN THE ALTERNATIVE, FOR SUMMARY JUDGMENT. FEBRUARY 13, 1974.

PRELIMINARY STATEMENT

Relying on the provisions of the Freedom of Information Act, 5 U.S.C. 552, plaintiff seeks by this action to compel disclosure of the transcript of the January 27, 1964 executive session of the Warren Commission. That Commission was established by Executive Order No. 11130, 28 Fed. Reg. 12789 (1963), to investigate the assassinations of President Kennedy and Lee Harvey Oswald. Congress also passed Public Law 88-202, approved December 13, 1963, authorizing the Commission to require attendance of witnesses and production of evidence. The particular transcript which plaintiff seeks in this action has been and remains classified "Top Secret" pursuant to Executive Order 10501, as amended (3 C.F.R. 280), and more recently, pursuant to Executive Order 11652, 37 Fed. Reg. 5209, March 10, 1972.

ARGUMENT

I.   The Freedom of Information Act Does Not Apply to Matters Which Are Required to Be Kept Secret in the Interest of National Defense or Foreign Policy

The Public Information Section of the Administrative Procedure Act, which section is known as the Freedom of Information Act, is expressly made inapplicable to matters that are "specifically required by Executive Order to be kept secret in the interest of the national defense or foreign policy." 5 U.S.C. 552 (b) (1). Thus, "Congress chose the Executive's determination in these matters and that choice must be honored." Environmental Protection Agency v. Mink. 410 U.S. 73, 81 (1973). In Mink, the Supreme Court gave unequivocal support to this exemption and stated that:

> [w]hat has been said thus far makes wholly untenable any claim that the Act intended to subject the soundness of executive security classifications to judicial review at the insistence of any objecting citizen. It also negates the proposition that Exemption 1 authorizes or permits in camera inspection of a contested document bearing a single classification so that the court may separate the secret from the supposedly nonsecret and order disclosure of the latter. The Court of Appeals was thus in error. The Irwin affidavit stated that each of the six documents for which Exemption 1 is now claimed "are and have been classified" Top Secret and Secret "pursuant to Executive Order No. 10501" and as involving "highly sensitive matter that is vital to our national defense and foreign policy." The fact of those classifications and the documents' characterizations have never been disputed by respondents. Accordingly, upon such a showing and in such circumstances, petitioners had met their burden of demonstrating that the documents were entitled to protection under Exemption 1 and the duty of the District Court under 552(a)(3) was therefore at an end. 410 U. S. at 84.

In other words:

> the only "matter" to be determined de novo under 552 (b)(1)
> is whether in fact the President has required by Executive
> Order that the documents in question are to be kept secret.
> Under the Act as written, that is the end of a court's inquiry.
> 410 U.S. at 95 (Opinion of Justice Stewart, concurring).

The attached affidavit of Dr. James B. Rhoads, Archivist of the United States (Government Exhibit 1), as well as Dr. Rhoads' answers to plaintiff's interrogatories 1-3, clearly establish that the document plaintiff seeks, the transcript of the January 27, 1964 executive session of the Warren Commission, is classified pursuant to Executive Order in the interest of national security. In short, under the controlling principles enunciated by the Supreme Court in Mink, supra, the instant action should be dismissed. See also Wolfe v. Froehlke, 358 F.Supp. 1318 (D.D.C. 1973).

While defendant respectfully submits that its reliance upon 5 U.S.C. 552 (b) (1) is dispositive of this action, it contends that the document plaintiff seeks is also exempt from compelled disclosure by reason of 5 U.S.C. 552 (b) (5) and (7).

II. The Freedom of Information Act Does Not Apply to Interagency or intra-agency memoranda embodying the Governmental Deliberative Process

The document plaintiff seeks is the transcript of the January 27, 1964 executive session of the Warren Commission. Such executive sessions were patently part of the deliberative process from which the Warren Report evolved, and the transcript of the session necessarily embodies and reflects this process. For this reason, the document falls within 5 U.S.C. 552 (b)(5) which exempts from compelled disclosure "inter-agency or intra-agency memorandums or letters which would not be available by law to a party other than an agency in litigation with the agency." The Courts have recognized that:

> the Congress intended that Exemption (5) was to reflect the
> privilege, customarily enjoyed by the Government in its litiga-
> tions, against having to reveal those internal working papers in
> which opinions are expressed and policies formulated and
> recommended.

The basis of Exemption (5), as of the privilege which ante-dated it, is the free and uninhibited exchange and communica-tion of opinions, ideas, and points of view—a process as essen-tial to the wise functioning of a big government as it is to any organized human effort. In the Federal establishment, as in General Motors or any other hierarchical giant, there are enough incentives as it is for playing it safe and listing with the wind; Congress clearly did not propose to add to them the threat of cross-examination in a public tribunal. Ackerly v. Ley, 420 F.2d 1336, 1341 (D.C. Cir. 1968).

Since plaintiff seeks disclosure of a document which is part of the Govern-ment's "deliberative processes", the disclosure should be denied. Internation-al Paper Company v. F.P.C. 438 F.2d 1349, 1359 (2d Cir. 1971).

Furthermore, in K.C. Wu v. National Endowment for Humanities, 460 F. 2d 1030 (5th Cir. 1972), cert. denied, 93 S. Ct. 1352 (1973), the Court held that:

We do not think the fact that one or more of the five [consul-tants who submitted memoranda] either included some fac-tual material in his memorandum or stated to the Endowment that he was able to refute appellant's arguments transforms these opinions into factual material within the meaning of the "purely factual" rule. 460 F.2d at 1033.

Similarly, in Mink, supra, the Supreme Court has plainly stated that Exemp-tion 5 protects documents such as those involved here:

The formulation [in drafts of the Information Act] was se-verely criticized, however, on the ground that it would permit compelled disclosure of an otherwise private document simply because the document did not deal "solely" with legal or policy matters. Documents dealing with mixed questions or fact, law and policy would inevitably, under the proposed ex-emption, become available to the public. As a result of this criticism, Exemption 5 was changed to substantially its present form. But plainly, the change cannot be read as suggesting that all factual material was to be rendered exempt from compelled disclosure. Congress sensibly discarded a wooden exemption that could have meant disclosure of manifestly private and confidential policy recommendations simply because the document containing them also happened to contain factual data.   410 U. S. at 90-91

For the above reasons, therefore, defendant submits that the transcript which plaintiff seeks falls squarely within the rationale of Exemption 5.

III.   The Freedom of Information Act is Inapplicable to Investigatory Files Compiled for Law Enforcement Purposes

In any event, the transcript plaintiff seeks is clearly exempt from com- pelled disclosure since it could only be part of "investigatory files compiled for law enforcement purposes" not available by law to a party other than an agency and therefore within the exclusion set forth at 5 U.S.C. 552 (b) (7). Thus, when it is demonstrated that the files in questions (1) were investiga- tory in nature; and (2) were compiled for law enforcement purposes, then "such files are exempt from compelled disclosure." Weisberg v. U.S. Depart- ment of Justice, No. 71-1026 (D.C. Cir., October 24, 1973) (en banc), slip opinion at 6. Since the Warren Commission was appointed to investigate the assassinations of President Kennedy and Lee Harvey Oswald (see Answer of Dr. Rhoads to plaintiff's interrogatory No. 7), it is apparent that the Com- mission's files, including the transcript plaintiff seeks, were investigatory in nature and compiled for law enforcement purposes.

The whole thrust of exemption 7 is to protect from disclosure all files which the Government compiles in the course of law enforcement investiga- tions which may or may not lead to formal proceedings. Barceloneta Shoe Corp. v. Compton, 271 F. Supp. 591, 592-593 (D. PR. 1967); Clement Brothers Co. v. NLRB, 282 F. Supp. 540 (N.D. Ga. 1968) approved, NLRB v. Clement Brothers Co., 407 F.2d 1027, 1031 (5th Cir. 1969); Benson v. United States, 309 F. Supp. 1144 (D. Neb. 1970); Evans v. Department of Transportation, 446 F. 2d 871 (5th Cir. 1971).

The rationale of the decision in Aspin v. Department of Defense, No. 72-2147 (D.C. Cir., November 26, 1973), slip opinion at 13-14, applies equally here:

> It is clear that if investigatory files were made public subse- quent to the termination of enforcement proceedings, the ability of any investigatory body to conduct future investi- gations would be seriously impaired. Few persons would re- spond candidly to investigators if they feared that their remarks would become public record after the proceedings. Further, the investigative techniques of the investigating body would be disclosed to the general public.

We note also that the recent en banc decision of this court in
Weisberg v. U.S. Department of Justice, supra, is consistent
with our decision in this case. While the court in Weisberg expressly limited the question there to the application of the
§ 7 exemption to "Federal Bureau of Investigation files"
(slip op. at 8), the point remains that a § 7 exemption was
there unheld as applied to files almost ten years old where no
prosecution was ever conducted. This squarely rebuts appli-
cant's broad argument that when there is no longer any pros-
pect for future enforcement proceedings (necessitated in
Weisberg by the death of the only suspect) the § 7 exemption from disclosure must terminate as well.

We therefore hold that an exemption under § 552 (b) (7), as
investigatory files compiled for law enforcement purposes,
remains available after the termination of investigation and
enforcement proceedings.

It is clear, then, that documents such as the transcipt plaintiff seeks are
exempted from the purview of the Information Act. It is "necessary for the
very operation of our Government to allow it to keep confidential certain
material, such as the investigatory files of the Federal Bureau of Investigation." Mink, supra, at 80, n.6 (1973) (quoting Senate Report No. 813,
89th Cong., 1st Sess., p. 3). See also, Harbolt v. Alldredge, 454 F.2d 1243,
1244 (10th Cir. 1972), cert. denied, 409 U.S. 1025 (Regulations of the Department [of Justice which] protect the confidentiality of investigatory
files compiled for law enforcement purposes except the extent available by
law to a party held to be valid); Moore v. Administrator, Veterans Administration, 475 F.2d 1283, 1286 (D.C. Cir. 1973) ("In general, it is well
established that no right to a preliminary investigatory file exists in administrative law.")

Finally, the Court of Appeals en banc decision in Weisberg, supra,
slip opinion 14-15, sets forth the controlling principles:

Where the district court can conclude that the Attorney General's designation and classification are correct, the Freedom
of Information Act requires no more. Here the record over-
whelmingly demonstrates how and under what circumstances
the files were compiled and that indeed they were "investigatory files compiled for law enforcement purposes." When the

District Judge made that determination, he correctly perceived
that his duty in achieving the will of Congress under the Freedom of Information Act was at an end.

Defendant respectfully contends, therefore, that the Court may readily conclude from the circumstances surrounding the establishment of the Warren
Commission as well as from the Warren Report itself that Commission files
including the transcript of the January 27, 1964 executive session, are investigatory and were compiled for law enforcement purposes.

CONCLUSION

For the foregoing reasons, defendant respectfully requests the Court to
grant its motion to dismiss or, in the alternative, for summary judgment, and
to dismiss the instant action.

/s/ _____
EARL J. SILBERT
United States Attorney

/s/ _____
ARNOLD T. AIKENS
Assistant United States Attorney

/s/ _____
MICHAEL J. RYAN
Assistant United States Attorney

STATEMENT OF MATERIAL FACTS AS TO WHICH THERE IS NO GENUINE ISSUE.

In support of its motion for summary judgment and pursuant to Local
Rule 1-9 (g), defendant submits the following statement of material facts as
to which it contends there is no genuine issue:

1.   The Warren Commission was established under Executive Order
and recognized by statute to investigate the assassinations of President
Kennedy and Lee Harvey Oswald. (Answer to Plaintiff's Interrogatory No. 7)

2.   The transcript of the January 27, 1964 Warren Commission Executive Session has been and continues to be classified "Top Secret" pursuant to Executive Order. (Government Exhibit 1) The transcript was originally classified under the provisions of Executive Order 10501, as amended (3 C.F.R., 1949-1953 Comp.), and is presently classified under the provisions of Executive Order 11652 (37 Fed. Reg. 5209, March 10, 1972). (Answers to Plaintiff's Interrogatories 1-3)

3.   By letter of May 4, 1968, addressed to Dr. James B. Rhoads, Archivist of the United States, plaintiff renewed a previous request for disclosure of the January 27, 1964 transcript (Complaint Exhibit A).

4.   By letter of May 20, 1968, Dr. Rhoads denied plaintiff's request (Complaint Exhibit B).

5.   By letter of June 21, 1971, Herbert E. Angel, then Acting Archivist, informed plaintiff of those transcripts, including the January 27, 1964 transcript, or parts of transcripts which were being withheld under the exemptions of the Freedom of Information Act (Complaint Exhibit C).

6.   By letters of January 6, 1972, plaintiff appealed the denial of his request for disclosure of the January 27, 1964 transcript (Complaint para. 12; Complaint Exhibit D).

7.   By letter of February 8, 1972, Mr. Richard Q. Vawter, Director of Information, General Services Administration, responded to plaintiff's letters of January 6, 1972 (Complaint Exhibit D).

8.   On November 13, 1973, plaintiff filed the instant suit under the Freedom of Information Act, 5 U.S.C. 552, in the United States District Court for the District of Columbia to compel disclosure of the transcript of the January 27, 1964 executive session of the Warren Commission.

/s/ _____

EARL J. SILBERT
United States Attorney

/s/ _____

ARNOLD T. AIKENS
Assistant United States Attorney

/s/ _____

MICHAEL J. RYAN
Assistant United States Attorney

Government Exhibit 1.

AFFIDAVIT OF DR. JAMES B. RHOADS. JANUARY 10, 1974.

DISTRICT OF COLUMBIA)
                                               ss.:
CITY OF WASHINGTON   )

    I, JAMES B. RHOADS, Archivist of the United States, National Archives and Records Service, General Services Administration, Eighth and Pennsylvania Avenue, N. W., Washington, D. C., living at 6502 Cipriano Road, Lanham, Maryland, do hereby solemnly swear:

    1.   I have read and am familiar with the allegations contained in the plaintiff's complaint in the case of Weisberg v. General Services Administration, Civil Action No. 2052-73, United States District Court for the District of Columbia.

    2.   At all times relevant to the circumstances of the complaint, I have served in the position of Archivist of the United States.

    3.   In accordance with Executive Order, at all times since the document in question, the transcript of the January 27, 1964 executive session of the Warren Commission, has been in the custody of the National Archives and Records Service, General Services Administration, it has been and continues to be classified "Top Secret."

    I have read the above statement, consisting of one page, and it is true and complete to the best of my knowledge and belief. I understand that the information I have given is not to be considered confidential and that it may be shown to the interested parties.

/s/ _____

(Affiant's Signature)

    Subscribed and sworn to before me at Eighth and Pennsylvania Avenue, N. W., Washington, D. C., on this 10th day of January, 1974.

/s/ _____

(Notary Public)

6.
ANSWERS TO INTERROGATORIES

JAMES B. RHOADS, Archivist of the United States, having been first duly sworn, under oath, deposes and says that it is upon his personal knowledge and belief that he gives the following information in answer to interrogatories propounded by plaintiff:

1. Yes.

2. The transcript was originally classified under the provisions of Executive Order 10501, as amended (3 CFR, 1949-1953 Comp.) It is presently classified under the provisions of Executive Order 11652.

3. 37 F.R. 5209, March 10, 1972.

4. Defendant objects to this interrogatory on the grounds that it is not relevant to the subject matter involved in the instant action, and divulgence of the information sought would be contrary to the jurisdictional requisites set forth at 5 USC 552.

5. Not applicable (N/A) in light of the previous answer.

6. The transcript is withheld as falling within certain exemptions from mandatory disclosure cited at 5 U.S.C. 552 (b) (1970).

7. The Warren Commission was established under Executive Order and recognized by statute to investigate the assassinations of President Kennedy and Lee Harvey Oswald.

8. The defendant is not aware of any such proceedings.

9. Not applicable (N/A) in light of previous answer.

10. The defendant is not aware of any contemplated future proceedings in this respect.

11. N/A

Filed with 5. Defendant's Motion to Dismiss.

12.   N/A

13.   N/A

14.   N/A

15.   Defendant objects to this interrogatory on the grounds that it is not relevant to the subject matter involved in the instant action. The General Services Administration has made no such recommendation.

16.   Defendant objects to this interrogatory on the grounds that it is not relevant to the subject matter involved in the instant action. The General Services Administration has made no such recommendation.

17.   Defendant objects to this interrogatory on the grounds that it is not relevant to the subject matter involved in the instant action. The General Services Administration has made no such recommendation.

18.   No.

19.   No.

20.   The only Federal agencies which have examined a copy of the transcript other than the defendant General Services Administration are the Central Intelligence Agency and the Federal Bureau of Investigation.

21.   Mr. Vawter's comment to "recent developments in the state of the law" in his letter of February 8, 1972, merely refers to an examination of newly issued judicial decisions on the Freedom of Information Act and the anticipated issuance of Executive Order 11652.

/s/ _____

JAMES B. RHOADS
Archivist of the United States

Subscribed and sworn to before me this 16th day of January, 1974. My Commission expires the 31st day of August, 1974.

/s/ _____

Notary Public

7.
PLAINTIFF'S MOTION FOR EXTENSION OF TIME WITHIN WHICH TO OPPOSE DEFENDANT'S MOTION TO DISMISS OR FOR SUMMARY JUDGMENT

Plaintiff respectfully moves the Court pursuant to Rule 6(b)(1) of the Federal Rules of Civil Procedure for an extension of time to March 12, 1974, within which to oppose the defendant's Motion to Dismiss or for Summary Judgment.

In support of this motion, plaintiff submits herewith a Memorandum of Points and Authorities.

/s/ _____
JAMES HIRAM LESAR
1231 Fourth Street, S. W.
Washington, D. C. 20024
Attorney for Plaintiff

MEMORANDUM OF POINTS AND AUTHORITIES IN SUPPORT OF PLAINTIFF'S MOTION FOR AN EXTENSION OF TIME WITHIN WHICH TO OPPOSE DEFENDANT'S MOTION TO DISMISS OR FOR SUMMARY JUDGMENT. FEBRUARY 22, 1974.

Under Rule 1-9 (d) of the Rules of the United States District Court for the District of Columbia and Rule 6 (e) of the Federal Rules of Civil Procedure, plaintiff has until February 26, 1974, to file a Memorandum of Points

<hr>

Filed: February 22, 1974.

30

and Authorities in opposition to the defendant's Motion to Dismiss or For Summary Judgment. In order to adequately oppose the defendant's motion, it is necessary for plaintiff's attorney to confer with the plaintiff, examine certain documentary evidence in his client's possession, and prepare an affidavit. Thus, proper preparation of the opposition to the defendant's motion requires that the undersigned attorney meet with his client in Frederick, Maryland, where the client lives. Plaintiff's attorney has not yet been able to make this trip, but if he can obtain gasoline, he hopes to be able to make this trip to Frederick on February 22, 1974.

Plaintiff regrets this delay and will endeavor to file his opposition to the defendant's motion at the earliest possible date. Plaintiff feels constrained to point out that on January 3, 1974, the day after the defendant's answers to plaintiff's interrogatories were due, plaintiff's attorney orally agreed to an extension of time until January 14, 1974, the date on which the defendant's Answer was also due. On January 14 the defendant parlayed the extension stipulated to by plaintiff's counsel into a court-granted further extension, citing as grounds a "delay in the preparation and transmittal of materials necessary for the preparation of such a motion" experienced by "the agency involved". Plaintiff notes, however, that the affidavit sworn to by Dr. Rhoads and submitted as Exhibit 1 to the Answer is dated January 10, 1974. Similarly the answers to plaintiff's interrogatories were sworn to by Dr. Rhoads on January 16, 1974. Had the defendant served the answers to the interrogatories on plaintiff at the time they were sworn to instead of waiting until the last possible day, February 13,1974, the extension of time requested herein would be unnecessary.

/s/ _____

JAMES HIRAM LESAR
1231 Fourth Street, S. W.
Washington, D. C. 20024
Attorney for Plaintiff

CERTIFICATE OF SERVICE.

This is to certify that service of the foregoing Motion for Extension of Time and the Memorandum of Points and Authorities and proposed Order attached thereto has been made upon the defendant by mailing a copy thereof to its attorney, Assistant United States Attorney Michael J. Ryan, United States Courthouse, Room 3421, Washington, D. C., 20001, on this 22nd day of February, 1974.

/s/ _____
JAMES HIRAM LESAR

8.
ORDER

Upon consideration of Plaintiff's Motion for Extension of Time Within Which to Oppose Defendant's Motion to Dismiss or for Summary Judgment and the entire record herein, it is by the Court this 25th day of February, 1974,

ORDERED that the Plaintiff's time to oppose Defendant's Motion to Dismiss or, in the alternative, For Summary Judgment, be and hereby is extended to March 12, 1974.

/s/ _____
GERHARD GESELL
UNITED STATES DISTRICT JUDGE

Filed: February 25, 1974.

9.
PLAINTIFF'S SECOND SET OF INTERROGATORIES

Under Rule 33 of the Federal Rules of Civil Procedure, plaintiff addresses the following interrogatories, numbered in continuation from his first set, to the defendant:

22.   Did the January 27, 1964 Warren Commission Executive Session transcript bear a classification stamp when the Warren Commission delivered it to the National Archives?

23.   If the answer to interrogatory 22 is yes, what was that classification, who classified the transcript, and what title and position did the classifier hold?

24.   On what date was the January 27 transcript first classified pursuant to Executive Order 10501?

25.   Who first classified the transcript pursuant to Executive Order 10501, what agency did he represent, and what was his title and position within that agency?

26.   Was the person identified in the above interrogatory authorized to classify documents Top Secret? By what authority?

27.   On what date was the transcript classified Top Secret under Executive Order 11652?

28.   Who classified the transcript Top Secret under Executive Order 11652, what agency did he represent, and what was his title and position within that agency?

Filed: February 27, 1974.

29. Was the person identified in interrogatory 28 authorized to classify documents Top Secret? By what authority?

30. On what dates did the representatives of the Central Intelligence Agency and the Federal Bureau of Investigation referred to in the answer to plaintiff's interrogatory number 20 examine the January 27 transcript?

31. What are the names of the representatives of the CIA and FBI who have examined the transcript and what titles and positions did they hold?

32. Were the persons identified in the answer to interrogatory number 31 authorized to classify documents Top Secret?

33. Were the persons identified in response to interrogatory number 31 asked to show their security clearances before being allowed to examine the January 27 transcript?

34. Does the January 27 transcript indicate on its face whether it is subject to the General Declassification Schedule? Is it?

35. If the transcript is exempt from the General Declassification Schedule, which exemption is claimed?

36. How many pages long is the transcript and is the entire transcript classified Top Secret or only parts of it?

37. Do the verbatim quotes contained in Chapter One of Gerald Ford's Portrait of the Assassin come from the January 27 transcript?

38. If the answer to the above interrogatory is yes, how many pages of the January 27 transcript are quoted from in Chapter One of Gerald Ford's Portrait of the Assassin?

39. Did disclosure of the parts of the transcript quoted in Gerald Ford's Portrait of the Assassin cause any harm to the national defense or foreign policy of the United States? If the answer is yes, what harm?

40. Did any of the United States Attorneys representing the General Services Administration in this case examine the January 27 transcript prior to February 13, 1974? If the answer is yes, which ones, and on what dates?

41. Executive Order 11652 states that: "The test for assigning 'Top Secret' classification shall be whether its unauthorized disclosure could reasonably be expected to cause exceptionally grave damage to the national security." Which of the following criteria for determining "exceptionally grave damage to the national security" (listed in Section 1(A) of Executive Order 11652) were used as a basis for classifying the January 27, 1964 transcript "Top Secret":

a) armed hostilities against the United States or its allies?

b)   disruption of foreign relations vitally affecting the national security?

c)   the compromise of vital national defense plans or complex cryptologic and communications intelligence systems?

d)   the revelation of sensitive intelligence operations?

e)   the disclosure of scientific or technological developments vital to national security?

42.   Referring to classified information, Executive Order 11652 states: "Wrongful disclosure of such information or material is recognized in the Federal Criminal Code as providing a basis for prosecution." Which provisions of the Federal Criminal Code establish a basis for prosecuting those who wrongfully disclose classified information?

43.   Would disclosure of the January 27 transcript constitute a violation of the Federal Criminal Code provisions cited in response to the above interrogatory?

44.   Would disclosure of the January 27 transcript be detrimental to the administration and enforcement of the laws and regulations of the United States and its agencies?

45.   If the answer to the above interrogatory is yes, which specific laws or regulations?

46.   Would disclosure of the January 27 transcript reveal the identity of confidential sources of information and impede or jeopardize future investigations by precluding or limiting the use of the same or similar sources in the future?

Please note that under Rule 33 of the Federal Rules of Civil Procedure you are required to serve upon the undersigned, within 30 days after service of this notice, your answers in writing and under oath to the above interrogatories.

/s/_____

JAMES HIRAM LESAR
1231 Fourth Street, S. W.
Washington, D. C. 20024

CERTIFICATE OF SERVICE.

I hereby certify that service of the foregoing has been made upon the defendant by mailing a copy thereof to its attorney, Assistant United States Attorney Michael J. Ryan, United States Courthouse, Room 3421, Washington, D. C. 20001, on this 27th day of February, 1974.

/s/_____

JAMES HIRAM LESAR

10.
MOTION TO STRIKE AFFIDAVIT OF DR. JAMES B. RHOADS

Plaintiff moves the court to strike the affidavit of Dr. James B. Rhoads, dated January 10, 1974, attached to defendant's Motion to Dismiss Or, In the Alternative, For Summary Judgment, on the ground that said affidavit does not comply with Rule 56(e) of the Federal Rules of Civil Procedure, in that said affidavit was not made on personal knowledge, does not set forth such facts as would be admissible in evidence, and does not show affirmatively that Dr. Rhoads is competent to testify to the matters stated in the affidavit.

/s/ _____
JAMES HIRAM LESAR
1231 Fourth Street, S. W.
Washington, D. C. 20024

MEMORANDUM OF POINTS AND AUTHORITIES IN SUPPORT OF PLAINTIFF'S MOTION TO STRIKE AFFIDAVIT OF DR. JAMES B. RHOADS.

In support of its motion for summary judgment the defendant has submitted Government Exhibit 1, an affidavit by Dr. James B. Rhoads, Archivist of the United States. The only pertinent part of this affidavit, paragraph 3, reads:

Filed: March 7, 1974.

3.   In accordance with Executive Order, at all times since the document in question, the transcript of the January 27, 1964 executive session of
the Warren Commission, has been in the custody of the National Archives and
Records Service, General Services Administration, it has been and continues
to be classified "Top Secret."

Rule 56(e) of the Federal Rules of Civil Procedure requires that affidavits made in support of a summary judgment motion:

... shall be made on personal knowledge, shall set forth such facts as
would be admissible in evidence, and shall show affirmatively that the affiant
is competent to testify to the matters stated therein.

Plaintiff contends that Dr. Rhoads' affidavit should be stricken because
it fails to meet the standards set forth by Rule 56(e). In the first place, Dr.
Rhoads' affidavit does not affirmatively show that he is competent to state
that the January 27 transcript has been classified Top Secret "in accordance
with Executive Order." Dr. Rhoads does not state that he is the person who
classified the January 27 transcript or even that he is authorized to classify
documents Top Secret. It is clear that under Executive Order 10501, upon
which the defendant relies, Dr. Rhoads has no such authority. Executive
Order 10501 provides:

Sec. 2. Limitation of Authority to Classify. The authority to classify
defense information or material under this order shall be limited in the departments and agencies of the executive branch as hereinafter specified.
Departments and agencies subject to the specified limitations shall be designated by the President:

(a)   In those departments and agencies having no direct responsibility for national defense there shall be no authority for original classification of information or material under this order. [Emphasis added.]

Similarly, under Executive Order 11652, also relied upon by the defendant,
the National Archives is omitted from the list of federal agencies and departments authorized to classify information Top Secret.

Plaintiff contends that only persons with authority to classify documents Top Secret under Executive Order 10501 or 11652 are competent to
assert that the January 27 transcript has been classified Top Secret in accordance with executive order. Dr. Rhoads does not state in his affidavit that he
has such authority and Executive Orders 10501 and 11652 eliminate the possibility.

Plaintiff also contends that Dr. Rhoads' affidavit is not made on personal knowledge and does not set forth facts such as would be admissible in evidence. Dr. Rhoads' affidavit does not state that he viewed the January 27 transcript. Nor does Dr. Rhoads state that the transcript bears on its face a Top Secret stamp. Nor does Dr. Rhoads name the person or persons who classified the transcript or the dates on which it was classified Top Secret. If the transcript was in fact classified Top Secret by authorized persons acting pursuant to Executive Order 10501 and Executive Order 11652, such facts are easily ascertainable by any National Archives file clerk. However, Dr. Rhoads' affidavit attests not to facts admissible in evidence, but only to a conclusion. Since Dr. Rhoads did not attach a copy of the cover or face sheet of the January 27 transcript to his affidavit, as required by Rule 56(e), it is not possible to tell from the text of the affidavit itself whether Dr. Rhoads' conclusion is based upon personal knowledge of admissible facts or upon hearsay or fraudulent misrepresentation. Rule 56(e) forbids the use of such affidavits in support of a motion for summary judgment:

> When affidavits are offered in support of a motion for summary judgment, they must present admissible evidence, and must not only be made on the personal knowledge of the affiant, but must show that the affiant possesses the knowledge asserted. When written documents are relied on, they must be exhibited in full. The statement of the substance of written instruments or of affiant's interpretation of them or of mere conclusions of law or restatements of allegations of the pleadings are not sufficient. Walling v. Fairmont Creamery Co., 139 F. 2d 318, 322 (CA 8, 1943).

In accord with this decision is the opinion of the United States Court of Appeals for the District of Columbia Circuit in Jameson v. Jameson, 176 F. 2d 58 (1949). Thus, there is clear authority supporting plaintiff's motion to strike the affidavit submitted by Dr. Rhoads.

Government affidavits are of critical importance in Freedom of Information Act suits. Recognizing this, the United States Court of Appeals for the District of Columbia Circuit discussed the problem at great length in Vaughn v. Rosen, 484 F. 2d 820 (1973). In recommending that the district court take certain measures to safeguard against "governmental obfuscation and mischaracterization," the Court of Appeals said:

> The problem of assuring that allegations of exempt status are adequately justified is the most obvious and the most easily remedied flaw in current procedures. It may be corrected by assuring government agencies that courts

will simply no longer accept conclusory and generalized allegations of exemptions . . . but will require a relatively detailed analysis in manageable segments.
[Emphasis added] Vaughn, supra, at 826.

Plaintiff believes that implementation of the Vaughn decision in this
case can best be achieved by granting his motion to strike the Rhoads' affidavit.

/s/ _____
JAMES HIRAM LESAR
1231 Fourth Street, S. W.
Washington, D. C. 20024

CERTIFICATE OF SERVICE.

I hereby certify that service of the foregoing Motion to Strike Affidavit
of Dr. James B. Rhoads and the Memorandum of Points and Authorities in
support of that motion has been made upon the defendant by mailing a copy
thereof to its attorney, Mr. Michael J. Ryan, Assistant United States Attorney,
United States Courthouse, Room 3421, Washington, D. C. 20001, on this 7th
day of March, 1974.

/s/ _____
JAMES HIRAM LESAR

ORDER.

Upon consideration of Plaintiff's Motion to Strike Affidavit of Dr.
James B. Rhoads and the entire record herein, it is by the Court this_____
day of_____ , 1974,
ORDERED that the affidavit of Dr. James B. Rhoads be and hereby
is stricken on the grounds that said affidavit does not comply with Rule 56(e)
of the Federal Rules of Civil Procedure.

_____
UNITED STATES DISTRICT JUDGE

11.
OPPOSITION TO DEFENDANT'S MOTION TO DISMISS OR, IN THE ALTERNATIVE, FOR SUMMARY JUDGMENT

This action involves a suit brought under the provisions of the Freedom of Information Act, 5 U.S.C. § 552, for disclosure of the transcript of an Executive Session of the Warren Commission held on January 27, 1964. The Complaint stated that the defendant, the General Services Administration, was withholding the January 27 transcript on the grounds that it was protected by two exceptions to the Freedom of Information Act, 5 U.S.C. § 552 (b)(1), which exempts from disclosure information "specifically required by Executive order to be kept secret in the interest of the national defense or foreign policy," and 5 U.S.C. § 552 (b)(7), which exempts "investigatory files compiled for law enforcement purposes except to the extent available by law to a party other than an agency." Plaintiff alleged, however, that the transcript was improperly classified, and that even if it had been properly classified, any justification for the continued suppression of the transcript was negated by the extensive use of verbatim quotes from the transcript by Warren Commission member Gerald Ford in his book Portrait of the Assassin.

Three months later the General Services Administration responded by filing a Motion to Dismiss Or, In The Alternative, For Summary Judgment. The GSA attempted to justify its suppression of the transcript by invoking three of the Act's exemptions, (b)(1), (b)(5), and (b)(7). The newly added ground for withholding, (b)(5), exempts from disclosure "inter-agency or

---

Filed: March 12, 1974.

intra-agency memorandums or letters which would not be available by law to a party other than an agency in litigation with the agency."

The GSA did not address the question of whether any or all of these defenses were waived by use of quoted material from the transcript in Portrait of the Assassin. Nor did the GSA submit any affidavits or other evidentiary materials in support of its claim that the transcript is protected from disclosure by Exemptions 5 and 7. However, the defendant did submit an affidavit in support of its Exemption 1 claim of immunity. For that reason, plaintiff begins with a discussion of that claim.

I.   THE DEFENDANT HAS NOT MET ITS BURDEN OF DEM—
      ONSTRATING THAT THE TRANSCRIPT IS ENTITLED TO
      PROTECTION UNDER EXEMPTION 1

      A. THE DEFENDANT HAS NOT SHOWN THAT THE TRAN-
          SCRIPT IS CLASSIFIED TOP SECRET PURSUANT TO AN
          EXECUTIVE ORDER

The Freedom of Information Act, 5 U.S.C. § 552, provides:

> (a)(3) . . . each agency on request for identifiable records . . . shall make the records promptly available to any person. On complaint, the district court of the United States . . . has jurisdiction to enjoin the agency from withholding agency records improperly withheld from the complainant. In such a case the court shall determine the matter de novo and the burden is on the agency to sustain its action. [Emphasis added]

In Environmental Protection Agency v. Mink, 410 U.S. 73 (1973), the Supreme Court discussed the agency's burden and the Act's provision for de novo review as they relate to claims of Exemption 1 immunity. EPA v. Mink involved a suit for the disclosure of recommendations and a report made by an inter-departmental committee on the advisibility of conducting an underground nuclear test at Amchitka Island, Alaska. In response to the complaint, the EPA moved for summary judgment on the grounds that the documents sought were protected by Exemptions 1 and 5. In support of its summary judgment motion, the EPA submitted a detailed affidavit by Under Secretary of State John N. Irwin. The affidavit firmly established the competency of

Mr. Irwin to invoke the protection of Exemption 1, reciting that he had been appointed by President Nixon as Chairman of an "Under Secretaries Committee" which was part of the National Security Council system organized by the President "so that he could use it as an instrument for obtaining advice on important questions relating to our national security." In discussing the Irwin affidavit, the Supreme Court said:

> The Irwin affidavit stated that each of the six documents for which Exemption 1 is now claimed "are and have been classified" Top Secret and Secret "pursuant to Executive Order 10501" and as involving "highly sensitive matter that is vital to our national defense and foreign policy." The fact of those classifications and the documents characterizations have never been disputed by respondents. Accordingly, upon such a showing and in such circumstances, petitioners had met their burden of demonstrating that the documents were entitled to protection under Exemption 1, and the duty of the District Court under §552 (a)(3) was therefore at an end. [Emphasis added] EPA v. Mink, supra, at 84.

The italicized portions of the quoted passage distinguish this case from Mink. The plaintiff in Mink did not dispute the government's claim that the documents sought had been lawfully classified pursuant to Executive Order 10501. Nor did the plaintiff in Mink dispute the characterization of the suppressed documents as "highly sensitive matter that is vital to our national defense and foreign policy." But in the present case plaintiff denies both the government's assertion that the January 27 transcript was originally classified Top Secret pursuant to Executive Order 10501 and that this transcript can be fairly characterized as involving "highly sensitive matter that is vital to our national defense and foreign policy."

The basis for plaintiff's denials is established by his affidavit and its exhibits, which are attached hereto. The Weisberg affidavit and its exhibits show that the January 27, 1964 transcript was originally classified Top Secret by Ward & Paul, a private court reporter which was hired to provide stenographic services for the Warren Commission. Plaintiff's affidavit and exhibits further show that, for internal bureaucratic reasons having nothing to do with the content of the Warren Commission transcripts or their putative danger to "national defense" or "foreign policy", Ward & Paul routinely classified all Commission transcripts Top Secret during the period from January 21 through March 4, 1964. [See attached affidavit of Harold Weisberg and Exhibits A through H.]

In short, the situation here is exactly opposite that in Mink. The defendant has not shown that the January 27 transcript was classified Top Secret pursuant to Executive Order 10501, or that if so classified, the classification was done by an authorized individual. Nor has the defendant asserted that the Warren Commission was authorized to classify documents Top Secret under the terms of Executive Order 10501. True, the defendant has filed a conclusory affidavit by Dr. James B. Rhoads, Archivist of the United States, which asserts that the transcript has been classified Top Secret "in accordance with Executive Order" ever since it came into the custody of the National Archives, but even this inadequate statement is unsupported by any evidence. If the January 27 transcript was originally classified in accordance with Executive Order 10501, evidence in support of that claim could have been obtained by the defendant and submitted along with the Rhoads' affidavit. For example, the defendant could have submitted a copy of the transcript's face sheet, which, if properly classified, is required to show the level of classification, the office of origin, the date of preparation and classification, and the identity of the person who classified the transcript. By not eliciting such facts, the defendant has failed to show that the transcript is lawfully classified Top Secret pursuant to Executive Order. Accordingly, the defendant has not met the burden placed upon it by the Freedom of Information Act of demonstrating that the transcript is entitled to protection under Exemption 1.

B.   THE DEFENDANT HAS NOT SHOWN THAT THE JANU-
     ARY 27 TRANSCRIPT INVOLVES HIGHLY SENSITIVE IN-
     FORMATION THAT IS VITAL TO OUR NATIONAL DE-
     FENSE OR FOREIGN POLICY

Executive Order 10501 limits all classification to "defense information." Top Secret information is, of course, even more restricted, as is shown by the text of Section 1(a):

Top Secret. Except as may be expressly provided by statute, the use of the classification Top Secret shall be authorized, by appropriate authority, only for defense information or material which requires the highest degree of protection. The Top Secret classification shall be applied only to that information or material the defense aspect of which is paramount, and the unauthorized disclosure of which could result in exceptionally grave damage to the Nation such as leading to a definite break in diplomatic relations affecting the defense of the United States, an armed attack against the United States or its allies, a war, or the compromise of military or defense plans, or intelligence operations, or scientific or technological developments vital to the national defense.

The substance of the January 27, 1964 transcript is well-known, in part because it is extensively quoted in Chapter One of Portrait of the Assassin. In his affidavit, plaintiff has described the content of this executive session:

18.   The January 27 executive session dealt with the rumor that Lee Harvey Oswald had been an undercover agent for the FBI. Although this rumor had been withheld from the members of the Commission, it was not news when it reached them on January 27, 1964. This rumor had previously appeared in print in Texas and Pennsylvania. Indeed, both the FBI and the Secret Service had conducted investigations of it a month and a half earlier. The FBI and Secret Service reports pertaining to their investigations of this rumor were never classified or withheld. In fact, affiant has many such reports in his possession. [Emphasis in the original. See attached affidavit of Harold Weisberg]

On the basis of both Chapter One of Portrait of the Assassin, attached hereto as Exhibit I, and plaintiff's affidavit, the Court can properly conclude that the January 27 Executive Session had nothing to do with information which was required to be classified Top Secret as that term is defined under Executive Order 10501. Moreover, other considerations add to the circumstances which dispute any attempt to characterize the January 27 transcript as involving information required to be classified in the interests of the national defense or foreign policy. Thus, when Gerald Ford testified before the Senate Rules Committee about his authorship of Portrait of the Assassin with John R. Stiles, he stated:

. . . we wrote the book, but we did not use in that book any material other than the material that was in the 26 volumes of testimony and exhibits that were subsequently made public and sold to the public generally. [Hearings on the Nomination of Gerald R. Ford of Michigan to be Vice President of the United States, Committee on Rules and Administration, United States Senate, p. 89]

Clearly, Gerald Ford is under the impression that Chapter One of Portrait of the Assassin did not disclose classified information. Nor is Gerald Ford alone in that regard. Apparently no government official has accused Ford of leaking or disclosing classified information in connection with his book. Yet government heads have an affirmative obligation to take action if unauthorized disclosure of classified information occurs. Section 13(B) of Executive Order 11652 provides:

> The head of each Department is directed to take prompt and stringent administrative action against any officer or employee of the United States, at any level of employment, determined to have been responsible for any release or disclosure of national security information or material in a manner not authorized by or under this order or a directive of the President issued through the National Security Council. Where a violation of criminal statutes may be involved, Departments will refer any such case promptly to the Department of Justice.

It is evident that no such action has been taken with regard to Gerald Ford's disclosure of lengthy verbatim quotes from the January 27 transcript. The obvious explanation for this is that the transcript does not contain information which is required to be kept secret in the interest of national defense or foreign policy. This conclusion is fortified by the fact that neither the defendant nor anyone else has claimed that the national security suffered "exceptionally grave damage" as a result of the publication of segments of the January 27 transcript. It is simply preposterous to claim that today, more than nine years after Gerald Ford and John R. Stiles "declassified" parts of the transcript on their own hook, disclosure of the transcript could result in armed hostilities and the like.

As discussed in the preceding section, the decision of the Supreme Court in Mink was conditioned on the fact that the plaintiff there had not disputed either the fact of classification or "the documents' characterizations." In the case at bar, the plaintiff disputes both. Plaintiff believes that Mink stands for the proposition that a failure to comply with the requirements of Executive Orders 10501 and 11652 precludes the government from asserting the applicability of Exemption 1. On the present record, the very least that can be said is that the defendant has failed to affirmatively show that the transcript is classified in compliance with either Executive Order 10501 or 11652. As a consequence, the defendant cannot properly invoke the protection of Exemption 1.

II.   DEFENDANT HAS NOT MET ITS BURDEN OF DEMON-
STRATING THAT THE TRANSCRIPT SOUGHT IS ENTITLED TO PRO-
TECTION UNDER THE INVESTIGATORY FILES EXEMPTION

The defendant has also sought to invoke the protection of Exemption 7,
which excepts from disclosure "investigatory files compiled for law enforcement purposes except to the extent available by law to a party other than an
agency." With regard to Exemption 7, the United States Court of Appeals for
the District of Columbia Circuit has held that:

The threshold question . . . is whether the files sought . . . relate to anything that can fairly be characterized as an enforcement proceeding. Bristol-
Myers v. F.T.C., 424 F. 2d 935, 939.

In Aspin v. Department of Defense, 348 F. Supp. 1081 (1972), the District Court applied this test to a suit to compel the Army to release the Peers
Commission Report on its investigation into the My Lai incident. The Court
found that Exemption 7 applied because "the affidavits of Mr. Robert Berry,
General Westmoreland, and Colonel George Ryker clearly indicate that the
Report was in fact the basis for the bringing of charges under the Code
against both officers and enlisted men." Aspin, supra, at 1082.

In reviewing the Aspin decision in the aftermath of Weisberg v. Department of Justice, No. 71-1026 (D.C. Cir., October 24, 1973), the Court of
Appeals again quoted the Bristol-Myers test:

The trial court's duty in FOIA cases is clear. It must examine the total record to determine "whether the files sought . . . relate to anything that
can fairly be characterized as an enforcement proceeding." Aspin v. Department of Defense, No. 72-2147 (D.C. Cir., November 26, 1973), slip op. at 8.

In the instant case, the defendant has not submitted any affidavits in
support of its Exemption 7 claim of immunity. In the instant case, unlike
Aspin, the defendant is unable to name a specific law or statute which the
transcript was or will be used to enforce. Unable to name a specific law enforcement purpose to which the transcript relates, the defendant has been
forced to admit that it is unaware of any court proceedings which have been,
or, in the future, may be initiated with respect to its unnamed law enforcement purpose. [See defendant's answers to plaintiff's interrogatories, Numbers 6-10] Also very damaging to the defendant's claim of Exemption 7

immunity is the defendant's admission, in response to interrogatories 18 and 19, that the transcript has never been made available to any court or law enforcement agency or officer of the State of Texas. These Texas officials are the only authorities established to have had a law enforcement purpose, the trials of Lee Harvey Oswald and Jack Ruby, but the transcript was not made available to them, nor does the defendant claim that it was ever intended that it would be made available to them.

In its Memorandum of Points and Authorities in support of its summary judgment motion, the defendant has contended that:

... the Court may readily conclude from the circumstances surrounding the establishment of the Warren Commission as well as from the Warren Report itself that Commission files including the transcript of the January 27, 1964 executive session, are investigatory and were compiled for law enforcement purposes. [Memorandum, pp. 7-8]

The defendant did not venture to put into the record any of these "circumstances", nor did it even mention any. Since plaintiff believes that the Court may just as readily reach the opposite conclusion from the actual facts as it can reach the defendant's desired conclusion from its vacuum of "circumstances," plaintiff calls attention to the Executive Order which established the Warren Commission and which set forth the express, specific, and limited purposes for which the Commission was convened:

The purposes of the Commission are to examine the evidence developed by the Federal Bureau of Investigation and any additional evidence that may hereafter come to light or be uncovered by federal or state authorities; to make further investigations as the Commission finds desirable; to evaluate all the facts and circumstances surrounding such assassination, including the subsequent violent death of the man charged with assassination, and to report to me its findings and conclusions. [Emphasis added. Executive Order 11130, November 29, 1963, attached hereto as Exhibit J]

There is not a word in Executive Order 11130 which indicates that the Commission had a law enforcement purpose. The Commission's task was to prepare a report to the President, not to apprehend or prosecute assassins. (The only alleged assassin, it must be remembered, was already dead.) The Commission's purpose is not to gather evidence for a grand jury but to ascertain the truth about the assassination and prepare a report for the President who would then make it public.

Thus, on the basis of the evidence which now comprises the total record in this case, the Court must conclude that the defendant has failed to meet its burden of demonstrating that the transcript which plaintiff seeks relates to anything which "can fairly be characterized as an enforcement proceeding." The transcript is, therefore, not protected from disclosure by Exemption 7.

III. THE DEFENDANT HAS FAILED TO SHOW THAT THE JANUARY 27 TRANSCRIPT IS ENTITLED TO PROTECTION UNDER EXEMPTION 5

The defendant has also invoked Exemption 5, which exempts from disclosure "inter-agency or intra-agency memorandums or letters which would not be available by law to a party other than an agency in litigation with an agency." In its correspondence with plaintiff, the defendant had not previously claimed Exemption 5 as a grounds for withholding the January 27 transcript. Presumably it has now been added because of the weakness of Exemptions 1 and 7 as grounds for avoiding disclosure.

The obvious ground for objecting to the invocation of Exemption 5 is that plaintiff is seeking a transcript not a letter or memorandum. Again, the defendant has not submitted any affidavit or other evidence in support of its Exemption 5 claim, nor has the defendant specified the policy deliberated at the January 27, 1964 executive session.

In Ackerly v. Ley, 420 F. 2d 1336 (D.C. Cir., 1969), the Court of Appeals had occasion to interpret the underlying legislative history of Exemption 5:

That history, looked at in more detail, only confirms the view of it expressed by us in Seligson, and we accept the Commissioner's contention that the Congress intended that Exemption (5) was to reflect the privilege, customarily enjoyed by the Government in its litigations, against having to reveal those internal working papers in which opinions are expressed and policies formulated and recommended. Ackerly, supra, at 1341. [Emphasis added]

The legislative history which the Court of Appeals had examined states in part:

It was pointed out in the comments of many of the agencies that it would be impossible to have any frank discussion of legal or policy matters in writing if all such writings were to be subjected to public scrutiny. It was argued, and with merit, that efficiency of Government would be greatly hampered if, with respect to legal and policy matters, all Government agencies were <u>prematurely</u> forced to "operate in a fishbowl." The Committee is convinced of the merits of this general proposition, <u>but it has attempted to delimit the exception as narrowly as consistent with efficient Government operation.</u> S. Rep. No. 813, at 9. [Emphasis added]

The present case does not involve a situation in which the government agency could assert the privilege "customarily enjoyed by the government in its litigations." The government agency involved, the Warren Commission, is no longer in existence and never was involved in litigation. Nor has the defendant shown that the January 27 transcript deals with "legal and policy matters." And, in any event, it cannot be said that plaintiff's request that the transcript be disclosed nearly ten years after the Commission went out of existence is forcing the Commission to "operate in a fishbowl" prematurely.

Nor has the defendant shown that release of the transcript is in any way inconsistent with efficient Government operation. This the defendant is required to do. As the Supreme Court said in <u>Mink</u>:

But the privilege that has been held to attach to intragovernmental memoranda clearly has finite limits, even in civil litigation. In each case, the question was whether production of the contested document would be "injurious to the consultative functions of government that the privilege of nondisclosure protects." <u>Mink</u>, <u>supra</u>, at 87, quoting <u>Kaiser Aluminum & Chemical Corp. v. United States</u>, 157 F. Supp. 939, 946 (Ct. of Cl. 1958)

Thus, even assuming for the purposes of argument that the transcript is properly described as an inter- or intra-agency memorandum or letter, the defendant has failed to establish that its release would be "injurious to the consultative functions of the government."

Finally, even if the transcript is an intra-agency memorandum, any claim to Exemption 5 immunity for it has been waived by: 1) the Warren <u>Report's</u> express denial of the rumor that Oswald had worked for the FBI, and 2) the publication, in <u>Portrait of the Assassin</u>, of lengthy parts of the transcript by a member of the Commission. The principle that public reliance on an internal memorandum operates as a waiver of Exemption 5 immunity was established by the United States Court of Appeals for the District of Columbia in <u>American Mail Line, Ltd.</u> v. <u>Gulick</u>, 411 F. 2d 696, 703 (1969).

CONCLUSION

For the reasons stated above, it is clear that the defendant has not met its burden of demonstrating that any of the cited exemptions protect the January 27, 1964 transcript from disclosure. In addition, it must be pointed out that in denying plaintiff access to this transcript after it has been extensively used by other persons for literary and commercial purposes, the defendant is arbitrarily violating plaintiff's First Amendment rights. It is a well-established constitutional principle that while regulation of protected First Amendment activity may itself be proper, such regulation must be even-handed to a fault. Niemotko v. Maryland, 340 U.S. 268 (1951), Fowler v. Rhode Island, 345 U.S. 67 (1953), Edwards v. South Carolina, 373 U.S. 229 (1963). Denying plaintiff access to the January 27 transcript after it has been commercially exploited by others is not "even-handed" treatment. Rather it is an arbitrary denial of First Amendment rights which violates the very constitutional premises upon which the Freedom of Information Act was based. As President Johnson commented on signing the Act:

This legislation springs from one of our most essential principles: a democracy works best when the people have all the information that the security of the Nation permits . . . 2 Weekly Compilation of Presidential Documents 895, July 11, 1966.

Accordingly, plaintiff requests that the defendant's Motion to Dismiss Or, In The Alternative, For Summary Judgment be denied. In addition, plaintiff wishes to state that after the defendant has answered plaintiff's Second Set of Interrogatories, plaintiff will probably file a Cross Motion For Summary Judgment.

/s/_____

JAMES HIRAM LESAR
1231 Fourth St., S. W.
Washington, D. C.
Attorney for Plaintiff

CERTIFICATE OF SERVICE.

I hereby certify that service of the foregoing Opposition and its attached exhibits has been made upon the defendant by mailing a copy thereof to its attorney, Mr. Michael J. Ryan, Esquire, Assistant United States Attorney, United States Courthouse, Room 3421, Washington, D. C. 20001, on this 12th day of March, 1974.

/s/_____
JAMES HIRAM LESAR

AFFIDAVIT OF HAROLD WEISBERG.

1.   I am an author. I live at Route 8, Frederick, Maryland.
2.   For the past ten years I have devoted myself to an intensive study of political assassinations. I am author of four published books on the investigation into President Kennedy's assassination: Whitewash: The Report on the Warren Report; Whitewash II: The FBI-Secret Service Coverup; Photographic Whitewash: Suppressed Kennedy Assassination Pictures; and Oswald in New Orleans: Case For Conspiracy with the CIA. I have also written one book on the assassination of Dr. Martin Luther King: Frame-Up: The Martin Luther King-James Earl Ray Case.
3.   In the 1930's I was an investigator for and editor of the record of a subcommittee of the Senate Labor Committee. After Pearl Harbor I served in the OSS, where my primary responsibilities were as an intelligence analyst. I have also worked with the FBI and several divisions of the Department of Justice in connection with my work for the Senate Labor Committee or through my writing.
4.   As an intelligence analyst for the OSS and Senate editor and investigator, I am familiar with the handling of the transcripts of official proceedings. I have handled such transcripts myself and had them printed. I have served as a Department of Justice expert on such transcripts and testified on them in court.
5.   I am familiar with government classification procedures. During my government service I was supplied with an assortment of stamps for stamping classifications on documents, but I was never given any meaningful standards or guidelines to use in determining which classification label to apply. There was no review of any classifications I affixed to documents.

6.   Having spent thousands of hours examining the records of the Warren Commission, I am familiar with the Commission's work, including its record-keeping and filing systems.

7.   I am the plaintiff in Weisberg v. General Services Administration, Civil Action No. 2052-73, United States District Court for the District of Columbia. I have read the defendant's Motion To Dismiss Or, in the Alternative, For Summary Judgment, and the Statement of Material Facts and Memorandum of Points and Authorities in support of that motion, as well as the Affidavit and Answers to Interrogatories sworn to by Dr. James B. Rhoads, Archivist of the United States.

8.   In his affidavit Dr. Rhoads swears that: "In accordance with Executive Order, at all times since . . . the transcript of the January 27, 1964 executive session of the Warren Commission . . . has been in the custody of the National Archives . . ., it has been and continues to be classified 'Top Secret'." (Paragraph 3 of Government Exhibit 1) In his answer to interrogatory number two, Dr. Rhoads further swears that the January 27 transcript "was originally classified under the provisions of Executive Order 10501" and is presently classified under the provisions of Executive Order 11652.

9.   The inference to be drawn from Dr. Rhoads' sworn statements is that the January 27 transcript was originally and lawfully classified Top Secret pursuant to Executive Order 10501. This is false. The January 27 transcript was originally classified Top Secret by an employee of Ward & Paul, the privately-employed court reporter for the Warren Commission. Affiant believes that the wording of Dr. Rhoads' affidavit and Answers to Interrogatories was deliberately framed so as to deceive the court on this point.

10.   Before the Warren Commission hired the commercial reporting services of Ward & Paul, a private firm, the Department of Justice itself provided these services. The Department of Justice did not classify these transcripts. Nor did the National Archives classify them thereafter. Attached hereto as Exhibits A and B are the first two pages of the first Warren Commission executive session, held in the National Archives on December 5, 1963. The December 5, 1963 session was reported and transcribed by Oakie Dyer of the Office of the United States Attorney for the District of Columbia. Although the December 5 executive session discussed some questions of utmost sensitivity, no classification stamp was ever affixed to the transcript, either at the time it was transcribed or later.

11.   Attached hereto as Exhibit C is the first of a series of Ward & Paul worksheets itemizing the work which that firm did for the Warren Com-

mission. In the upper right-hand corner this sheet bears the designation "File No. PC-2." This is the designation for the Warren Commission's "housekeeping file." The sheet was prepared by Ward & Paul. As the face of Exhibit C shows, Ward & Paul stamped even its housekeeping records Top Secret.

12.   This worksheet also shows that all twenty-one entries on it are classified Top Secret. Thus, each transcript of all executive sessions held between January 21 and March 4, 1964 was classified Top Secret by Ward & Paul. As the third entry on this sheet reflects, this specifically includes the January 27, 1964 transcript whose disclosure I seek.

13.   Further evidence that the January 27 transcript was classified Top Secret by Ward & Paul as a matter of routine and without regard to content is shown by Ward & Paul Receipt No. 3013, attached hereto as Exhibit D. This receipt reflects that the January 27 transcript was delivered to the Secretary to the General Counsel for the Warren Commission, who signed for it at 9:10 a.m. on January 28, prior to a reading of it by any member or employee of the Commission and after it had been classified Top Secret by Ward & Paul.

14.   The Warren Commission disregarded the Top Secret labels which Ward & Paul routinely affixed to all the transcripts listed on this worksheet. In fact, nearly all of the Top Secret transcripts recorded on this worksheet were published by the Warren Commission itself.

15.   The Ward & Paul practice of routinely classifying all the transcripts Top Secret was not followed by Department of Justice employees who prepared and handled these transcripts. Attached hereto as Exhibit E is a letter of April 20, 1964 from Louis LaCour, then United States Attorney for the Eastern District of Louisiana, to Ward & Paul. Although the transcripts of the testimony of five of the witnesses deposed in New Orleans were forwarded with this letter, the letter bears no classification stamp. One of the transcripts which the United States Attorney forwarded to Ward & Paul contained the testimony of Julian Evans, who had been an elderly neighbor of the Oswalds when Lee Harvey Oswald was a boy. When this previously unclassified transcript of Mr. Evans' recollections of Oswald as a young kid reached Washington, Ward & Paul promptly classified it Top Secret, as shown by Exhibit F. But Exhibits G and H, the Preface and Table of Contents to Volume VIII of the Warren Commission Hearings, show that the Commission ignored Ward & Paul's Top Secret label and published Julian Evans' testimony anyway.

16.   The Ward & Paul practice of classifying all transcripts Top Secret had nothing to do with national defense or foreign policy. In fact, at a later date Ward & Paul downgraded its classifications from Top Secret to Confidential. The result of this downgrading was internal chaos: without the Top Secret stamp the Ward & Paul bureaucracy was unable to keep track of the various copies of the transcripts it prepared.

17.   The substance of the January 27, 1964 transcript is well-known. When Vice-President Ford was a congressman and member of the Warren Commission, he put his campaign manager on his payroll and had him ghost the book they co-authored, Portrait of the Assassin. Chapter One of Portrait is entirely devoted to the substance of the January 27 executive session and contains many verbatim quotes from the transcript. In this manner, parts of the transcript denied to affiant were sold to Simon & Schuster and Ballantine Books for a total of $13,000.

18.   The January 27 executive session dealt with the rumor that Lee Harvey Oswald had been an undercover agent for the FBI. Although this rumor had been withheld from the members of the Commission, it was not news when it reached them on January 27, 1964. This rumor had previously appeared in print in Texas and Pennsylvania. Indeed, both the FBI and the Secret Service had conducted investigations of it a month and a half earlier. The FBI and Secret Service reports pertaining to their investigations of this rumor were never classified or withheld. In fact, affiant has many such reports in his possession.

/s/_____

HAROLD WEISBERG

FREDERICK COUNTY, MARYLAND

Before me this_____day of March, 1974, deponent Harold Weisberg has appeared and signed this affidavit, first having sworn that the statements made therein are true.

My commission expires_____.

/s/_____

NOTARY PUBLIC IN AND FOR
FREDERICK COUNTY, MARYLAND

EXHIBIT A.

Outside Cover Sheet of December 5, 1963, Warren Commission Executive Session.

PRESIDENTIAL COMMISSION
TO INVESTIGATE THE ASSASSINATION
OF PRESIDENT KENNEDY

5 December 1963
National Archives
Washington, D. C.

Reported and Transcribed by
Oakie Dyer
Reporter
Office of the United States Attorney
Washington, D. C.

EXHIBIT B.

Inside Cover Sheet of December 5, 1963 Warren Commission Executive Session.

PRESENT:

Chief Justice Earl Warren - Chairman

Senator Richard B. Russell

Senator John Sherman Cooper

Representative Hale Boggs

Representative Gerald R. Ford

Mr. Allen W. Dulles

Mr. John J. McCloy

Mr. Nicholas deB. Katzenbach, Deputy Attorney General (Present from 10:00 AM to 11:22 AM, approximately).

PLACE:

Conference Room
National Archives
Washington, D. C.

TIME:

Approximately 10:00 AM to 12:45 PM, 5 Dec 1963

EXHIBIT C.

Ward & Paul Worksheet. January 21 - March 4, 1964.

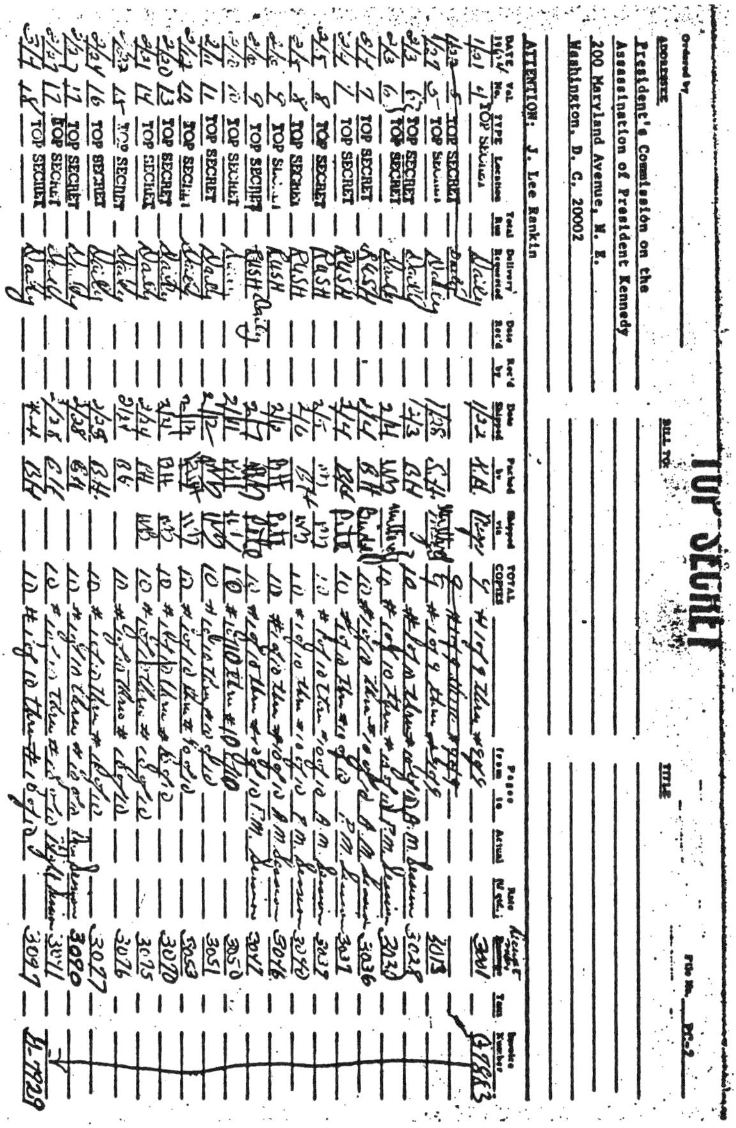

TOP SECRET

Ordered by ____ File No. PC-2

ADDRESSEE
President's Commission on the
Assassination of President Kennedy
200 Maryland Avenue, N. E.
Washington, D. C. 20002

BILL TO:

TITLE

ATTENTION: J. Lee Rankin

DATE 1964	Vol. No.	TYPE	Location	Total Run	Delivery Requested	Date Rec'd	Rec'd by	Date Shipped	Packed by	Shipped via	TOTAL COPIES	Pages from to	Actual	Rate N qtd.	Receipt Number	Tax	Invoice Number
1/21	4	TOP SECRET			Daily			1/22	K.H.		9	#1 of 9 thru #9 of 9			3001		G7883
~~1/23~~	~~5~~	~~TOP SECRET~~			~~Daily~~						~~9~~	~~#1 of 9 thru #9 of 9~~					
1/27	5	TOP SECRET			Daily			1/28	S.H.		9	#1 of 9 thru #9 of 9			3013		
2/3	6	TOP SECRET			Daily			2/3	BH		10	#1 of 10 thru #10 of 10 A.M. Session			3028		
2/3	6	TOP SECRET			Daily			2/4	WB		10	#1 of 10 thru #10 of 10 P.M. Session			3030		
2/4	7	TOP SECRET			RUSH			2/4	BH		10	#1 of 10 thru #10 of 10 A.M. Session			3036		
2/4	7	TOP SECRET			RUSH			2/4	BH	Pete	10	#1 of 10 thru #10 of 10 P.M. Session			3037		
2/5	8	TOP SECRET			RUSH			2/5			10	#1 of 10 thru #10 of 10 A.M. Session			3039		
2/5	8	TOP SECRET			RUSH			2/6	BH	WB	10	#1 of 10 thru #10 of 10 P.M. Session			3040		
2/6	9	TOP SECRET			RUSH			2/6	BH	Pete	10	#1 of 10 thru #10 of 10 A.M. Session			3046		
2/6	9	TOP SECRET			RUSH Daily			2/7		Pete	10	#1 of 10 thru #10 of 10 P.M. Session			3047		
2/10	10	TOP SECRET			Daily			2/11			10	#1 of 10 thru #10 of 10			3050		
2/11	11	TOP SECRET			Daily			2/12	WB	WB	10	#1 of 10 thru #10 of 10			3051		
2/12	12	TOP SECRET			Daily			2/17			10	#1 of 10 thru #10 of 10			3053		
2/20	13	TOP SECRET			Daily			2/21	BH	WB	10	#1 of 10 thru #10 of 10			3070		
2/21	14	TOP SECRET			Daily			2/24	BH	WB	10	#1 of 10 thru #10 of 10			3075		
2/23	15	TOP SECRET			Daily			2/24	BB		10	#1 of 10 thru #10 of 10			3076		
2/24	16	TOP SECRET			Daily			2/25	B.H.		10	#1 of 10 thru #10 of 10			3077		
2/27	17	TOP SECRET			Daily			2/28	BH		10	#1 of 10 thru #10 of 10 Day Session			3090		
2/27	17	TOP SECRET			Daily			2/28	BH		10	#1 of 10 thru #10 of 10 Night Session			3091		
3/4	18	TOP SECRET			Daily			3-4	BH		10	#1 of 10 thru #10 of 10			3097		H-7929

EXHIBIT D.

Ward & Paul Receipt No. 3013.

Receipt No. 3013

WARD & PAUL
SHORTHAND REPORTERS
917 G Street, N. W.
WASHINGTON, D. C. 20001

JESSE L. WARD, JR.   OFFICIAL REPORTERS FOR
ALMA PAUL WICK   CONGRESSIONAL COMMITTEES
WAYNE BIRDSELL

Date_____ January 28, 1964_____

Received from WARD & PAUL__NINE__copies of transcript of proceedings
before President's Commission on the Assassination of President Kennedy
in re TOP SECRET
held at Washington, D. C. on_____ January 27, 1964_____
     No. 1 of 9 thru No. 9 of 9

also, Reporter's notes, master sheets, carbon paper and waste.

To   President's Commission on the
       Assassination of President Kennedy
       200 Maryland Avenue, N. E.
       Washington, D. C. 20002   By /s/_____
                                      Released by Jesse L. Ward, Jr.
                                      1/28/64 at 9$\frac{10}{}$

EXHIBIT E.

Letter from United States Attorney Louis C. LaCour to Jesse Ward, Ward & Paul, Inc., April 20, 1964.

Registry 82328

United States Department of Justice

UNITED STATES ATTORNEY
EASTERN DISTRICT OF LOUISIANA
NEW ORLEANS XX LOUISIANA 70130

April 20, 1964

CERTIFIED MAIL
RETURN RECEIPT REQUESTED
AIR MAIL

Mr. Jesse Ward
Ward and Paul, Inc.
917 "G" Street, N. W.
Washington, D. C.

Dear Mr. Ward:

Enclosed [TS251(81)] please [TS249(79)] find the depositions [TS252(82)] of [TS250 (80)] Edward Voebel [T.S. 248(78)], Julian Evans, Charles Hall Steele, Jr., Charles Hall Steele, Sr., and Charles Murrett, taken before Mr. Albert E. Jenner of the President's Commission on the Assassination of President John F. Kennedy. Also attached is the statement of George S. Thomas Co. for the depositions taken by reporter Robert L. Lee.

I have retained in this office the carbon copies of these depositions for inspection of the witnesses or their counsel, in accordance with Mr. J. Lee Rankin's letter of April 3, 1964.

Sincerely,
/s/
LOUIS C. LaCOUR
United States Attorney

LCL/ab
Encl.

EXHIBIT F.

Ward & Paul Receipt No. 3237. April 22, 1964.

Receipt No. 3237
T. S. 249 (79)

WARD & PAUL
SHORTHAND REPORTERS
917 G STREET, N. W.
WASHINGTON, D. C. 20001

JESSE L. WARD, JR.   OFFICIAL REPORTERS FOR
ALMA PAUL WICK   CONGRESSIONAL COMMITTEES
WAYNE BIRDSELL

Date _____ April 22, 1964 _____

Received from WARD & PAUL ___8___ copies of transcript of proceedings
before President's Commission on the Assassination of President Kennedy
in re TOP SECRET — Deposition of: Julian Evans
held at W̶a̶s̶h̶i̶n̶g̶t̶o̶n̶,̶ ̶D̶.̶C̶. New Orleans on _____ April 7, 1964
copies No. 1 of 8 thru No. 8 of 8
Herewith original copy from which copies were made Pages 1 thru 30

To   President's Commission on the
      Assassination of President Kennedy
      200 Maryland Avenue, N. E.
      Washington, D. C. 20002 _____ By /s/ _____

                                Released by /s/ _____

                                Date 4/24/64 Time_____

EXHIBIT G.

Preface to Warren Commission Volume VIII.

Preface

The testimony of the following witnesses is contained in volume VIII: Edward Voebel, William E. Wulf, Bennierita Smith, Frederick S. O'Sullivan, Mildred Sawyer, Anne Boudreaux, Viola Peterman, Myrtle Evans, Julian Evans, Philip Eugene Vinson, and Hiram Conway, who were associated with Lee Harvey Oswald in his youth; Lillian Murret, Marilyn Dorothea Murret, Charles Murret, John M. Murret, and Edward John Pic, Jr., who were related to Oswald; John Carro, Dr. Renatus Hartogs and Evelyn Grace Strickman Siegel, who came into contact with Oswald while he was in New York during his youth; Nelson Delgado, Daniel Patrick Powers, John E. Donovan, Lt. Col. A. G. Folsom, Jr., Capt. George Donabedian, James Anthony Botelbo, Donald Peter Camarata, Peter Francis Connor, Allen D. Graf, John Rene Heindel, David Christie Murray, Jr., Paul Edward Murphy, Henry J. Roussel, Jr., Mack Osborne, Richard Dennis Call, and Erwin Donald Lewis, who testified regarding Oswald's service in the Marine Corps; Martin Isaacs and Pauline Virginia Bates, who saw Oswald when he returned from Russia; and Max E. Clark, George A. Bouhe, Anna N. Meller, Elena A. Hall, John Raymond Hall, Mrs. Frank H. Ray (Valentina); and Mr. and Mrs. Igor Vladimir Voshinin, who became acquainted with Oswald and/or his wife after their return to Texas in 1962.

EXHIBIT H.

Contents to Warren Commission Volume VIII.

Contents

EXHIBIT I.

Chapter One of Portrait of the Assassin.

PORTRAIT
OF THE
ASSASSIN

BY

GERALD R. FORD
AND
JOHN R. STILES

SIMON AND SCHUSTER · NEW YORK

FIRST PRINTING

LIBRARY OF CONGRESS CATALOG CARD NUMBER: 65-18886
MANUFACTURED IN THE UNITED STATES OF AMERICA
BY H. WOLFF BOOK MFG. CO., NEW YORK
DESIGNED BY EVE METZ

CHAPTER I

THE COMMISSION

GETS ITS FIRST SHOCK

NO SOONER had the Commission investigating President Kennedy's assassination assembled its staff and tentatively outlined methods of operation than it was plunged into an astounding problem. On Wednesday, January 22, the members of the Commission were hurriedly called into emergency session by the chairman. Mr. J. Lee Rankin, newly appointed General Counsel for the Commission, had received a telephone call from Texas. The caller was Mr. Waggoner Carr, the Attorney General of Texas. The information was that the FBI had an "undercover agent" and that that agent was none other than Lee Harvey Oswald, the alleged assassin of President Kennedy!

Prior to that day the newspapers had carried an inconspicuous article or two speculating on whether Oswald could have been an agent of any United States Government agency. Mrs. Marguerite Oswald had made statements that she thought her son must have been tied in with the CIA or the State Department. But now the alarm had been sounded by a high official; and the Dallas prosecutor, Mr. Henry Wade, who had also reported the rumor, was himself a former FBI man.

Individual members of the Commission got their first inkling of the seriousness of Carr's report when they met in emergency session late in the afternoon of the twenty-second of January. Each had received an urgent message to come at 5:30 P.M. to the Commission's offices in the Veterans of Foreign Wars Building. My secretary had contacted me immediately. I happened to be in a subcommittee hearing in connection with my normal duties on military appropriations. The other members of the Commission—Chief Justice Earl Warren, Senators Richard B. Russell and John Sherman Cooper, Congressman Hale Boggs, John J. McCloy and Allen W. Dulles—were going about their busy schedules.

On the arrival of the members, each took his place around the (p.14) eight-foot oblong table. The late hour and the complete disruption of everyone's personal plans added to the atmosphere of tension. I was already overdue to leave the office, go home, change to evening clothes and attend the dedication of the new Museum of History and Technology. The Chief Justice had the same problem. He was the scheduled speaker at this important event.

J. Lee Rankin, General Counsel of the Commission, then reported the startling allegations to the members. They looked at one another in amazement.

The session that followed lasted until after seven. I cannot recall attending a meeting more tense and hushed.

The Commission made the decision to ask the Texas Attorney General, District Attorney Wade and any other Dallas officials who had knowledge of these allegations to come at once to Washington and secretly present what they had heard. There should be absolutely no publicity.

PORTRAIT OF THE ASSASSIN

The Texas officials slipped into the nation's capital with complete anonymity. They met with Lee Rankin and other members of the staff and told what they knew. The information was that Lee Oswald was actually hired by the FBI; that he was assigned the undercover-agent number 179; that he was on the FBI payroll at two hundred dollars a month starting in September 1962 and that he was still on their payroll the day he was apprehended in the Texas Theatre after having gunned down Officer J. D. Tippit! The officials returned to Dallas after their visit on Friday, January 24. Their presence in Washington was unknown to the press or the public.

Meantime, a story broke over the weekend in The New York Times. The Times had got wind of part of the speculation that Oswald was an agent and point-blank asked the FBI if it was true. The FBI denied any possible connection with Oswald.

Then Harold Feldman's article in The Nation magazine hit the newsstands at the moment the Dallas officials were consulting with the Commission on Friday. No one could have known the consternation among the Texas officials and the President's Commission, but Mr. Feldman had laid down four pages of hard-to-answer questions in his article, "Oswald and the FBI," in the January 27, 1964, issue. Fortunately, the public did not know how serious the matter appeared to be at the moment. Although the speculations in Feldman's article were enough to arouse a good deal of public interest, the (p. 15) theories had no official basis and they did not create the panic they might have if it had been known that even the Attorney General of Texas was afraid that some of them might have a basis in fact. The Commission itself had no grounds at the moment for rejecting or accepting. Members simply knew that the whole business was a most delicate and sensitive matter involving the nation's faith in its own institutions and one of the most respected federal agencies. Harold Feldman set forth a formidable sequence of circumstantial evidence pointing to the same things the Attorney General and Mr. Wade had brought up in telephone conversations with Lee Rankin. His speculations were elaborate.

Feldman began his hypothesis with the observation that the day after the assassination the Dallas chief of police had stated on television that the FBI had interviewed Oswald about a week earlier and had failed to inform the Dallas authorities of the fact. If this was true—that the FBI had interviewed Oswald a week before the shooting—why would they have failed to let the agencies in charge of the President's security know that this dangerous man was near Dallas?

"In Washington the FBI denied they had interrogated Oswald recently," Feldman said.

Oswald had taken a mysterious trip to Mexico City in October and had returned on the third of that month. Feldman pointed out that William M. Kline, chief of the U. S. Customs Bureau investigative services in Laredo, Texas, stated on November 25 that Oswald's movements when he went to Mexico were watched at the request of a "federal agency at Washington."

The Commission Gets Its First Shock

It was very apparent that the FBI knew a good deal about this former defector Lee Harvey Oswald. How could they be keeping such close tabs on him and still overlook the fact that he was working in the Texas School Book Depository Building, directly on the route of the President's motorcade?

Feldman went on to gather more of the published material that made the circumstances curious. He cited an article by one Joe Golden in the Philadelphia Inquirer of December 8, 1963, two weeks after Kennedy's death, that flatly stated:

"The FBI attempt to recruit Oswald as an informant, an informed law enforcement official said, was made in September, just after he had moved to Dallas from New Orleans.

(p. 16) "Oswald's mother said an 'agent named Hosty' came to the Irving house and talked to the young man at length in his car.

"An FBI agent named Joseph Hosty handles investigations of subversives for the Dallas field office.

"The source said he did not know if the FBI succeeded in hiring Oswald; and the federal agency would not discuss the matter."

In addition to the above article by reporter Golden, Harold Feldman cited another important story. It was an article written by Lonnie Hudkins in the Houston Post on January 1, 1964, "Oswald Rumored as Informant for U.S." There was indeed an agent Hosty in Dallas, and Hudkins alleged that Oswald knew him. William Alexander, an assistant prosecutor to Henry Wade, apparently affirmed this, because he stated that during the interrogation of Oswald which he attended after the assassination it had been brought out that in his address book Oswald had both the phone number of Hosty's office and the license number of his car. Why? In Hudkin's article he quoted Wade as commenting on the possibility of Oswald's connection with the FBI, "It may be true, but I don't think it will ever be made public."

Seeming to justify this point of view, Feldman pointed out that the FBI had asked witnesses not to talk to reporters about evidence they might have given that agency. In many cases witnesses later contacted by reporters did refuse to talk and, when asked why, were reputed to have said, "Well, the FBI told me to keep my mouth shut."

Shortly after the assassination a story gained currency in Dallas that Oswald had lived well for a man who couldn't hold a job. He was reputed to have had money to spend on projects his salary couldn't justify. Then a story was printed that the Western Union office had received small but regular money orders from an unrevealed source for Lee Harvey Oswald. Could this be the FBI's way of paying him off for his reputed "undercover" work? Reporters who tried to run this down collided with a brick wall. Western Union refused to make any of its records public—this could be done only by an order from Washington. Again, had the FBI told Western Union to bottle up the truth? Whom were they trying to protect if not themselves?

PORTRAIT OF THE ASSASSIN

Despite the fact the FBI allegedly told witnesses to clam up and (p. 17) that they refused information to reporters, major news leaks were deliberately let out not by the FBI but by even higher federal authorities. It was as if they first opened the hatch to let out a puff of smoke and then suddenly slapped it down again. Two examples of this Feldman found tantalizing. It was said that Marina Oswald knew her husband kept a rifle in the Paine garage and that she noted it was missing the morning of the assassination. Then this was denied. Next the story was allowed to leak out that Marina knew Oswald had taken a "pot shot" at Major General Edwin A. Walker; the FBI was even said to have a document in Oswald's own handwriting admitting it. This information could only have come from some official source, but when reporters asked to see the document the matter was quickly cloaked in mystery and the FBI wasn't talking.

On the subject of the Walker shooting and the Kennedy assassination, had the authorities wanted to give the impression that the same gun was used in both cases? Feldman pointed out in this instance what would seem to be an inconsistency. The "experts" had said at the time the general was shot at that the bullet dug out of the wall had been fired from a .30-06 rifle. The rifle found in the Texas School Book Depository, after considerable contradiction, was reputed to be a 6.5 millimeter gun, equivalent to about .270 caliber. Someone had his "facts" mixed up or again there was a deliberate effort to confound the truth.

Going deeper into the subject of Oswald's income and the freewheeling way he seemed to spend money, he was supposed to have earned eighty rubles a month while he was in Russia. According to authorities, this would be a bare subsistence level, and still he was able to raise the cash to come back to America in 1962 with a wife and child. A single passage from Moscow would be expensive enough; somehow he managed to pay the boat fare for three and then fly from New York to Fort Worth.

And what about the $1,500 he was reputed to have put aside during his enlistment in the Marine Corps? It was this money he was supposed to have used to pay for his trip to Helsinki when he defected to the Communists. This was, to be sure, a substantial savings for an ordinary soldier, and one shouldn't overlook the possibility that he was subsidized in some way by the Soviets, or perhaps by the CIA and the FBI working together to plant an observer in Russia. There had been a fair number of American GIs who had "defected" (p. 18) to Russia. Likewise, some Russian defectors to the United States were suspected of posing as defectors in order to gain inside positions in this country. Turn about is fair play, and it would be hard to devise a more logical way to put a man behind the Iron Curtain.

Feldman pointed out that Oswald paid Miss Pauline Bates, a public stenographer, to type parts of a manuscript he was writing about his experiences in the Soviet Union. This was money he could ill afford to spend. He "hinted he had gone to the Soviet as a U.S. Secret Agent." Furthermore, he

The Commission Gets Its First Shock

was alleged to have told her, "When the State Department granted my visa, they stipulated they could not stand behind me in any way," which could imply that they knew he was taking a desperate chance acting as an agent and would have to repudiate him if he was caught.

His activities in the Fair Play for Cuba Committee must have been costly. He was rumored to have rented at his own expense an office for thirty dollars a month; he arranged to have leaflets printed and recruited helpers to distribute them; and when he was arrested he promptly came up with payment of his fine. These activities did not sound like the work of a "loner."

The police were said to have found $150 in his room when he was arrested for the shooting of Officer Tippit. Some time previously he had purchased a rifle with a telescopic sight and a revolver and had supposedly spent other money on rifle-range practice and bore sighting of the weapon. Practice rifle shooting is not inexpensive.

And where did he get the money for a quick trip to Mexico City? His meanderings around the world sounded more like the journeys of a well-heeled globetrotter than the restricted life of a sometimes employed laborer without a skill. It was said that if he had obtained a visa from the Cuban Embassy in Mexico City he intended to junket over to Havana and then perhaps on to Moscow once more for a little sight-seeing. This was almost too much to believe. Pravda had recently explained it by stating that without a doubt Oswald had been an American spy from the beginning. Again there was the possibility he could have been a CIA agent, perhaps trained by the FBI, and upon returning to the USA was used to penetrate such groups as the Fair Play for Cuba Committee. With his background as a defector, he could have made a perfect counteragent to spy on Castro's supporters.

Feldman recalled that on November 30 the Dallas Times Herald (p. 19) had carried this Associated Press dispatch—again the allegation that Oswald had received money via Western Union: "Someone telegraphed small amounts of money to Lee Harvey Oswald for several months before the assassination of President Kennedy, it was reported today. The unidentified sender telegraphed Oswald $10 to $20 at a time."

The writer of "Oswald and the FBI," after examining some of the threads in the web, stated what every American would agree to: "The Warren Commission should, if possible, tell us how President Kennedy was killed, who killed him, and why. But beyond that it must tell us if the FBI or any other government intelligence agency was in any way connected with the alleged assassin, Lee Harvey Oswald." The same day on which the Commission was confronted with this challenge by Attorney General Carr, Feldman summed up the impressions of most laymen with the observation, "At this moment the possibility of such associations in the young man's life is intolerably a subject for speculation."

Discussions among members of the Commission on Monday, January 27, indicated they couldn't agree more—but just how to go about uncovering the facts was not an easy matter.

PORTRAIT OF THE ASSASSIN

Because of the background of Mr. Allen Dulles, other members turned to him for suggestions on how best to handle this touchy matter. What were they to do with a story like this?

"This is a terribly hard thing to disprove," he told the others.

"Let's take a specific case," Representative Hale Boggs suggested. "That fellow Powers was one of your men."

"Oh yes, but he was not an agent. He was an employee."

"There was no problem in proving he was employed by the CIA?"

"No, we had a signed contract."

In the case of the U-2 incident and Powers, he was not an undercover agent, as Mr. Dulles pointed out. The problem was far more difficult with a true undercover agent, where there is nothing in writing.

Mr. Boggs observed with some uneasiness, "What you do is to make out a problem, if this be true—make our problem utterly impossible, because you say this rumor can't be dissipated under any circumstance."

These observations by Allen Dulles pinpointed the difficulty the (p. 20) Commission would face in dealing not only with the possibility that Oswald might be an FBI agent but also with all the myriad rumors that the imaginations of thousands of writers would create in the next thousand years. They dramatized the complexity of the Commission's charge. A free society must have some secret agencies to defend itself against the deception of its potential enemies. On the other hand, secrecy is the enemy of truth, and the Commission was appointed by the President of the United States to find out all the circumstances surrounding the assassination of President Kennedy.

Mr. Rankin, chief counsel for the Commission, explained why Dallas' District Attorney Wade was so troubled. Wade had told Rankin about his wartime experiences as a former FBI man.

"He did say he had considerable experience with the FBI and knew their practices, that he handled as much as $2,000 a month during the war period in which he paid off informers and undercover agents in South America, and he knew that it wasn't revealed on any records he ever handled who he was paying it to and he never got any receipts, and it wasn't the practice to get receipts; that he would have a list of numbers in his office—that was one of the most closely guarded records that he had—and he would put down the amount he paid off.

"He was frank, however, about stating that he didn't know whether that practice continued; he didn't know how they were doing it; that was a long time ago and how the FBI would handle any such transaction now, he didn't know.

"He thought that the postal box was an ideal way to handle such transactions and was a way he had used at various times in the past too.

"He didn't indicate that he was sure this was the case at all. He just indicated that it was a possibility, and some of the things that happened he thought were curious."

The Commission Gets Its First Shock

In mentioning the use of postal boxes, Wade was thinking of the habit Oswald had of using these blind addresses wherever he went—again, why?

The dilemma of the Commission was how to go about checking the allegation that the FBI was involved in this matter. For more than thirty years the FBI had been one of the most highly respected agencies of the United States Government. Not that the members of the Commission would be awed by the prestige of the bureau or of (p. 21) its almost legendary director, J. Edgar Hoover, but certainly it would not be justified in plunging into the matter in some irresponsible manner that might jeopardize the effectiveness of an important agency's future operations.

The President's order creating the Commission implicitly authorized it to look into the security policies of the Secret Service. Every intelligence agency of the Government also had to be scrutinized. The Commission would have to devise an approach that was independent of all these agencies, and yet obviously the President's Commission could not create a "scientific crime bureau" of its own just for the purpose of this inquiry. They would need trained men from the CIA, the Secret Service, local police and certainly the FBI. They would need fingerprint experts, ballistics experts, handwriting analysts and dozens of other professional helpers. Thus the matter of determining at the outset how to handle the rumor that Oswald was connected with the FBI was a test of the ability of the Commission to execute its mission. Its members approached this challenge carefully. Senator Russell asked chief counsel Lee Rankin, "What steps, if any, have we taken to clear up this matter, Mr. Rankin, if it can be cleared up, to determine whether there is anything to this or not?"

Mr. Rankin: "Well, we have discussed various possibilities—that is, the Chief Justice and myself have—and I want to tell you about them, and I think you will have to instruct us what you want us to do.

"We thought, first, about approaching the Department with a request that the Attorney General inform us as to the situation, not only as to what he would say about whether Oswald was or was not an undercover agent, but also with the supporting data that the Commission could rely upon.

"I suggested the possibility for the Commission to consider that I should go over and see Edgar Hoover myself and tell him this problem and that he should have as much interest as the Commission in trying to put an end to any such speculations, not only by his statement, which I would be frank to tell him I would think would not be sufficient, but also if it was possible to demonstrate by whatever records and materials they have that it just couldn't be true, and see if we couldn't get his cooperation to present that with the understanding that the Commission—and stated understanding, at the time—the Commission would have to feel free to make such other inves- (p. 22) tigation and take testimony if it found it necessary, in order to satisfy the American people that this question of an undercover agent was out of the picture."

PORTRAIT OF THE ASSASSIN

Representative Boggs asked, "What other alternatives are there?"

Mr. Rankin replied, "Well, the other alternative would be to examine Hudkins, the reporter. Also to examine Hosty, the FBI agent who was working in that area, and to examine the Special Agent in charge of the area, and to examine Mr. Hoover, under oath, right up the line.

"We do have a dirty rumor that is very bad for the Commission, the problem, and it is very damaging to the agencies that are involved in it and it must be wiped out insofar as it is possible to do so by this Commission.

"So it seemed to me in light of the way I would treat it, if I were in their position, would be to have someone approach me, tell me the problem and see what I frankly could do to clear my skirts, if there was a way to do it, and as long as the Commission didn't agree not to go further, if they felt that would not satisfy them, I don't see how the Commission would be prejudiced."

Chairman Warren: "Well, Lee and I both agreed that we shouldn't leave this thing in this present posture, that we should go ahead and try to clear the matter up as best we can.

"Now, my own suggestion was to Lee that we find out first from these people as far as we can if there is any substance to it or whether it is just plain rumor.

"It may be that Hudkins would claim privilege. If he did, I thought that after we tried to get him to see that it was in the interest of his country to state the facts that we might go to the publisher of his paper and see if we couldn't get—enlist him to have this man tell us where he got his information.

"Lee, on the other hand, felt it would be the better part of cooperation to go over and see Mr. Hoover and tell him frankly what the rumor was, state that it is pure rumor—we haven't evaluated the facts—but ask him, first, if it is true, and secondly if he can supply us with information to establish that these facts are not true, and they are inconsistent with what would be the way of operation of their bureau."

Mr. McCloy observed, "If we got a statement from the Department that the Attorney General and perhaps from Mr. Hoover, or (p. 23) from Mr. Hoover himself, which said, 'I am telling you that this man was not in any way employed by the FBI,' or in the case of John McCloy or the CIA, I think that probably stops us, unless we run into something . . ."

Mr. Rankin: "Allen, how would you feel about it, if you were head of the CIA now, and the same claim was made and this Commission was worried about the claim being believed by the public, and they would ask you, would you want the Commission to come to you directly?"

Mr. Dulles: "Oh, yes, certainly I would."

Mr. Rankin: "Or would you want us to go out and examine witnesses first?"

Mr. Dulles: "I think I would want you to come so I could give you leads as to how you could examine witnesses if you wanted to."

The Commission Gets Its First Shock

Mr. Rankin: "If you had us out examining witnesses about whether you had the man in your employ, would you feel that we were not very fair to you?"

Mr. Dulles: "No. I don't think I would."

Mr. Rankin: "That wouldn't bother you."

Mr. Dulles: "No."

Senator Russell: "There is no man in the employ of the Federal Government who stands higher in the opinion of the American people than J. Edgar Hoover."

Mr. Dulles: "That is right."

Senator Russell: "Of course, we can get an affidavit from Mr. Hoover and put it in this record and go on and act on that, but if we didn't go any further than that, and we don't pursue it down to Hudkins or whoever it is, there still would be thousands of doubting Thomases who would believe this man was an FBI agent and you just didn't try to clear it up and you just took Hoover's word.

"Personally, I would believe J. Edgar Hoover. I have a great deal of confidence in him."

Mr. Dulles: "I do, too."

Senator Russell: "But the other people—I would believe, a simple statement as Holy Writ, this one statement without being under oath, but you can't try cases that way, and you can't base the conclusions of this Commission on that kind of material."

Senator Cooper: "I would like to have your idea about what I suggested."

(p. 24) Mr. McCloy: "State it again."

Senator Cooper: "We know these people have been here, so this speculation or rumor is somewhat official—we will not say it has their approval, but they don't disapprove it."

Mr. McCloy: "They have taken cognizance of it."

Senator Cooper: "That being true, since we are under a duty to see what Hudkins says about it, where he got that information, my suggestion was we do that but apprise Mr. Hoover about the facts—where this information comes from, that we have to inquire into it, that we will inquire into it, and then later talk to him further about it and see if there are any facts which he ought to know about, and it would be a matter of justice to him instead of having him disprove it from the beginning."

Mr. McCloy: "What is your objection, John, to going to Hoover or the Department of Justice, or the CIA, John McCone, or Under Secretary of Defense—he has an intelligence unit too—ask them if they can give us any information which would prove or disprove this rumor?"

Senator Cooper: "I haven't got any objection to it, but even if—if we are dealing with the FBI now—if Mr. Hoover makes his statement, I think still by reason of the fact you have heard these people and they have said that Hudkins does have some information about the truth of it, whether it is so or not, you still are under a duty to examine them."

PORTRAIT OF THE ASSASSIN

Chairman Warren: "We must go into this thing from both ends, from the end of the rumormongers and from the end of the FBI, and if we come into a cul de sac—well, there we are, but we can report on it.

"Now that is the way it would appeal to me. These are things where people can reasonably disagree. Whatever you want to do I am willing to approach it in that manner."

Mr. Rankin: "Would it be acceptable to go ahead and find out what we could about these—"

Mr. McCloy: "Hudkins' sources."

Mr. Rankin: "Then if he [J. Edgar Hoover] reacts and says, 'I want to show you that it couldn't be,' or something like that, beforehand, what about that kind of an approach?"

Chairman Warren: "Well, Lee, I wouldn't be in favor of going to any agency and saying, 'We would like to do this.' I think we ought (p. 25) to know what we are going to do, and do it, and take our chances one way or the other.

"I don't believe we should apologize or make it look that we are in any way reticent about making any investigation that comes to the Commission."

Mr. Rankin: "I don't think the country is going to be satisfied with the mere statement from, not to use Mr. Hoover's name, but just examine about any intelligence agency that Oswald wasn't hired, in light of this kind of an accusation, a rumor.

"I think that the country is going to expect this Commission to try to find out the facts as to how those things are handled to such an extent that this Commission can fairly say, 'In our opinion, he was or was not an employee of any intelligence agency of the United States.' "

It was the consensus of all seven men that the only way to proceed was to conduct extensive and thorough hearings of as many witnesses as was necessary to exhaust not just this rumor but dozens of other rumors. Where doubts were cast on any United States agency, independent experts would be hired and the investigation conducted in such a way as to avoid reliance on a questioned authority. No matter what the cost in time or money, every facet of the events in Dallas had to be explored. The Commission drew up an exhaustive list of witnesses and collected for analysis all pertinent books and magazines and newspaper articles. The staff compiled a directory of names of all persons said to have had any part in the matter. Then began months of hearings, hours of taking sworn testimony, which led from one skein of facts to another. Seldom has a crime appeared to be more complicated and mysterious. Never has a crime been so thoroughly investigated. From that investigation comes this biography of an assassin.

EXHIBIT J.

Executive Order No. 11130. November 29, 1963.

IMMEDIATE RELEASE   NOVEMBER 30, 1963
               Office of the White House Press Secretary

                              THE WHITE HOUSE
                              EXECUTIVE ORDER
                              NO. 11130

         APPOINTING A COMMISSION TO REPORT UPON THE
         ASSASSINATION OF PRESIDENT JOHN F. KENNEDY

         Pursuant to the authority vested in me as President of the United States,
I hereby appoint a Commission to ascertain, evaluate and report upon the
facts relating to the assassination of the late President John F. Kennedy and
the subsequent violent death of the man charged with the assassination. The
Commission shall consist of—
         The Chief Justice of the United States, Chairman;
         Senator Richard B. Russell;
         Senator John Sherman Cooper;
         Congressman Hale Boggs;
         Congressman Gerald R. Ford;
         The Honorable Allen W. Dulles;
         The Honorable John J. McCloy.
         The purposes of the Commission are to examine the evidence developed
by the Federal Bureau of Investigation and any additional evidence that may
hereafter come to light or be uncovered by federal or state authorities; to
make such further investigation as the Commission finds desirable; to evaluate
all the facts and circumstances surrounding such assassination, including the
subsequent violent death of the man charged with the assassination, and to
report to me its findings and conclusions.
         The Commission is empowered to prescribe its own procedures and to
employ such assistants as it deems necessary.
         Necessary expenses of the Commission may be paid from the "Emer-
gency Fund for the President".
         All Executive departments and agencies are directed to furnish the
Commission with such facilities, services and cooperation as it may request
from time to time.

                              LYNDON B. JOHNSON
THE WHITE HOUSE
November 29, 1963.

12.
DEFENDANT'S OPPOSITION TO PLAINTIFF'S MOTION TO STRIKE THE AFFIDAVIT OF DR. JAMES B. RHOADS

By this action brought under the Freedom of Information Act, 5 U.S.C. 522, plaintiff seeks to compel disclosure of the transcript of the January 27, 1964 executive session of the Warren Commission. Defendant has filed a motion to dismiss or, in the alternative, for summary judgment which is supported by the affidavit of Dr. James B. Rhoads, Archivist of the United States. In that affidavit, Dr. Rhoads testifies that the transcript in question, during the entire time of its custody by GSA, has been and continues to be classified "Top Secret" pursuant to Executive Order. Plaintiff has now moved to strike Dr. Rhoads' affidavit for non-compliance with Rule 56(e) on the alleged grounds that the affidavit was not made on personal knowledge, does not set forth such facts as would be admissible in evidence, and does not show affirmatively that Dr. Rhoads is competent to testify to the matters stated in the affidavit. Defendant submits that plaintiff's motion is wholly without merit and should be denied.

Initially, defendant notes that Dr. Rhoads' affidavit is not a pleading or part of a pleading and does not contain an insufficient defense, or any redundant, immaterial, impertinent or scandalous matter within the purview of Rule 12(f), Federal Rules of Civil Procedure. Further, as Dr. Rhoads testifies in his affidavit, he is the Archivist of the United States, National Archives and Records Service, General Services Administration, and has held that position at all times relevant to the circumstances of the complaint. Thus, he is particularly competent to testify with respect to the status of documents in the

---

Filed: March 20, 1974.

custody of the National Archives and Records Service, for which he serves as the head agency official. Furthermore, it is beyond peradventure that Dr. Rhoads is in a position to have personal knowledge of the status of documents under his control and his affidavit clearly reflects that he has familiarized himself with plaintiff's allegations and that he has personal knowledge of the status of the transcript which plaintiff seeks. Plaintiff is particularly not in a position to deny that Dr. Rhoads has personal knowledge regarding that transcript, and an affidavit may not be controverted by such representations in a legal memorandum. Sardo v. McGrath, 90 U.S. App.D.C. 195, 198, 196 F.2d 20, 23 (1952). Moreover, Dr. Rhoads' personal knowledge of the classification of the documents clearly does not depend upon his own ability to classify the document, nor should the sufficiency of his affidavit depend upon an involved recitation of how his personal knowledge was acquired. In a Freedom of Information Act matter, where it is disclosure of the document itself which is sought, defendant submits that it is not practicable to attach copies of the document to the affidavit.

As the Supreme Court held in Environmental Protection Agency v. Mink, 410 U.S. 73 (1973), the Freedom of Information Act did not intend to permit judicial review of the soundness of executive security classifications, and the only matter to be determined is whether the document sought has been classified pursuant to Executive Order. 410 U.S. at 81. See also Wolfe v. Froehlke, 358 F. Supp. 1318 (D.D.C. 1973). Vaughn v. Rosen, 484 F.2d 820 (1973), alluded to by plaintiff in his legal memorandum, dealt with different Freedom of Information Act issues and is clearly inapplicable to the First Exemption under the Act.

Conclusion

For the foregoing reasons, defendant respectfully requests the Court to deny plaintiff's motion to strike the affidavit of Dr. James B. Rhoads.

/s/ _____

EARL J. SILBERT
United States Attorney

/s/ _____

ARNOLD T. AIKENS
Assistant United States Attorney

/s/
_____

MICHAEL J. RYAN
Assistant United States Attorney

CERTIFICATE OF SERVICE.

I HEREBY CERTIFY that service of the foregoing Defendant's Opposition to Plaintiff's Motion To Strike The Affidavit Of Dr. James B. Rhoads and proposed Order has been made upon plaintiff by mailing a copy thereof to his attorney, James H. Lesar, Esquire, 1231 Fourth Street, S. W., Washington, D. C. 20024, on this 20th day of March, 1974.

/s/
_____

MICHAEL J. RYAN
Assistant United States Attorney
U. S. Courthouse
Room 3421
Washington, D. C. 20001
426-7375

ORDER.

Upon consideration of plaintiff's motion to strike the affidavit of Dr. James B. Rhoads, defendant's opposition thereto, and the entire record herein, it is by the Court this_____day of_____, 1974,

ORDERED that plaintiff's motion be and the same hereby is denied.

_____
UNITED STATES DISTRICT JUDGE

13.
ANSWERS TO INTERROGATORIES

JAMES B. RHOADS, Archivist of the United States, National Archives and Records Service, General Services Administration, Eighth and Pennsylvania Avenue, N.W., Washington, D.C., having been first duly sworn, under oath, deposes and says that it is upon his personal knowledge and belief that he gives the following information in answer to interrogatories propounded by Plaintiff:

22.   Yes.

23.   Top Secret. The National Archives contains a copy of the letter from J. Lee Rankin, General Counsel of the Warren Commission, ordering the firm which transcribed the executive sessions of the Commission to classify all such transcripts, "Top Secret."

24.   The above-mentioned letter is dated May 1, 1964.

25.   Based only on the above-mentioned letter, it is my assumption that Mr. Rankin, General Counsel of the Warren Commission, classified the transcript.

26.   I do not know.

27.   The transcript was not subject to declassification or reclassification because of the issuance of Executive Order 11652. Its classification under Executive Order 10501 automatically carried over upon the effective date of Executive Order 11652, i.e., June 1, 1972.

28.   Not applicable (N/A) in light of answer to No. 27.

29.   N/A

Filed: April 1, 1974.   Deposer's initials   _/s/_____

30.   The Central Intelligence Agency examined the transcript in 1967 and again in December 1972. The Department of Justice examined the transcript in 1967-68 and again in 1972.

31.   Arthur Dooley, title and position unknown, examined the transcript for the CIA. Martin Richman, Fredericka Pass and Mary Eastwood, acting in behalf of the FBI, examined the transcript for the Department of Justice. Each identified himself or herself as an attorney in Justice's Office of Legal Counsel.

32.   I do not know.

33.   No. Each was held out as possessing such a security clearance.

34.   No. It is not subject to the General Declassification Schedule.

35.   Because the transcript was not originally classified under the provisions of Executive Order 11652, there is no requirement that one of that Order's exemptions from the General Declassifications Schedule appear on its face. The transcript is presently undergoing a mandatory classification review. Should it remain classified after the completion of the review, one of these exemptions is required to appear on the face of the document as the basis for its continuing classification.

36.   The transcript contains eighty-six pages, each of which is classified "Top Secret."

37.   Defendant objects to this interrogatory on the grounds that it is not relevant to the subject matter involved in the instant action.

38.   Defendant objects to this interrogatory on the grounds that it is not relevant to the subject matter involved in the instant action.

39.   Defendant objects to this interrogatory on the grounds that it is not relevant to the subject matter of the instant action.

40.   No.

41.   The transcript was classified under the provisions of Executive Order 10501, and, as was stated in No. 27, was not reclassified under the provisions of Executive Order 11652. I do not know the basis for classification relied upon by the classifier in 1964, other than the provisions of Executive Order 10501.

42.   Section 798 of title 18, United States Code.

43.   Defendant objects to this interrogatory on the grounds that it is not relevant to the subject matter of the instant action.

44.   Defendant objects to this interrogatory on the grounds that it is not relevant to the subject matter of the instant action. Moreover, the

Deposer's initials   /s/

interrogatory calls for a conclusion that I am not qualified to provide.

    45.   N/A

    46.   Defendant objects to this interrogatory on the grounds that it is not relevant to the subject matter of the instant action. Moreover, the interrogatory calls for a conclusion that I am not qualified to provide.

I have read the answers above, and they are true and complete to the best of my knowledge and belief.

/s/ _____

JAMES B. RHOADS

Archivist of the United States

Subscribed and sworn to before me at Eighth and Pennsylvania Avenue, N.W., Washington, D.C., on this 22nd day of March, 1974.

/s/ _____

    (Notary Public)

My commission expires: August 14, 1974

14.
OBJECTIONS TO INTERROGATORIES

Defendant, through its attorney, the United States Attorney for the District of Columbia, and pursuant to Rule 33, Federal Rules of Civil Procedure, hereby notes its objections to plaintiff's second set of interrogatories as set forth in defendant's Answers to Interrogatories filed herewith.

/s/_____
EARL J. SILBERT
United States Attorney

/s/_____
ARNOLD T. AIKENS
Assistant United States Attorney

/s/_____
MICHAEL J. RYAN
Assistant United States Attorney

Filed: April 1, 1974.

CERTIFICATE OF SERVICE.

I HEREBY CERTIFY that service of the foregoing Answers to Interrogatories and Objections to Interrogatories was made upon plaintiff by mailing a copy thereof to his attorney, James H. Lesar, Esq., 1231 Fourth Street, S. W., Washington, D. C. 20024 on this 1st day of April, 1974.

/s/ _____

MICHAEL J. RYAN
Assistant United States Attorney
U. S. District Courthouse
Room 3421
Washington, D. C. 20001
Telephone: 426-7375

15.
MEMORANDUM AND ORDER

Plaintiff brought this action under the Freedom of Information Act, 5 U.S.C. § 552, seeking disclosure of the transcript of the January 27, 1964, executive session of the Warren Commission, which is presently in the custody of the United States General Services Administration and its National Archives and Records Service. Defendant G.S.A. has moved for dismissal or summary judgment on the ground, inter alia, that the transcript is exempted from disclosure as a document "specifically required by Executive Order to be kept secret in the interest of the national defense or foreign policy." 5 U.S.C. § 552 (b)(1). In support of its motion, defendant has filed the affidavit of Dr. James B. Rhoads, Archivist of the United States, who states under oath that the disputed transcript "has been and continues to be classified 'Top Secret'." Plaintiff opposes summary judgment and has moved to strike Dr. Rhoads' affidavit on the ground that it contains information beyond the personal knowledge of the affiant.

The Court finds that the affidavit is perfectly proper—as far as it goes. Dr. Rhoads clearly has personal knowledge of the transcript's present classified status, and his statement with regard to that issue can be considered by the Court in deciding defendant's motion. Although Dr. Rhoads may well lack personal knowledge as to whether or not the transcript was properly classified under the procedures set forth in Executive Order 11652, his affidavit contains no assertions on that issue. Plaintiff's motion to strike is therefore denied.

Filed: April 4, 1974.

As plaintiff notes, however, procedural irregularities may well be an issue in this case. While the Court will not review the wisdom or propriety of an Executive decision classifying a particular document for national defense or foreign policy reasons, Environmental Protection Agency v. Mink, 410 U.S. 73 (1973), it can require the Government to make the elementary showing that such classification was ordered by an individual authorized to do so under duly prescribed procedures. See Wolfe v. Froehlke, 358 F. Supp. 1318, 1320 (D.D. C. 1973); Epstein v. Resor, 296 F. Supp. 214, 217-18 (N.D. Cal. 1969), aff'd, 421 F. 2d 930 (9th Cir. 1970), cert. denied, 398 U.S. 965 (1970). The affidavit of Dr. Rhoads, while perfectly proper in and of itself, does not fully satisfy defendant's burden of establishing procedural regularity.

Defendant shall therefore file with the Court by April 17, 1974, proof competent under Rule 56 of the Federal Rules of Civil Procedure that the transcript at issue has been properly classified under Executive Order 11652. Past classification procedures need not be considered unless they are relevant to the legality of the present classification. Plaintiff will have until April 26, 1974, to reply. The Court will then decide defendant's motion for dismissal or summary judgment on the record before it.

SO ORDERED.

/s/ _____

GERHARD GESELL
UNITED STATES DISTRICT JUDGE

April 4, 1974.

16.
DEFENDANT'S MEMORANDUM PURSUANT TO ORDER OF THE COURT

Defendant, by its attorney, the United States Attorney for the District of Columbia, in supplemental support of its motion to dismiss or, in the alternative, for summary judgment, and pursuant to the Court's Memorandum and Order of April 4, 1974, respectfully submits the attached affidavit of J. Lee Rankin, former General Counsel of the Warren Commission. Defendants submit that this affidavit fully complies with the said Memorandum and Order of the Court.

The Warren Commission was established by Executive Order 11130, 28 Fed. Reg. 12789 (1963) to investigate the assassinations of President Kennedy and Lee Harvey Oswald. In view of the subject matter of its undertaking, the Warren Commission plainly had authority to classify documents pursuant to Executive Order 10501, promulgated November 5, 1953, 3 C.F.R. 979 (1949-1953 Comp.). Executive Order 11652, 3 C.F.R. 375 (1973 Supp.) superseded Executive Order 10501 only as of June 1, 1972. See Executive Order 11652, Sections 14 and 15. In this connection, the Supreme Court, in Environmental Protection Agency v. Mink, 410 U.S. 73 (1973), upheld the nondisclosure of documents classified pursuant to Executive Order 10501, notwithstanding the effectiveness of Executive Order 11652. Defendants submit, therefore, that the document sought in the instant case has been properly classified under applicable procedures.

Filed: April 17, 1974.

For the foregoing reasons, therefore, as well as those included in defendant's motion to dismiss or, in the alternative, for summary judgment, defendant respectfully requests the Court to grant its said motion and to dismiss the instant action.

/s/ _____
EARL J. SILBERT
United States Attorney

/s/ _____
ARNOLD T. AIKENS
Assistant United States Attorney

/s/ _____
MICHAEL J. RYAN
Assistant United States Attorney

CERTIFICATE OF SERVICE.

I HEREBY CERTIFY that service of the foregoing Defendant's Memorandum Pursuant to Order of the Court has been made upon plaintiff by mailing a copy thereof to his attorney, James H. Lesar, Esquire, 1231 Fourth Street, S. W., Washington, D. C. 20024 on this 17th day of April, 1974.

/s/ _____
MICHAEL J. RYAN
Assistant United States Attorney
U. S. District Courthouse
Room 3421
Washington, D. C. 20001
Telephone: 426-7375

AFFIDAVIT OF J. LEE RANKIN.

I, J. LEE RANKIN, living at 35 Sutton Place, New York, New York, do hereby solemnly swear:

1.   From December 8, 1963, I served as General Counsel of the President's Commission on the Assassination of President Kennedy (Warren Commission).

2.   Shortly after I had assumed the duties of General Counsel of the Commission, I was instructed by the Commission that among my duties was the responsibility to security classify at appropriate levels of classification those records created by the Commission in its investigation and report that should be security classified under existing Executive order. The Commission's authority to classify its records and its decision to delegate that responsibility to me existed pursuant to Executive Order 10501, as amended.

3.   As agreed to by the Commission, I ordered that the transcripts of certain of the Commission executive sessions, including that of January 27, 1964, be classified "Top Secret," and I communicated the fact of said classification to Ward & Paul, transcribers of the executive sessions (see attached copies of correspondence between Ward & Paul and me).

I have read the above statement, consisting of two pages, and it is true and complete to the best of my knowledge and belief. I understand that the information I have given is not to be considered confidential and that it may be shown to the interested parties.

/s/ _____
J. LEE RANKIN

Subscribed and sworn to before me
at New York, New York
on this 8th day of April, 1974.

/s/ _____

[Rankin Affidavit Letter A]

Letter of Earl Warren to Bernard L. Boutin, General Services Administration.

JLR/jte   December 21, 1964

Honorable Bernard L. Boutin
Administrator, General Services
        Administration
Washington, D. C.

Dear Mr. Boutin:

Pursuant to Executive Order 11130 of November 29, 1963, the Members of the President's Commission to Investigate the Assassination of President Kennedy, at a meeting of the Commission on December 6, 1963, agreed to solicit the services of J. Lee Rankin as General Counsel for the Commission. Mr. Rankin officially accepted the appointment on December 8, 1963.

                          Sincerely,
                          /s/
                          Chairman

[Rankin Affidavit Letter B]

Letter of Jesse Ward to J. Lee Rankin.

WARD & PAUL
SHORTHAND REPORTERS
917 G STREET, N. W.
WASHINGTON 1, D. C.

628-4266

JESSE L. WARD
ALFRED C. PAUL
(1933-1962)

JESSE L. WARD, JR.

OFFICIAL REPORTERS FOR
CONGRESSIONAL COMMITTEES

January 7, 1964

Hon. J. Lee Rankin, General Counsel,
Presidential Commission on the
        Assassination of President Kennedy,
200 Maryland Avenue, N. E.,
Washington, D. C. 20002.

Dear Sir: Re: Stenographic Reporting

        Pursuant to our conversation of yesterday, in which a general outline of reporting services and needs was discussed, and at which time you asked for a statement of prices for work performed, I am happy to submit the following schedule of charges:

Original and two copies	$1.65 per page	(Total)
4th copy	.15 per page	$1.80
5th copy	.15 per page	1.95
6th copy	.15 per page	2.10
7th copy	.15 per page	2.25
8th copy	.15 per page	2.40
9th copy	.10 per page	2.50
10th to 20th copies	.05 per page	3.05
21st to 25th copies	.02 per page	3.15

The first eight copies are at the current Congressional rate for closed sessions, no sales permitted; the ninth and succeeding copies reflect a multiple copy rate with decreasing costs due to higher production of copies.

It is contemplated that the reporting services will be performed in Washington, D. C., and that transcription and duplication will be in the premises of Ward & Paul at the address given above. The work will be given Top Secret or Secret classification, so marked on each volume, volumes numbered in accordance with security regulations, and receipts obtained for material passing between the Commission and our firm. If desired, notes, waste paper and other materials will be delivered to the Commission daily, with the delivery of each transcript, or they can be retained by us, under security, and destroyed from time to time. I would suggest that all waste material be destroyed weekly, and the notes be turned over to the Commission at the end of each week, this for possible reexamination of any necessary page or phrase which might need it.

All reporting will be done on a Daily Copy basis, that is, work reported on one day will be delivered by 9:00 a.m. the following day, unless there is a night session, in which case the portion reported during the day will be delivered as indicated, and the night session delivered during the following day.

Only personnel having the full necessary clearance will be used in any phase of handling the work of the Commission.

In event reporting services are needed outside of the City of Washington, we will be able to service the hearing with reporter and typist, prepared to deliver a minimum number of copies in the field, perhaps an original and one copy, and forward the necessary copy back to Washington for duplication and delivery to the Commission as early as possible. Travel and other such expenses will be borne by the Commission in this event, to be thoroughly vouchered by the personnel involved.

Please excuse this lengthy letter, but we feel that it is better to lay a proper groundwork for mutual understanding of the different phases of work involved.

Please allow me to thank you, sir, for the time you took to talk with me, and for the understanding of our problems. It is our hope that we may be chosen to serve the Commission, and that we may do so in a manner that will reflect credit on those who have been kind enough to suggest our firm for the work.

Respectfully submitted,

WARD & PAUL

By: /s/ _____
Jesse L. Ward, Jr.

[Rankin Affidavit Letter C]

Letter of J. Lee Rankin to Jesse Ward.

HPW:al
t 1/7/64   Jan. 8, 1964

Mr. Jesse L. Ward, Jr.
Ward & Paul
917 G Street, N. W.
Washington 1, D. C.

Dear Mr. Ward:

Thank you for your letter of January 7, 1964, setting forth the schedule of charges for your reporting service.

The arrangements set forth in your letter are satisfactory to me and I am confident that your organization will be of great assistance to this Commission. I would like you to handle the reporting of the meetings of the Commission as well as any hearings outside the city which may be held by the Commission. I shall advise you of the date of the next Commission meeting as soon as possible.

Thank you for your promptness in supplying me with this information.

Sincerely,

/s/
J. Lee Rankin
General Counsel

[Rankin Affidavit Letter D]

Letter of J. Lee Rankin to Ward & Paul.

JLR/bh   May 1, 1964

Ward & Paul
917 G Street, N. W.
Washington, D. C. 20001

Gentlemen:

This is to inform you that as of this date all depositions and testimony handled by your firm for the Commission will be classified as confidential rather than top secret. The meetings of the Commissioners will
continue to be classified top secret.

                              Very truly yours,

                              /s/
                              J. Lee Rankin
                              General Counsel

17.
SUPPLEMENT TO DEFENDANT'S MEMORANDUM
PURSUANT TO ORDER OF THE COURT

Defendant, by its attorney, the United States Attorney for the District of Columbia, respectfully informs the Court that since preparation and filing of Defendant's Memorandum Pursuant to Order of the Court, counsel's attention has been called to the letter of November 23, 1964 from President Johnson to Earl Warren, Chairman of the Warren Commission, 3 C.F.R. 376 (1964-1965 Comp.). Defendant therefore supplements its earlier memorandum with this reference as additional evidence of the authority of the Warren Commission to classify documents pursuant to Executive Order 10501.

/s/_____
EARL J. SILBERT
United States Attorney

/s/_____
ARNOLD T. AIKENS
Assistant United States Attorney

/s/_____
MICHAEL J. RYAN
Assistant United States Attorney

Filed: April 22, 1974.

CERTIFICATE OF SERVICE.

I HEREBY CERTIFY that service of the foregoing Supplement to Defendant's Memorandum Pursuant to Order of the Court has been made upon plaintiff by mailing a copy thereof to his attorney, James H. Lesar, Esquire, 1231 Fourth Street, S. W., Washington, D. C. 20004 on this 22nd day of April, 1974.

/s/ _____

MICHAEL J. RYAN
Assistant United States Attorney
United States Courthouse
Room 3421
Washington, D. C. 20001
Telephone: 426-7375

18.
PLAINTIFF'S MEMORANDUM PURSUANT TO ORDER OF THE COURT

In its order of April 4, 1974, the Court directed the defendant to file with the Court "proof competent under Rule 56 of the Federal Rules of Civil Procedure that the transcript at issue has been properly classified under Executive Order 11652. Past classification procedures need not be considered unless they are relevant to the legality of the present classification."

In response to the Court's order, the defendant submitted an affidavit by Mr. J. Lee Rankin, former General Counsel for the Warren Commission, which asserts that in accordance with instructions given him by the Commission, he ordered "certain" Executive Session transcripts classified, including that of January 27, 1964, which is sought by plaintiff. Mr. Rankin also alleged that the Warren Commission had authority to classify its records under Executive Order 10501, as amended.

The defendant made no attempt to show that the transcript at issue has been properly classified under Executive Order 11652. Nor did defendant explain why Executive Order 11652 is not relevant to the present action.

Plaintiff disputes that the transcript was ever classified pursuant to Executive Order 10501. Attached hereto are the Supplemental Affidavit of Harold Weisberg and several exhibits which contradict the assertions of Mr. J. Lee Rankin.

Plaintiff maintains, however, that in addition to showing valid classification under Executive Order 10501, defendant also has the burden of demonstrating that the transcript is properly withheld under the guidelines

Filed: April 26, 1974.

97

set forth in the Attorney General's Memorandum of April 13, 1965, [see Memorandum Exhibit H] and the provisions of Executive Order 11652. The reasons for this are elaborated upon below.

I.   The Warren Commission did not have authority to classify its records pursuant to Executive Order 10501.

The defendant represents that the Warren Commission had authority to classify documents pursuant to "Executive Order 10501, as amended," and Mr. Rankin has executed an affidavit to that effect. The defendant has not specified which amendments to Executive Order 10501 authorized the Warren Commission to classify its records.

Executive Order 10901 amended Section 2 of Executive Order 10501 as follows:

Sec. 2. LIMITATION OF AUTHORITY TO CLASSIFY. The authority to classify defense information or material under this order shall be limited in the departments, agencies, and other units of the executive branch as hereinafter specified.

* *

(c) Any agency or unit of the executive branch not named herein, and any such agency or unit which may be established hereafter, shall be deemed not to have authority for original classification of information or material under this order, except as such authority may be specifically conferred upon any such agency or unit hereafter. [Emphasis added]

The defendant has not claimed that the authority to classify defense information or material under Executive Order 10501 was specifically conferred upon the Warren Commission by the Executive. There is no mention of any such authority in Executive Order 11130 which created the Commission. [See Opposition Exhibit J] Nor do the Commission's own Rules of Procedure refer to any such authority. [See Memorandum Exhibit C] Indeed, in suggesting that "In view of the subject matter of its undertaking, the Warren Commission plainly had authority to classify documents pursuant to Executive Order 10501," [See Defendant's Memorandum Pursuant to Order of the Court, p. 1] defendant in effect admits that no such authority was ever specifically conferred upon the Warren Commission.

Four days before plaintiff's Memorandum was due, counsel for plaintiff received a "Supplement to Defendant's Memorandum" which cited "as additional evidence of the authority of the Warren Commission to classify documents pursuant to Executive Order 10501" a letter from President Johnson to Earl Warren dated November 23, 1964. Since the defendant did not attach a copy of this letter, plaintiff quotes the text of it here:

The procedures set forth in Section 5(i) of Executive Order No. 10501 with respect to the declassification of material shall have no application to the Report of the President's Commission on the Assassination of President Kennedy and the exhibit volumes thereto.

The heading above this letter in the Federal Register is "Non-applicability of Declassification Procedures," and that aptly sums up the essence of Section 5(i) to which the letter refers. Since agencies which do not have authority to originally classify defense information do sometimes have authority to declassify, the National Archives being one such, no inference can be drawn that, ergo, the Warren Commission had authority to classify defense information under 10501. All this letter did was to protect the Warren Commission against the charge that in publishing its Report and exhibit volumes the Commission had released information validly classified by federal agencies authorized to so classify it without following the declassification procedures prescribed by Executive Order 10501. Having been drafted for that purpose, the President's letter specified only the Commission's Report and exhibit volumes, not the remaining volume of the Commission's records, including its Executive Session transcripts.

II.   Classification procedures required by Executive Order 10501 were not followed in the classification of documents generated by the Warren Commission.

Executive Order 10501 sets forth numerous guidelines and procedures for classifying defense information. Some of the most important are set forth in the following provisions:

Sec. 3.   CLASSIFICATION. Persons designated to have authority for original classification of information or material which requires protection in the interests of national defense under this order shall be responsible for its proper classification in accordance with the definitions of the three categories in section 1, hereof. Unnecessary classification and over-classification shall be scrupulously avoided. The following special rules shall be observed in classification of defense information or material:

(a) DOCUMENTS IN GENERAL. Documents shall be classified according to their own content and not necessarily according to their relationship to other documents. References to classified material which do not reveal classified defense information shall not be classified.

As plaintiff stated in his first affidavit, Ward & Paul routinely classified all transcripts, whether of witness testimony or of Warren Commission Executive Sessions. Indeed, Ward & Paul even classified transcripts which were sent to it unclassified by the United States Attorney. [See Affidavit of Harold Weisberg, P. 15] Under the terms of Executive Order 10501, this was totally unnecessary classification. Under the terms of the Ward & Paul bureaucracy, however, it was vitally necessary. When, on May 1, 1964, Mr. Rankin ordered the transcripts of witness testimony "declassified" from Top Secret to Confidential "so the printers can handle it," [See Memorandum Exhibit J], it brought internal chaos to Ward & Paul. [See Affidavit of Harold Weisberg, P. 16]

The defendant's own exhibits and answers to interrogatories establish that rather than documents being classified "according to their own content," as required by Executive Order 10501, they were classified in a blanket fashion by Ward & Paul. Transcripts were ordered classified into the indefinite future without exception. [See letter of May 1, 1964, attached to affidavit of Mr. Rankin]

This, of course, defeats the purposes of Executive Order 10501, which requires that the potential damage to the national defense be weighed against the public's right to know and measured against explicit criteria for determining whether defense considerations are present. The United States District Court for the Eastern District of Virginia - Alexandria Division has recently addressed this issue in a case in which the CIA insisted, on national security grounds, that some 339 deletions be made from Victor Marchetti's book, The CIA and the Cult of Intelligence. In refusing to uphold certain of these deletions, the court said:

The result of this may be to release some sensitive information; however the rationale underlying the fixing of classification as the dividing line between what could be revealed and what could not was the assumption that, at the time the determination was made to classify, there had been a weighing of the competing interests of national defense and foreign relations on the one hand and the public's right to know on the other hand. Alfred A. Knopf, Inc. v. William Colby, et al., Civil Action No. 540-73-A, slip opinion, p. 7.

It is both apparent and undenied by the defendant that no such "weighing" took place at the time the January 27, 1964, Executive Session transcript was classified Top Secret.

Other violations of security regulations make it evident that the Executive Session transcripts were not classified out of a concern for national security. All transcripts of witness testimony and Executive Sessions done by Ward & Paul were classified Top Secret until May 1, 1964. But the firm of Ward & Paul sold copies of Top Secret witness testimony before it was declassified. [See Memorandum Exhibit E] The sale of classified transcripts was authorized by the Commission's rules. [See Memorandum Exhibit C] The Commission was aware that this would enable the press to obtain copies of it. [See Memorandum Exhibit D]

With respect to Executive Session transcripts, one member of the Commission and his campaign manager personally profited from the sale and publication of parts of the classified January 27 transcript which plaintiff seeks. No action was taken to halt the publication of this classified information or to bring sanctions against those who disclosed it. The reason why is obvious: the January 27 transcript was not classified pursuant to Executive Order 10501, did not contain defense information, and the responsible authorities, including Mr. Rankin, knew it.

In this connection, it is noted that Section 4 (j) of Executive Order 10501 (as amended) requires that "when classified material affecting the national defense is furnished authorized persons, in or out of Federal Service, other than those in the executive branch," the following notation is to be placed on such material:

This material contains information affecting the national defense of the United States within the meaning of the espionage laws, Title 18, U.S.C., Secs. 793 and 794, the transmission or revelation of which in any manner to an unauthorized person is prohibited by law.

No such notation was placed on the material classified by Ward & Paul.

III.   The defendant has not shown that it has complied with the President's guidelines on the public availability of Warren Commission records.

In January, 1965, in response to a grass roots protest of the National Archives' attempt to suppress Warren Commission records, [See Memorandum Exhibit F], the White House directed the Attorney General to make a study with a view towards changing the announced policy of the defendant. As directed by the White House, the Department of Justice solicited the views of Chief Justice Earl Warren on the public availability of the Commission's records. The Attorney General's Memorandum of April 13, 1965, states:

The Chief Justice has informed me in a letter dated April 5, 1965, that the President's Commission has concluded, after full consideration, that the public availability of the Commission's records was a matter to be resolved by the Attorney General and the originating agencies in accordance with established law and policies of the Government. According to the Chief Justice, the Commission assumed that these determinations would be made in light of 'the overriding consideration of the fullest possible disclosure.' Moreover, the Commission did not desire to restrict access to any of its working papers except those classified by other agencies. [Emphasis added. See Memorandum Exhibit H.]

Counsel for plaintiff has attempted to obtain a copy of Chief Justice Warren's April 5, 1965, letter, but the National Archives has stated that it does not have a copy and the defendant's attorney has advised him that he may only obtain a copy through a motion for discovery or a separate Freedom for Information suit.   Accordingly, plaintiff will file a discovery motion for this letter. As restated by the Attorney General, however, the letter seems to flatly contradict the defendant's attempts to suppress the January 27 transcript.

Furthermore, the guidelines set by the Attorney General for the disclosure of Warren Commission records were approved by the White House and the Archives was directed to implement them. In testifying before the House Foreign Operations and Government Information Subcommittee on May 11, 1972, Dr. Rhoads was asked to submit a statement in regard to the availability of Warren Commission records. In that statement Dr. Rhoads says:

The reviews of the records provided for in the guidelines were held in 1965, 1967, and 1970. A large number of the documents withheld from research as a result of the 1965 review were made available by the 1970 review. The five year review of the records withheld from research as a result of the 1967 review is now being conducted. This review includes a survey of the security classified documents among the Commission's records to determine whether they should be declassified or down graded under the provisions of Executive Order 11652 . . . [Emphasis added. Hearings, House Foreign Operations and Government Information Subcommittee, 92nd Cong., 2nd Sess., Part 7, page 2610]

Plaintiff contends that before the defendant can meet the burden of justifying nondisclosure imposed upon it by the Freedom of Information Act it must show that the January 27 transcript has been withheld as a result of the reviews it was required to make and in compliance with the guidelines set forth in the Attorney General's Memorandum. This would include the 1972 review to see whether or not the transcript should be declassified under Executive Order 11652.

IV. Defendant's Motion For Dismissal Or Summary Judgment must be denied because material facts are in dispute and the defendant has not met its burden of showing that it is entitled to invoke the protection of Exemption 1.

The function of summary judgment is to avoid a useless trial. A trial is not useless, but is in fact absolutely necessary, where there is a genuine issue as to a material fact. As the Supreme Court has stated:

Rule 56 should be cautiously invoked to the end that parties may always be afforded a trial where there is a bona fide dispute of facts between them.

Associated Press v. United States, 326 U.S. 1, 6 (1945). See Adickes v. S. H. Kress & Co., 398 U.S. 144, 153-61 (1970); National Cable Television Ass'n, Inc. v. FCC, 479 F. 2d 183, 186 (1973) (when summary judgment is appropriate in FOIA cases). In this regard, all "inferences to be drawn from the underlying facts contained in such materials must be viewed in the light most favorable to the party opposing the [summary judgment] motion." United States v. Diebold, Inc., 369 U.S. 654, 655 (1962). And it is the Government which has the burden of proving the applicability of an exemption from disclosure. 5 U.S.C. §552 (a)(3). See Vaughn v. Rosen, 484 F. 2d 820,

823-826 (1973), <u>cert. denied</u>, 42 U.S.L.W. 3523. Furthermore, the courts are entirely in agreement that the moving party for summary judgment has the burden of showing the absence of any genuine issue as to material fact, which under applicable principles of substantive law, entitle him to judgment as a matter of law. Nothing may be assumed, and there may be no real doubt as to any material fact. <u>Adickes</u>, <u>supra</u>, at 157.

The Freedom of Information Act places the burden of proof upon the government to demonstrate not only that a document is classified, but that the procedure of classification was proper. <u>Environmental Protection Agency</u> v. <u>Mink</u>, 410 U.S. at 84, <u>Wolfe</u> v. <u>Froehlke</u>, 358 F. Supp. at 1318. That has not been done in this case. Plaintiff's affidavits and exhibits place in dispute all of the important material facts in this action. That being so, defendant's motion for summary judgment must be denied.

DATED: April 26, 1974   /s/ _____

                                         JAMES HIRAM LESAR
                                         1231 Fourth Street, S. W.
                                         Washington, D. C. 20024
                                         Attorney for Plaintiff

EXHIBIT A.

Supplemental Affidavit of Harold Weisberg.

    1.   I am the plaintiff in the above-entitled action.

    2.   In the affidavit which I executed in support of the Opposition to defendant's Motion to Dismiss Or For Summary Judgment, I have already set forth my qualifications as an expert on the Warren Commission's investigation into the assassination of President Kennedy.

    3.   I am familiar with the transcripts of all Warren Commission Executive Sessions except for the four which are withheld <u>in toto</u> and the excized portions of three other transcripts which are withheld in part.

    4.   I have read the affidavits of Dr. James B. Rhoads and Mr. J. Lee Rankin which have been submitted by the defendant in this cause.

    5.   In his affidavit Mr. Rankin states: "Shortly after I had assumed the duties of General Counsel of the Commission, I was instructed by the Commission that among my duties was the responsibility to security classify at appropriate levels of classification those records created by the Commission in its investigation and report that should be security classified under

existing Executive Order. The Commission's authority to classify its records and its decision to delegate that responsibility to me existed pursuant to Executive Order 10501."

6.   Read together with the correspondence attached to it, Mr. Rankin's affidavit implies that before Ward & Paul was chosen as the Commission's reporter, the Commission instructed Rankin to direct Ward & Paul to classify all work done by it for the Commission.

7.   I have carefully examined the files of the Warren Commission relating to the Commission's Executive Sessions. I know of no document in the Commission's files directing Mr. Rankin to classify the Executive Session transcripts pursuant to Executive Order 10501. The defendant has produced no such document. Under date of July 20, 1971, I asked Dr. James B. Rhoads, the Archivist of the United States, for a copy of any Executive Order which he regarded as relevant to the withholding of the Warren Commission's Executive Session transcripts. Dr. Rhoads never provided me with a copy of any such Executive Order.

8.   Mr. Rankin states that he began work as General Counsel for the Commission on December 8, 1963. No transcript of an Executive Session held before that date was ever classified. In fact, those Executive Session transcripts made by the Department of Justice both before and after that date were never classified, neither at the time by the Department of Justice, nor subsequently by the National Archives.

9.   The first Executive Session reported by Ward & Paul was that of January 21, 1964. No transcript of an Executive Session held between December 8, 1963 and January 21, 1964, was ever classified. The first transcript of an Executive Session to be classified was that of January 21, 1964, the date on which Ward & Paul became the Commission's reporter.

10.   I have read all of the Executive Session transcripts not still withheld. At no point is there a directive from the Commission to Mr. Rankin ordering him to classify the Executive Session transcripts pursuant to Executive Order 10501. Nor was there even any discussion of classifying Executive Session transcripts pursuant to Executive Order 10501.

11.   The only Executive Session at which the Commission could have ordered Mr. Rankin to classify its Executive Session transcripts is that of December 16, 1963. That transcript is unclassified and a casual reading of its beginning pages discloses that the Commission was not concerned with and did not address any of the concerns of Executive Order 10501. [See Memorandum Exhibit B]

12.   In addition to the actual physical safety and integrity of its files, the Commission's specific and articulated concern throughout its existence was over news leaks.

13.   Neither Executive Order 11130, which created the Commission, nor Senate Joint Resolution 137, which gave it the power to subpoena witnesses and compel the production of evidence, authorized the Commission to classify documents pursuant to Executive Order 10501. [Executive Order 11130 is reproduced as Opposition Exhibit J. S. J. Res. 137 is reprinted in the Warren Report, pp. 473-474]

14.   Although the testimony of all witnesses transcribed by Ward & Paul was routinely classified, the Commission's own procedures for the taking of testimony did not provide for this. The Commission's procedures, adopted at its Executive Session of March 16, 1964, were themselves classified Top Secret by Ward & Paul. Although the Commission's procedures were reprinted in the Warren Report, the National Archives did not declassify them until more than three years later. [The Commission's resolution adopting these procedures is attached hereto as Memorandum Exhibit C]

15.   Notwithstanding the fact that Ward & Paul classified all witness testimony, Commission Rule "I-C" permitted witnesses to purchase transcripts of their testimony. [See Memorandum Exhibit C] When discussing this provision at its January 21, 1964, Executive Session, Mr. Rankin pointed out that copies of witness transcripts might be sold to the press. Representative Hale Boggs stated: "A witness has the right to look at his own testimony. If the press wants to buy it, they can buy it." [See Memorandum Exhibit D] Mr. Rankin personally authorized the sale of classified witness transcripts. Attached hereto as Memorandum Exhibit E are Ward & Paul invoices reflecting the sale of classified transcripts to Mrs. Marina Oswald and news reporter Ike Pappas.

16.   After the Warren Commission went out of existence with the filing of its Report on September 27, 1964, the National Archives attempted to throw a 75-year cloak of secrecy over the Commission's records. An eloquent letter of protest from the Mayor of Cedar Rapids, Iowa to the President [See Memorandum Exhibit F] served as the instrument by which the Executive Branch initiated action intended to override the Archives' suppression of Warren Commission documents. The White House directed the Attorney General to make a study with a view towards changing the policy announced by the General Services Administration. [See White House "Memorandum For Acting Attorney General Katzenbach" attached hereto as Memorandum Exhibit G]

17.   As directed by the White House, the Department of Justice solicited the views of Chief Justice Earl Warren on the public availability of the Commission's records. The Attorney General's Memorandum of April 13, 1965, states: "The Chief Justice has informed me in a letter dated April 5, 1965, that the President's Commission has concluded, after full consideration, that the public availability of the Commission's records was a matter to be resolved by the Attorney General and the originating agencies in accordance with established law and policies of the Government. According to the Chief Justice, the Commission assumed that these determinations would be made in light of 'the overriding consideration of the fullest possible disclosure.' Moreover, the Commission did not desire to restrict access to any of its working papers except those classified by other agencies." [Emphasis added. See the Attorney General's Memorandum of April 13, 1965, attached hereto as Memorandum Exhibit H]

18.   The Attorney General's April 13 Memorandum outlined certain procedures to be followed in making Warren Commission records publicly available. The White House approved these guidelines and procedures on April 19, 1965, and directed the Department of Justice and the National Archives to implement them. [See Memorandum Exhibit I] In 1968 the National Archives wrote a student of the Warren Commission that: "We are not aware of any documents from the office of President Johnson on which the withholding of Warren Commission documents from research is based, except the memorandum of Mr. McGeorge Bundy of April 19, 1965, approving the procedures proposed by the Attorney General for making records of the Commission available for research."

19.   In the Memorandum and Order entered by the Court in this cause on April 4, 1974, the Court ordered the defendant to file with the Court "proof competent under Rule 56 of the Federal Rules of Civil Procedure that the transcript at issue has been properly classified under Executive Order 11652." No such proof has been submitted by the defendant.

20.   In response to interrogatory 2, which asked if there was any Executive Order which specifically requires the transcript of the January 27 Executive Session to be kept secret in the interest of the national defense or foreign policy, Dr. Rhoads stated that the transcript "is presently classified under the provisions of Executive Order 11652." Later, when pressed for specifics on the transcript's classification under Executive Order 11652, Dr. Rhoads stated that: "The transcript was not subject to declassification or reclassification because of the issuance of Executive Order 11652. Its classification under Executive Order 10501 automatically carried over upon the effective date of Executive Order 11652, i.e., June 1, 1972." [Answer to interrogatory 27]

21.   There is no evidence in the record showing that the January 27 transcript was in fact classified pursuant to Executive Order 10501. In addition, the answer to interrogatory 27 gives the impression that no review of the security classification of the January 27 transcript has been undertaken since it was classified by Ward & Paul on the day it was transcribed. This is not true. On May 11, 1972, Dr. Rhoads testified before the Foreign Operations and Government Information Subcommittee of the House of Representatives. In response to questions about the Warren Commission's records, Dr. Rhoads submitted a prepared statement. Referring to the guidelines drawn up by the Department of Justice and approved by the White House, Dr. Rhoads stated: "The reviews of the records provided for in the guidelines were held in 1965, 1967, and 1970. A large number of the documents withheld from research as a result of the 1965 review were made available by the 1970 review. The five year review of the records withheld from research as a result of the 1967 review is now being conducted. This review includes a survey of the security classified documents among the Commission's records to determine whether they should be declassified or downgraded under the provisions of Executive Order 11652 . . . " [Hearings, House Foreign Operations and Government Information Subcommittee, 92nd Cong., 2nd Sess., Part 7, page 2610]

22.   In his affidavit Mr. Rankin states: "As agreed to by the Commission, I ordered that the transcripts of certain of the Commission executive sessions, including that of January 27, 1964, be classified 'Top Secret,' and I communicated the fact of said classification to Ward & Paul, transcribers of the executive sessions (see attached copies of correspondence between Ward & Paul and me)." As I have pointed out above, there is no record of any such agreement by the Commission and the defendant has produced none. All evidence is directly to the contrary. In addition, rather than "certain" of the Executive Session transcripts being classified, the fact is that all Executive Session transcripts made by Ward & Paul were classified Top Secret. This is shown by the Ward & Paul worksheets. [One such worksheet is Opposition Exhibit C] These worksheets also show that all Executive Session transcripts were classified Top Secret by Ward & Paul as a matter of routine and utterly without regard to content.

23.   In answering interrogatories 23, 24, and 25, which ask when the January 27 transcript was classified, and by whom, Dr. Rhoads cites only a May 1, 1964, letter from Mr. Rankin to Ward & Paul. Although this letter postdates the date on which the January 27 transcript was actually classified by more than three months, it is attached to Mr. Rankin's letter as evidence

that he communicated the fact of classification to Ward & Paul. Mr. Rankin's affidavit and his May 1, 1964, letter to Ward & Paul leave the impression that in that letter he reissued a previous order to Ward & Paul to classify all Executive Session transcripts for reasons relating to national security. This impression is totally misleading. Mr. Rankin's letter relates to the Executive Session of the previous day, April 30, 1964, which had discussed the printing of the Commission's Report. The printing of the testimony of witnesses who had appeared before the Commission did not present a threat to the national defense but, for internal bureaucratic reasons, it was necessary to downgrade the witness testimony. As Mr. Rankin explained in making the motion to downgrade: "I think at this time we ought to take action on declassifying our transcript so the printers can handle it, from Top Secret to Confidential." [See Memorandum Exhibit J]

24.   In answer to interrogatory 36, Dr. Rhoads has stated that the January 27 transcript contains eighty-six pages, each of which is classified Top Secret. Attached hereto as Memorandum Exhibit K is a copy of the Agenda for the January 27 Executive Session. Having been prepared by the Commission staff rather than by Ward & Paul, it is unclassified. As I said in my October 13, 1968, letter to Dr. Rhoads, this agenda "makes it obvious that the entire transcript cannot properly be withheld." [See Memorandum Exhibit L] Dr. Rhoads never responded to this.

25.   Several years ago I discovered that a transcript of an Executive Session had been faked. Mr. J. Lee Rankin personally distributed the faked Executive Session transcript to the members of the Warren Commission.

26.   The Executive Session in question, held on September 18, 1964, had been forced by three members of the Warren Commission who raised objections to the Warren Report's conclusion that there had been no conspiracy to assassinate President Kennedy. The three dissenting Warren Commission members thought that a transcript of their objections was being made and would be kept as a historical record. Long after the end of the Commission's work and the publication of its Report, the Commission members were provided with a covering letter and what purported to be a transcript of this meeting. The first page of the faked transcript counterfeits the work of Ward & Paul. The first and succeeding pages of this faked transcript were numbered to make it appear that they were in proper sequence with all preceding Ward & Paul transcripts. However, this transcript is in fact a fake and does not include any verbatim report of the actual Executive Session. It also does not include the objections raised by Senator Russell and the other unsatisfied members of the Warren Commission.

27.   After I discovered the faked transcript, I met and corresponded with Senator Richard Russell about it. At first Senator Russell could not believe that the doubts and disagreements he had expressed at the September 18th Executive Session were not recorded. When, on June 5, 1968, I informed Senator Russell of what Dr. Rhoads had written me, that "No verbatim transcript of the executive session of September 18, 1964, is known to be among the records of the Commission," Senator Russell asked me to make a further inquiry. On June 14, 1968, I informed him of the National Archives' added responses: "All that we have for that session is the minutes, a copy of which was furnished you."

28.   Senator Russell was shocked to learn that the purported copy of the Executive Session transcript had indeed been faked. Not long before his death Senator Russell began to publicly voice his doubts about the conclusions which the Commission had reached in its Report. Privately Senator Russell told me that he was convinced that there were two areas in which Warren Commission members had been deceived by the Federal agencies responsible for investigating the assassination of President Kennedy. These two areas were: (1) Oswald's background; and, (2) the ballistics evidence. The first of these two areas was the principal subject discussed at the January 27, 1964, Executive Session.

/s/ _____
HAROLD WEISBERG

FREDERICK COUNTY, MARYLAND

Before me this 25th day of April, 1974, deponent Harold Weisberg has appeared and signed this affidavit, first having sworn that the statements made herein are true.

My commission expires_____.

/s/ _____
NOTARY PUBLIC IN AND FOR
FREDERICK COUNTY,
MARYLAND

EXHIBIT B.

Pages 1-12 of December 16, 1963 Warren Commission Executive Session Transcript.

PRESIDENTIAL COMMISSION
TO INVESTIGATE THE ASSASSINATION
OF PRESIDENT KENNEDY

16 December 1963
National Archives
Washington, D. C.

Reported and Transcribed by
Alex Dal Porto
Reporter
Office of the United States Attorney
Washington, D. C.

PRESENT:

Chief Justice Earl Warren - Chairman

Senator Richard B. Russell

Senator John Sherman Cooper

Representative Hale Boggs

Representative Gerald R. Ford

Mr. Allen W. Dulles

Mr. John J. McCloy

Associate Justice Stanley F. Reed
(Present to administer oath)

Mr. J. Lee Rankin
(General Counsel of the Commission)

PLACE:

Conference Room
National Archives
Washington, D. C.

TIME:

Approximately 2:00 PM to 4:30 PM, 16 Dec 1963

(p. 1)

CHAIRMAN: Gentlemen, the meeting is open. I have brought Justice Reed over to administer our oath.

JUSTICE REED: Would each of you hold up your right hand? (At this point all members of the Commission stood and raised their right hands.)

JUSTICE REED: I will support and defend the Constitution of the United States against all enemies foreign and domestic and I will bear true faith of allegiance to same. I take this obligation freely, without any mental reservation or purpose of evasion, and I will well and faithfully discharge the duties of the office which I am about to enter, so help you God.

(Chorus of "So help me God.")

CHAIRMAN: We'll sign them, Stanley, and we'll send them over to you. Thank you very much, Stanley.

(At this point, approximately 3:05 PM, Justice Reed left the conference room.)

CHAIRMAN: Gentlemen, I have tried to make up a little agenda here. We have had to make it on the run because we have been in a running operation here and we have been putting things on as they come to us. Gentlemen, I want to say that Mr. Rankin was able to accept our offer to become General Counsel of our Commission and he's been with me most of the time since our last meeting and we have been trying to tend to the housekeeping part of this thing so we will be in business.

I have no report of the minutes of the prior meetings as yet because they have not yet been written up. I have asked the Attorney General to write them up and send them to us and then we can have them approved at a later date.

As regards Number Three on the agenda, we have found some quarters which, I think, you will find nearly ideal for our (p. 2) purposes. They are located on the fourth floor of this little Veterans of Foreign Wars building, just a block or two away from here. The Government has leased ten thousand square feet of space in there. They have some other people in there but they were able to move them to give us the entire fourth floor of the building, and if we should need more space they tell us that they can give it to us on the floor below it. It is a brand new building. It's as clean as thistle and in all respects, I think, is adequate. We have a room on the fourth floor that is large enough for our Commission meetings, and if we need more space for more people to be in the room at one time we can use the meeting room of the

Veterans of Foreign Wars. They use it very seldom and they have said we can use that. This will give you an idea of the size of it. It will set up to two hundred people, in addition to the Commission, or we can divide it off into three rooms. So I think we have every facility that we need over there. We have office space for those who are out of the city, Mr. Dulles and Mr. McCloy. I think all told that they are about as nice quarters as we can get. They are close to everybody.

We only have one problem. We have a little problem of parking there. Senator, the parking lot of the new Senate building is directly across the street, and I wonder if we can get a little space for some of our people. I'm told you have a large lot and all of it is not used.

SEN. RUSSELL: I'm sure it can be arranged. If there is no unusual number I'm sure that can be arranged. I'd like to know how many spaces we'll need.

CHAIRMAN: We'll find out and let you know. The reason it's essential for us to have some space is that there are no other (p. 3) places around there possible for more parking space, and we're in the winter season. It gets dark now about four thirty or five o'clock, and I'm just afraid to have our women employees moving around that part of our city in the dark. I don't even let them go from our building over to our parking lot, which is a block away without officers being stationed there to look in their cars when they get there to see that there is no one around. I think you have had some experience.

SEN. RUSSELL: I think we have a policeman on duty at all times.

CHAIRMAN: Yes. So, if you like, the offices are open. We're in business over there. If we have time, and you'd like to do it, I'd like to have you go over and see it this afternoon, at the conclusion of the meeting. Are you in agreement that the place and everything is acceptable?

REP. FORD: I so move, if you want a resolution.

SEN. RUSSELL: I second it.

CHAIRMAN: Is there any further discussion?

(No response.)

CHAIRMAN: All in favor say "Aye"?

(Chorus of "Ayes.")

CHAIRMAN: Contrary minded?

(No response.)

CHAIRMAN: The "Ayes" have it.

REP. BOGGS: What's the address?

CHAIRMAN: 200 Maryland Avenue.

REP. BOGGS: That's right near the new Senate building.

CHAIRMAN: Right across the street from it.

MR. RANKIN: Do you want to give them the telephone number?

(p. 4) CHAIRMAN: 961-3365.

MR. RANKIN: We are going to have a switchboard put in so that we can take calls.

CHAIRMAN: We're in business over there. Now, it's set up with new furniture for us. We have an office manager. GSA sent one to us. He's on duty this morning. We have an expert on files, who we got from Mr. Grover, the archivist. These people should know the filing business about as well as anyone I'm told, and he says this is one of his very best men. Mr. Rankin is there with his secretary. And we have an arrangement made with GSA so we can borrow our secretarial help.

SEN. RUSSELL: Mr. Chief Justice, that brings to mind the matter of the reporter. Will we utilize the Department of Justice reporters all the way through or are we supposed to get other reporters from some of the reporting agencies.

CHAIRMAN: Mr. Rankin and I were talking about that today. We came to the conclusion that we would suggest to you that we get a reporting agency of our own.

SEN. RUSSELL: I think that would be highly advisable, where we can. At least we won't be criticized for things that could be brought in, as so often happens.

SEN. COOPER: What worries me is the security.

CHAIRMAN: There will be a man. Before we get to that may we just finish this about the reporters. Do any of you know reporting systems which should be used? After we got through talking to Mr. Katzenbach today he mentioned some firm. Perhaps you would know it from your legislative committees. I don't know.

MR. DULLES: There's a good one in the Armed Services.

SEN. RUSSELL: Ward and Paul. We had them during the MacArthur hearing. They're very good. I'm not trying to sell (p. 5) anyone. There are two or three different ones up on the Hill.

MR. RANKIN: Someone recommended the Alderson firm.

CHAIRMAN: Do any of you know that firm? Suppose Senator, you know these people, you have had a little more experience than any of us, suppose you let us know which one would be best to use.

SEN. RUSSELL: They all use practically the same system, if they're all cleared. Of course, our people have to have the very highest clearance over there.

CHAIRMAN: Who does your work over there?

SEN. RUSSELL: I think it's Ward and Paul.

MR. DULLES: That's familiar to me.

SEN. RUSSELL: They have been doing it ever since the Armed Services Committee was organized.

CHAIRMAN: Do any of the rest of you know any reporting firms? I don't know a reporting firm in the city. My recommendation wouldn't be worth anything. Will you be satisfied with that firm?

SEN. RUSSELL: Yes, indeed. I know they're topflight. The Appropriations Committee has a different firm. I think they're practically all cleared. I know this firm is cleared. We have some of the most sensitive hearings on the Hill and there have been no leaks at all.

CHAIRMAN: Is it agreeable to the rest of you to take the firm, whatever firm it is, that the Armed Services Committee has?

SEN. COOPER: I so move.

SEN. RUSSELL: I would prefer to have some staff get in touch with them and have them see Mr. Rankin. If that is agreeable I'll tell them to get in touch with Mr. Rankin.

(p. 6) CHAIRMAN: Is that agreeable with everyone? Very well, that will be done, and Mr. Rankin, you have the power to act after you discuss it with Senator Russell.

So I think that is about all we have on the housekeeping affairs. Can you think of anything?

MR. RANKIN: The question was asked about security clearance.

SEN. COOPER: Files, for example.

CHAIRMAN: Yes?

SEN. COOPER: You have to go in and get them, I suppose, go down there and get what you want to read and return it. What about the security investigation on whoever keeps those files?

CHAIRMAN: Well, of course, we wouldn't have anyone in there who doesn't have full clearance on top secret matters handling those files. We'll go through the Department of Justice and GSA on that. I'm hopeful that we won't have to have any investigations made, that we can borrow all of those people who have been already cleared, so that it won't take any time to do it. I would think, from what I've heard, that could be done. And then we have this whole floor, as I've told you, and GSA said they would have a guard on that floor twenty-four hours a day. So I think we're in pretty good shape from that standpoint, John. Does that answer your question?

SEN. COOPER: Yes.

MR. McCLOY: When you take those documents out, for example, they have a regular procedure. I wish they would do that. In my office they sent up somebody and they prescribed the type safe to have and where it should be located, and maybe you want to do the same thing.

(p. 7) MR. DULLES: I have a safe that meets the qualifications. I don't have a guard. I don't think that's necessary.

CHAIRMAN: I suppose we all have safes, most of us that are in the Government service.

SEN. RUSSELL: I only have a file safe. The only thing I have is a guard on duty. He's on duty twenty-four hours a day. I don't intend to keep out anything that is essential.

SEN. COOPER: For those of us that are here it is rather simple. We can go to these offices, take anything out, and return it.

MR. McCLOY: They have an FBI unit up there in New York that keeps a very close check. Lots of times they take them back at the end of the day and put them in their own safe.

MR. RANKIN: We can arrange to have a locked file cabinet in the office for you and Mr. Dulles, because you asked for offices here, and we can arrange with the FBI to check out any security.

MR. McCLOY: That office doesn't have to be too formal. Just a place to sit down.

MR. DULLES: A separate office isn't necessary. I have an office in my house.

CHAIRMAN: Very well.

MR. DULLES: I think that people that are in charge of the files should have Top Secret clearance.

CHAIRMAN: Yes. We won't deal with anything less than that.

MR. RANKIN: And for any of the members of the Congress we have a place over there where they can examine things.

MR. DULLES: What are you going to do about stenographic help?

(p. 8) CHAIRMAN: We hope to borrow all of that from secretarial help that has been cleared. It will enable us to start right in business. I have been given assurances that we would be able to get secretaries, without question, from the Department of Defense.

SEN. RUSSELL: I have one suggestion. If you can, get good ones.

MR. DULLES: I was trying to get you one from the CIA, one who had been in the CIA but who had to leave for maternity reasons. I think I can get one very quickly.

CHAIRMAN: Well, I would think, Mr. Rankin, you can confer with Mr. Dulles if you have any difficulty getting them from one of the departments here. But I hope we don't have to go out into the open market and employ anybody. That I don't want to do. I think it can be arranged without that.

MR. DULLES: We'll probably have to pay these, won't we?

MR. RANKIN: We hope they'll be given to us.

MR. DULLES: At least somebody else. I don't know.

REP. FORD: It might jeopardize this continuity of employment or service, Allen.

CHAIRMAN: It might.

MR. DULLES: That's true.

CHAIRMAN: So I would be inclined to try to borrow them and we'll see, if it creates any problem we'll come back to discussing some other way.

Gentlemen, you all have, I am sure, a copy of the FBI report. We just got today one copy of the State Department report, and we're asking them, of course, to make other copies and send a copy to each member of the Commission. That was just handed to Mr. Rankin shortly before noon today.

(p. 9) MR. DULLES: They'll be delivered to Mr. Rankin. Will they be held in the office for us? My copy of the FBI report got to me all right but I was surprised. It got there in a big box and I thought it was some more of my books. I shoved it aside and I didn't have it under any security at all.

MR. McCLOY: The FBI I thought was very particular in giving it to me. They delivered it in person.

MR. DULLES: If they're all delivered to you then we can pick it up from you.

MR. RANKIN: (Nods head.)

CHAIRMAN: We have been told that Mr. Rankin has been notified by the Secret Service that they'll perhaps have their report in before the end of the week. The CIA said that it has no big report to make but it has some communications that it wants to present to us and it will do so when Mr. Rankin tells them we're ready for it.

MR. DULLES: They have not seen the annexes to the FBI report. They do not have those. Their report could only be of value, in my opinion, unless they have something extraneous, after they have seen the FBI report.

MR. McCLOY: But they do have something that is extraneous.

MR. DULLES: That we ought to get.

CHAIRMAN: Yes. They have the trip down to Mexico, for one thing, I know. Where he went to the Cuban Embassy down there, and possibly some other agency. So whatever ones there are that come in to play we'll see that there are copies made for all of you. And I think we also ought to make a formal recommendation of the Texas people to send us their reports. I had proposed to (p. 10) talk to the Attorney General this afternoon, after our meeting, and invite him and his attorney, a man by the name of Jaworski, who bears an excellent reputation in his State for all purposes, and ask him to come down here and visit with us tomorrow and talk about the matter of liaison between the State of Texas and our Commission. From what I have learned from the Attorney General and from Mr. Jaworski I am satisfied that it will be forthcoming, we can do business with them on a very fine plane.

SEN. RUSSELL: Do you intend to ask about the police force or just go through the FBI?

CHAIRMAN: I have hoped, Senator, that we might be able, as far as Texas is concerned, to deal with the Attorney General of the State but, as you know, you're dealing with people who depend upon relationships between them, of which I'm not certain, and I felt it would be better if we could deal directly with the Attorney General of the State and get everything from him.

SEN. RUSSELL: I agree with that but I think it would be well for us to know if there are any independent files given by the State Police independent from that as kept by the Dallas Department of Police.

CHAIRMAN: We'll check that, Senator. If it is your desire we'll ask all of those agencies.

SEN. RUSSELL: I think you're exactly right in going through the Attorney General.

REP. BOGGS: In connection with this matter, prior to your arrival this afternoon, some of us inquired informally if there was any security with respect to Mrs. Oswald. She's a Russian citizen. She might just take off and leave.

MR. DULLES: I was rather worried about that. She's (p. 11) been in touch with the Embassy, that we know, and of course she might just take off and go to Mexico.

CHAIRMAN: The only thing that I heard was that the Secret Service took her into protective custody so that nothing would happen to her. Now, what they have done since that time I don't know. They were afraid that something might happen to her, as happened to her husband, so they took her to some unknown place, I think.

REP. FORD: It would be another bad flavor, I think.

CHAIRMAN: You're exactly right.

MR. McCLOY: There's another woman here that intrigues me and that is Mrs. Paine.

MR. DULLES: And her husband, too. I understand there's a report on that.

SEN. RUSSELL: There's nothing absolutely normal about any phase of it.

CHAIRMAN: Well, gentlemen, to be very frank about it, I have read that report two or three times and I have not seen anything in there yet that has not been in the press.

SEN. RUSSELL: I couldn't agree with that more. I have read it through once very carefully, and I went through it again at places I had marked, and practically everything in there has come out in the press at one time or another, a bit here and a bit there.

MR. DULLES: Some of the details of the annexes are not in the press.

SEN. RUSSELL: That's true.

MR. DULLES: I wish we could get from the FBI more readable annexes. There are three, four, or five annexes there and I think they ought to assume the responsibility of writing them (p. 12) so we can read them.

REP. FORD: I agree with you. I've had a terrible time trying to read some of the notes of Oswald and I think that, as a convenience to us, it would be very helpful if it was typewritten up so that it would be very readable.

MR. DULLES: His handwriting is very hard to decipher. They do a better job of deciphering the handwriting than we do.

MR. McCLOY: I think that you've got to bear in mind that they were under pressure to get this to us, and this only purports to be a summary. The grammar is bad and you can see they did not polish it all up. It does leave you some loopholes in this thing but I think you have to realize they put this thing together very fast.

REP. BOGGS: There's nothing in there about Governor Connally.

CHAIRMAN: No.

SEN. COOPER: And whether or not they found any bullets in him.

MR. McCLOY: This bullet business leaves me confused.

CHAIRMAN: It's totally inconclusive.

SEN. RUSSELL: They couldn't find where one bullet came out that struck the President and yet they found a bullet in the stretcher.

MR. McCLOY: I think you ought to have the autopsy documents.

CHAIRMAN: By all means we ought to have the medical reports. We ought to have them as part of this document here because they might play a very important part in it.

MR. McCLOY: I understand there are two. I may be wrong about this, but there's a report in Dallas by the surgeons who

EXHIBIT C.

Warren Commission Rules, Proceedings of Executive Session, March 16, 1964.

2732

TOP SECRET

PRESIDENT'S COMMISSION

ON THE

ASSASSINATION OF PRESIDENT KENNEDY

- - -

Washington, D. C.
Monday, March 16, 1964

The President's Commission met, pursuant to recess, at 5:47 p.m., in the Hearing Room, Fourth Floor, 200 Maryland Avenue, Northeast, Washington, D. C., Chief Justice Earl Warren, presiding.

PRESENT:

Chief Justice Earl Warren, Chairman
Senator John Sherman Cooper, Member
Representative Gerald R. Ford, Member
John J. McCloy, Member

- - -

J. Lee Rankin, General Counsel
Norman Redlich, Special Assistant to General Counsel

CLASSIFICATION CANCELLED
By authority of
Archivist of United States
By_*MMJ*_____
Date_*2/13/65*_Case_____

2733

PROCEEDINGS

The Chairman. Gentlemen, I wish to read the following resolution governing the questioning of witnesses by members of the Commission staff:

"Pursuant to Executive Order No. 11130, November 29, 1963, which authorizes this Commission 'to prescribe its own procedures', it is therefore

"Resolved, that the following are hereby adopted as the rules of this Commission for the questioning of witnesses by members of the Commission staff.

"I.   Sworn Depositions:

"A.   Individual members of the staff are hereby authorized to administer oaths and affirmations, examine witnesses, and receive evidence in the form of sworn depositions on any matter under investigation by the Commission.

"B.   Such sworn depositions may be taken only from witnesses designated in writing for questioning in this manner by the Commission, by a member of the Commission, or by the General Counsel of the Commission.

"C.   A stenographic verbatim transcript shall be made of all sworn depositions. Copies of the witness' testimony shall be available for inspection by the witness or his counsel. When approved by the Commission, said copies may be purchased by the witness or his counsel at regularly prescribed rates from the official reporter.

2734

"D.   Process and papers of the Commission issued under Paragraph (d) of Joint Resolution S.J. 137, 88th Congress, 1st Sess., shall be returnable no less than three days from the date on which such process or papers are issued, and shall state the time, place, and general subject matter of the deposition. In lieu of such process and papers, the Commission may request the presence of witnesses and production of evidence for the purpose of sworn depositions by written notice mailed no less than three days from the date of the deposition.

"E.   The period of notice specified in Paragraph D may be waived by a witness.

"F.   A witness at a sworn deposition shall have the right to be accompanied by counsel of his own choosing, who shall have the right to advise the witness of his rights under the laws and Constitution of the United States, and the State wherein the deposition shall occur, and to make brief objections to questions. At the conclusion of the witness' testimony, counsel shall have the right to clarify the testimony of the witness by questioning the witness.

"G. At the opening of any deposition a member of the Commission's staff shall read into the record a statement setting forth the nature of the Commission's inquiry and the purpose for which the witness has been asked to testify or produce evidence.

"H. Any witness who refuses to answer a question shall state the ground for so doing. At the conclusion of any (2735) deposition in which the witness refuses to answer a question the transcript shall be submitted to the General Counsel for review and consideration whether the witness should be called to testify before the Commission.

"II. Sworn Affidavits.

"A. Members of the Commission staff are hereby authorized to obtain sworn affidavits from those witnesses who have been designated in writing by the Commission, a member of the Commission, or the General Counsel of the Commission as witnesses whose testimony will be obtained in this manner.

"B. A copy of the affidavit shall be provided the affiant or his counsel."

Representative Ford. I move the adoption of the resolution.

Mr. McCloy. Second.

The Chairman. All in favor say aye.

(There was a chorus of "ayes".)

The Chairman. Opposed?

(No response.)

The Chairman. The motion is carried unanimously.

(Whereupon, at 5:50 p.m., the Commission adjourned, subject to the call of the Chair.)

EXHIBIT D.

Page 26 of Warren Commission Executive Session Transcript for January 21, 1964.

CLASSIFICATION CANCELLED
By authority of
Archivist of United States
By__*MMJ*_____
Date_*2/21/68*_Case_____

88

or inspect only the transcript of his testimony before the Commission."

Did you get that from other commissions?

Mr. Rankin. That is right. They could sell that to the press possibly.

The Chairman. Beg pardon?

Mr. Rankin. They could sell that to the press if they want to do that but that is the usual provision for the commissions.

Rep. Boggs. A witness has the right to look at his own testimony. If the press wants to buy it, they can buy it.

Mr. Dulles. Can I ask one question, Mr. Chairman?

The Chairman. Yes.

Mr. Dulles. Does this wording imply that the Commission or the Commissioners sitting are bound by the legal rules of evidence?

The Chairman. No. There is no such implication. In no sense. No.

Mr. Dulles. Because of this language?

The Chairman. No.

Mr. Dulles. Because if so we would be pretty badly tied up.

The Chairman. No, but what we are thinking of was so that the public would know that we are not letting our counsel browbeat someone in here, the Commissioners shall take care of the rights.

Mr. Dulles. I wanted to take care of that point. I am not enough of a trial lawyer to be able to answer that.

EXHIBIT E.

Ward & Paul Invoices for Transcript Sale.

WARD & PAUL, INC.
Stenotype Reporters

817 G STREET, N. W., WASHINGTON, D. C. 20001

NATIONAL { 8-4266 / 8-4267 / 8-4268 }

WA 4555

WHEN REMITTING PLEASE REFER TO THIS NUMBER

INVOICE TO: Mrs. Marina Oswald, 929 Belt Line Road, Richardson, Texas 75080

SHIPPED TO (SAME AS SOLD TO UNLESS OTHERWISE INDICATED): Same

Terms: NET CASH

INVOICE DATE	YOUR ORDER NO	ORDERED BY	SHIPPING DATE	SHIPPED VIA	DOCKET NO PLACE	W&P FILE NO
11-4-64	Letter of 10-23-64	Attorneys	11-2-64	FIRST CLASS MAIL REGISTERED		PC-2

BEFORE: President's Commission on the Assassination

NAME:

HEARING DATE	NO OF COPIES	DESCRIPTION	NO OF PAGES	PAGE RATE	AMOUNT
		TRANSCRIPT OF PROCEEDINGS as follows:			
Feb. 3	1	Taken at Washington, D. C.	65		
4	1	" " " "	65		
5	1	" " " "	101		
6	1	" " " "	107		
Jun 11	1	" " " "	55		
Sept 6	1	Taken at Dallas, Texas	104		
			497	15¢	89.85
		Amount of Invoice			$95.95
		Less check of 10-23			11.10
		Balance			84.85

DELIVERY CHARGES 6.10

TOTAL 95.95

Thanks Again! WE APPRECIATE YOUR BUSINESS

JOB FOLDER COPY

...ARD & PAUL, INC. / *Stenotype Reporters*

...G STREET, N.W., WASHINGTON, D.C. 20001

INVOICE NUMBER **WA 3752**

WHEN REMITTING PLEASE REFER TO THIS NUMBER

SHIPPED TO (SAME AS SOLD TO UNLESS OTHERWISE INDICATED)

C. Icarus M. Pappas
301 East 48th Street
New York, N. Y.

Terms: NET CASH

INVOICE DATE	YOUR ORDER NO	ORDERED BY	SHIPPING DATE	SHIPPED VIA
8-4-34			8-4-34	Reg-Registered

DOCKET NO
PLACE Washington, D.C.
WRP FILE NO   IC-2   cv

HEARING DATE	NO OF COPIES	DESCRIPTION	NO OF PAGES	PAGE RATE	AMOUNT
July 29	1	President's Commission on the Assassination of President Kennedy	40	.15	6.00
		TRANSCRIPT OF PROCEEDINGS as follows:			
		Deposition of Icarus M. Pappas			
			Postage		1.25
			DELIVERY CHARGES		
			TOTAL		7.25

Thanks Again!
WE APPRECIATE YOUR BUSINESS

EXHIBIT F.

Letter of Mayor Robert M. L. Johnson of Cedar Rapids, Iowa, to President Lyndon Johnson.

January 4, 1965

Mr. President:

As one who read and believed the Warren Report on the assassination of President Kennedy I am disturbed and chagrined that you would permit a government agency to dictate to you what will be done with testimony and exhibits for the next 75 years.

Knowing that you believe in the public's right to know—a statement you have often made—it intrigues me that you would permit a 75 year cloak of secrecy to fall over the facts involved in the Kennedy assassination.

The decision of the National Archives Bureau to withhold from the public "off the record testimony and exhibits of the Warren Commission for 75 years" is inexplicable and inexcusable and gives cause to doubt the veracity of the published Warren Commission report.

I believe in national security but I fail to see the relationship between the facts of the Kennedy assassination and the security of the nation at this time.

May I suggest that if there is true justification for withholding from the public the facts of one of the most tragic events of our time, it is also incumbent upon our national leadership to make it clear why.

Franklin D. Roosevelt said: "the only thing we have to fear is fear itself." Secrecy creates fear.

Respectfully submitted,

/s/

Robert M. L. Johnson
Mayor

The President
The White House
Washington 25, D. C.   RMLJ/bw

EXHIBIT G.

White House Memorandum for Acting Attorney General Katzenbach.

THE WHITE HOUSE

CONFIDENTIAL   WASHINGTON

January 18, 1965

MEMORANDUM FOR ACTING ATTORNEY GENERAL KATZENBACH

SUBJECT: PUBLIC DISCLOSURE OF WARREN COMMISSION REPORTS
           AND WORKING PAPERS

1.   Attached at TAB 1 is a copy of a letter which the President recently received from Mayor Robert Johnson of Cedar Rapids, Iowa, and which objects
rather strongly to a report that the National Archives will not make available
to the public, for 75 years, certain Warren Commission records. On receiving
this letter, we asked National Archives for a background memo on the subject
and for a suggested reply to Mayor Johnson.

National Archives has met our request and attached at TAB 2 is a copy of a
GSA memo, with enclosures, which recommends that Warren Commission
records be treated on the same basis as other investigative records and that,
generally speaking, they not be made available to the public for a period of
75 years.

2.   While the GSA memo seems to me to have some merit, in view of the
very special nature of the Warren Commission investigation and the desirability of the fullest possible disclosure of all the findings, I believe that a
further study should be made on the feasibility and advisability of making
an exception, in this particular case, to the normal 75-year disclosure procedure. In this regard, and because of the legal ramifications involved, I would
appreciate it very much if you would direct the Justice Department, in consultation with other appropriate agencies, to coordinate this study. The study
should include, but not necessarily be limited to answers to such questions as
the following:

(a)   What alternatives are there to the 75-year procedure which would meet the aim of "fullest possible disclosure" and, at the same time, not violate the national security or the dictates of good sense? For example, can some or most of the material be released in two years? Five years? Can certain categories of the public (e.g. scholars) receive special treatment?

(b)   How does the Warren Commission view this problem (particularly the Chief Justice and Lee Rankin)?

McGeorge Bundy

cc: Acting Administrator
      Knott, GSA

EXHIBIT H.

Attorney General's Memorandum of April 13, 1965 with Page One of the Attachment Thereto.

April 13, 1965

MEMORANDUM FOR: Honorable McGeorge Bundy
                  Special Assistant to the President

RE: Public Availability of Materials Delivered to the National Archives by the President's Commission on the Assassination of President Kennedy.

The Department of Justice has completed the study, requested by you in your memorandum of January 15, 1965, concerning the advisability of modifying the usual restrictions which would govern the availability to the public of materials delivered to the National Archives by the President's Commission on the Assassination of President Kennedy. In the course of this study, the Department of Justice has obtained the views of the President's Commission, the Archivist of the United States, the interested Federal Agencies, and the Dallas Police Department.

Under normal regulations governing access to materials deposited in the National Archives, materials are made available to any competent adult with a definite, serious reason for requesting access, unless there is in effect an overriding restriction on disclosure or disclosure would violate obvious requirements of public policy or propriety. With respect to investigative reports furnished to the President's Commission by Federal agencies, the relevant restriction is a rule of non-disclosure for a period of 75 years unless the agency in which the report originated authorizes disclosure.

The Chief Justice has informed me in a letter dated April 5, 1965, that the President's Commission concluded, after full consideration, that the public availability of the Commission's records was a matter to be resolved by the Attorney General and the originating agencies in accordance with established law and policies of the Government. According to the Chief Justice, the Commission assumed that these determinations would be made in light of "the overriding consideration of the fullest possible disclosure." Moreover, the Commission did not desire to restrict access to any of its working papers except those classified by other agencies.

Based on the views of the Commission and the recommendations of the Federal agencies involved (summarized in the Attachment to this letter), the Department of Justice believes that there should be some modification of the normal procedures of the National Archives. The Department recommends that the following procedures be adopted in order to accomplish the most complete disclosure consistent with other legitimate interests:

1.   All material furnished to the President's Commission by the Dallas Police Department and the Immigration and Naturalization Service should be made available to the public on a regular basis, since both agencies have authorized full disclosure.

2.   Investigative reports and related materials furnished to the President's Commission by other Federal agencies should be administered in accordance with the existing regulations of the National Archives. These agencies should be requested to examine the materials furnished by them with a view to authorizing the immediate disclosure on a regular basis of as much of the materials as possible. (Where materials originated with an agency other than the one furnishing them to the Commission, the decision regarding disclosure should be made by the originating agency.) The following guidelines should be applied:

   a.   Statutory requirements of non-disclosure should be observed;

   b.   Security classifications should be respected, but the agency responsible for the classification should consider whether the classification can be eliminated or graded down consistently with the national security;

   c.   All unclassified material which has been disclosed verbatim or in substance in the Report of the President's Commission or accompanying published documents should be made available to the public on a regular basis. (In this connection, it should be noted that the Archivist has advised that a final determination of which reports have been published in whole or in part, verbatim or in substance, will not be available before 1966.)

   d.   Unclassified material which has not already been disclosed in another form should be made available to the public on a regular basis unless disclosure

      1)   will be detrimental to the administration and enforcement of the laws and regulations of the United States and its agencies;

      2)   may reveal the identity of confidential sources of information or the nature of confidential methods of acquiring information, and thereby prevent or limit the use of the same or similar sources and methods in the future;

3) may lead to the incorrect identification of sources of information and thereby embarrass individuals or the agency involved;

4) would be a source of embarrassment to innocent persons, who are the subject or source of the material in question, because of the dissemination of gossip and rumor or details of a personal nature having no significant connection with the assassination of the President;

5) will reveal material pertinent to the criminal prosecution of Jack Ruby for the murder of Lee Harvey Oswald, prior to the final judicial determination of that case.

Where one of the above reasons for non-disclosure may apply, the agency involved should weigh such reason against the "overriding consideration of the fullest possible disclosure" in determining whether or not to authorize disclosure.

e. Except in special cases, documents should be withheld or disclosed in their entirety.

3. Classified and unclassified material which is not made available to the public should be reviewed by the agency concerned five years and ten years after the initial examination has been completed. The criteria applied in the initial examination, outlined above, should be applied to determine whether changed circumstances will permit further disclosure. Similar reviews should be undertaken at ten-year intervals during the remainder of the 75-year period of nondisclosure. The Archivist should undertake to arrange for such review at the appropriate times.

4. When a request for limited disclosure of particular unclassified documents or groups of documents is received by the Archivist, he should communicate such request to the agency concerned, which should consider the request in the light of the criteria outlined above and, wherever consistent with those criteria, authorize the limited disclosure requested. In the application of the criteria, consideration should be given to the qualifications of the person requesting disclosure and the purpose for which the request is made.

It should be noted that the Archivist has indicated that the arrangement and preparation of an inventory of the material turned over to the National Archives by the President's Commission will not be completed until June 1, 1965. Accordingly, it is unlikely that a review of the material turned over to the Commission by the various agencies can be undertaken before that date. It is suggested that the Archivist be asked to make arrangements with the various agencies for such review to be undertaken at the earliest possible date, to be carried out on an expedited basis.

The Archivist has advised that the disposition of materials originating with the President's Commission itself has been discussed with Mr. Rankin and that a final decision has been deferred until after June 1. He has advised also that pending a determination of the ownership of phyical exhibits, requests for access to them will be referred to the Department of Justice. While it is anticipated that the fullest possible disclosure of these portions of the record will be authorized, in accordance with the desires of the President's Commission, the Department believes that particular decisions as to them should not be made until information regarding them is complete.

If these procedures meet with your approval, this Department will prepare the necessary instructions.

Attorney General

Attachment

SUMMARY OF VIEWS OF INTERESTED FEDERAL AGENCIES CONCERNING THE DISCLOSURE TO THE PUBLIC OF MATERIALS DELIVERED TO THE NATIONAL ARCHIVES BY THE PRESIDENT'S COMMISSION ON THE ASSASSINATION OF PRESIDENT KENNEDY.

In response to inquiry by the Department of Justice, the federal agencies which submitted reports or other materials to the President's Commission expressed the following views regarding the disclosure of these materials to the public.

1.   FEDERAL BUREAU OF INVESTIGATION. The Federal Bureau of Investigation recognizes that materials furnished by it for use by the President's Commission, except those which were classified for reasons of national security, are in the public domain. Most of the material furnished by the Bureau was unclassified. Security classification was necessary in some instances to prevent the identification of confidential informants, to protect the secrecy of confidential investigative techniques, to avoid disclosure of information showing the Bureau's coverage of the Soviet Embassy in Washington, D. C., and to maintain the classification imposed by other agencies on information furnished by them to the Bureau. The Bureau believes that clas-

sified material should be disclosed only to persons having the necessary security clearance.

The Bureau believes that another problem is presented by unclassified material, some of which contains reports of rumor, gossip, and similar data involving innocent people. Some of this unclassified material contains the results of extensive investigations of Mrs. Marina Oswald and various associates of the Oswalds. Disclosure of such material, the Bureau believes, would be a source of unwarranted embarrassment to the people concerned. Some material contained in unclassified documents was furnished to the Bureau in confidence by sources such as banks and hotels. The records of these sources cannot be produced except pursuant to a court order. Public disclosure of this information might cause the Bureau to lose the cooperation of such sources in the future and might subject the sources to civil suit.

EXHIBIT I.

White House Memorandum by McGeorge Bundy Approving Attorney General's Guidelines for Disclosure of Warren Commission Records.

THE WHITE HOUSE

WASHINGTON

April 19, 1965

MEMORANDUM FOR THE ATTORNEY GENERAL

SUBJECT: Public Availability of Materials Delivered to the National Archives by the Warren Commission

1.   The procedures, described in your memorandum of April 13 about the above subject, have been approved.

2.   In coordination with Archives, please instruct the appropriate agencies (a) to conduct the review of documents in accordance with the guidelines set forth in your memorandum and (b) to complete this review by September 1, 1965.

3.   At the conclusion of this review, please inform us of the approximate percentage of the material in question which has been designated as available for public access.

/s/
McGeorge Bundy

cc: National Archives (Mr. Bahmer)

EXHIBIT J.

Page 20 of April 30, 1964, Warren Commission Executive Session Transcript.

20   5869

what happened to this man after he left the United States, went to Russia, came back—I think we ought to get in the record what the State Department knows about him.

What about De Mohrenschildt?

The Chairman. He has had a full deposition.

Off the record.

(Discussion off the record.)

The Chairman. Back on the record.

Mr. Rankin. I think at this time we ought to take action on declassifying our transcript so the printers can handle it, from Top Secret to Confidential.

The Chairman. Did I hear a motion?

Mr. McCloy. I move it.

Mr. Dulles. Seconded.

The Chairman. All in favor say aye.

(Chorus of aye)

The Chairman. Off the record.

(Discussion off the record.)

The Chairman. Back on the record.

The first item here is a report on printing of final report.

Mr. Rankin. We have been talking to the Budget people and GSA, and the printer, about the form of the report. And here is a draft that they have made up, first of the summary of the report, a form that they suggest that will be in a form that they can get out most reasonably and present it. And then the second

EXHIBIT K.

Agenda for January 27, 1964, Warren Commission Executive Session Transcript.

AGENDA FOR MEETING
OF
PRESIDENT'S COMMISSION ON THE
ASSASSINATION OF PRESIDENT KENNEDY

Monday, January 27, 1964 - 3 P. M.

I.   Proposed letters regarding security precautions.

        A.   Letters to Department of Justice and CIA (Attachment 1)

        B.   Letter to Department of the Treasury (Attachment 2)

        C.   Letter to Police Commissioners (Attachment 3)

II.   Allegations regarding Oswald as an undercover agent

        A.   Report on events since last meeting of Commission

        B.   Alternative courses of action

III.   Progress Report on the work of Commission Staff - General Counsel

IV.   Additional Materials

        A.   Statements of Lee Harvey Oswald after arrest

        B.   Chronology prepared by Secret Service

EXHIBIT L.

Letter to Dr. James B. Rhoads from Harold Weisberg.

October 13, 1968

Dr. James B. Rhoads
Archivist of the United States
National Archives and Records Service
Washington, D. C. 20408

Dear Dr. Rhoads:

The agenda of the Warren Commission executive session of January 27, 1964, makes it obvious that the entire transcript cannot properly be withheld. I therefore renew my request for it and for a list of any of the topics you may decide still to withhold. From the attachments to the agenda, it would seem that not even what relates to the protection of the President is subject to withholding.

Mr. Hoover's letter of February 11, 1964, in the GAI-FBI file, refers to several things I would like: The Lonnie Hudkins story in the Houston Post of 1/1/64; the FBI interview with him of 2/8/64 (and any others); the FBI interviews with Philadelphia Inquirer reporter Joe Goulden and his stories.

Mr. Hoover's letter of February 17, 1964, same file: the January 25, 1964, interview with Bill Alexander (and any others).

Mr. Hoover's letter of February 10, 1964, same file: the FBI interview February 8, 1964, with Henry Wade (and any others).

From these files it would seem there should be additional memoranda by Mr. Rankin and/or others, on their conferences relating to Oswald as government-connected. These should include those of his January 24 conference with the Texans and that of January 28 with Mr. Hoover. If there are any reports or memoranda of interviews with Dean Storey, I should like them, also.

There was no covering letter with the registered package of material I received yesterday, including those letters and what relates to the January 27,

1964, executive session. I presume you have not yet sent me all the material on Oswald as an agent.

In the PG-6 file is a memo saying there were to be subsequent staff meetings on this subject, including the Hosty matter. If there were, I would like copies of any records.

In the material supplied me, there are no affidavits denying Oswald was connected with either the Defense Intelligence Agency, the Office of Navy Intelligence or any Marine intelligence unit. Is there such evidence? If so, may I please have copies?

May I, please, have copies of Exhibits 706-9 and CD 1395, pp. 46-8.

If my account is getting low, if you will advise me, I will replenish it.

Sincerely,

/s/

Harold Weisberg

19.
REQUEST FOR PRODUCTION OF DOCUMENTS

Pursuant to Rule 34 of the Federal Rules of Civil Procedure, plaintiff requests that within 30 days the defendant produce and permit plaintiff to make copies of the following documents:

1.   The letter from former Chief Justice Earl Warren to the Attorney General of the United States dated April 5, 1965, and referred to at the bottom of page one of the Attorney General's April 13, 1965, Memorandum re "Public Availability of Materials Delivered to the National Archives by the President's Commission on the Assassination of President Kennedy."

2.   Any letters sent to members of the Warren Commission as a result of the January 18, 1965, White House directive to the Attorney General that he find out how the Warren Commission viewed the problem of the public availability of its records. Also, the response of any Warren Commission member to any such letters. [A copy of the January 18, 1965, directive is attached hereto]

3.   Any document purporting to give the Warren Commission authority to classify documents under Executive Order 10501.

4.   Any instruction from the Warren Commission to Mr. J. Lee Rankin ordering him to classify the January 27, 1964, Executive Session transcript or any other Executive Session transcript.

5.   Any document specifically ordering Ward & Paul to classify the January 27, 1964, Executive Session transcript or any other Executive Session transcript.

Filed: April 29, 1974.

139

6.   Any statement of views on the public availability of Warren Commission records solicited of the following agencies: The Federal Bureau of Investigation, the Secret Service, the Central Intelligence Agency, the Department of State, and the Department of Defense. Also, the letters soliciting these views from the foregoing agencies. [The statements of these agencies are summarized in the Attachment to the Attorney General's April 13, 1965 Memorandum referred to in Paragraph 1 above]

7.   The statement of views of Mr. Howard P. Willens of the Criminal Division of the Department of Justice referred to in the last paragraph of the January 15, 1965, letter from Lawson B. Knott, Jr. to Gordon Chance. [A copy of this letter is attached hereto]

8.   Any statement of views expressed by the agencies mentioned in the last paragraph of the January 15, 1965, letter from Lawson B. Knott, Jr. to Gordon Chance.

Plaintiff requests that copies of the above documents be mailed to his attorney within 30 days.

/s/ _____

JAMES H. LESAR
1231 Fourth Street, S. W.
Washington, D. C. 20024

CERTIFICATE OF SERVICE.

I hereby certify that service of the foregoing Request for the Production of Documents has been made upon the defendant by mailing a copy thereof to its attorney, Assistant United States Attorney Michael J. Ryan, Room 3421 United States Courthouse, Washington, D. C., on this 29th day of April, 1974.

/s/ _____

JAMES HIRAM LESAR

ATTACHMENT A.

Memorandum to Acting Attorney General Katzenbach from McGeorge Bundy.
January 18, 1965.

THE WHITE HOUSE

WASHINGTON

January 18, 1965
MEMORANDUM FOR ACTING ATTORNEY GENERAL KATZENBACH
SUBJECT: Public Disclosure of Warren Commission Reports and Working
Papers

1.   Attached at Tab 1 is a copy of a letter which the President recently received from Mayor Robert Johnson of Cedar Rapids, Iowa, and which objects
rather strongly to a report that the National Archives will not make available
to the public, for 75 years, certain Warren Commission records. On receiving
this letter, we asked National Archives for a background memo on the subject
and for a suggested reply to Mayor Johnson.

National Archives has met our request and attached at Tab 2 is a copy of a
GSA memo, with enclosures, which recommends that Warren Commission
records be treated on the same basis as other investigative records and that,
generally speaking, they not be made available to the public for a period of
75 years.

2.   While the GSA memo seems to me to have some merit, in view of the
very special nature of the Warren Commission investigation and the desirability of the fullest possible disclosure of all the findings, I believe that a
further study should be made on the feasibility and advisability of making an
exception, in this particular case, to the normal 75-year disclosure procedure.
In this regard, and because of the legal ramifications involved, I would appreciate it very much if you would direct the Justice Department, in consultation
with other appropriate agencies, to coordinate this study. The study should
include, but not necessarily be limited to, answers to such questions as the
following:

(a) What alternatives are there to the 75-year procedure which would
     meet the aim of "fullest possible disclosure" and, at the same
     time, not violate the national security or the dictates of good
     sense? For example, can some or most of the material be released
     in two years? Five years? Can certain categories of the public
     (e.g. scholars) receive special treatment?

(b) How does the Warren Commission view this problem (particularly
     the Chief Justice and Lee Rankin)?

McGeorge Bundy

cc: Acting Administrator
     Knott, GSA

ATTACHMENT B.

Memorandum to Gordon Chase from Lawson B. Knott, Jr. January 15, 1965.

Gordon Chase
The White House

The Acting Administrator

Proposed reply to Mayor Robert Johnson's letter to President Johnson concerning the records of the Warren Commission

As requested I am attaching a draft of a proposed reply to Mayor Robert
Johnson's letter to the President, January 4, 1965, in which he objected to
restrictions reportedly imposed on the use of the records of the Warren Commission. Mayor Johnson's letter was apparently inspired by press reports
(see attached clipping, Washington Post, December 22, 1964) quoting Deputy
Archivist, Robert H. Bahmer, to the effect that the Commission records
would be closed for 75 years. In point of fact Mr. Bahmer stated that the 75
year limitation was the general policy applied to the reports of investigatory
agencies and similar material and would be applied to the records of the Warren Commission unless an exception were made in this particular case.

The Warren Commission records were transferred to the National Archives on November 23, 1964, in accordance with the Commission's decision announced in the final paragraph of the foreword to its Report:

"The Commission is committing all of its reports and working papers to the National Archives, where they can be permanently preserved under the rules and regulations of the National Archives and applicable Federal law."

The records consist of some 300 cubic feet of material, much of it consisting of unfiled documents and extra copies of papers duplicated for the Commission's use. Several months will be required properly to arrange the records and prepare an inventory of them. In general the records consist of:

1. The administrative and business files of the Commission.
2. Documentary material gathered by or submitted to the Commission.
    a. Testimony given before the Commission.
    b. Depositions taken by officers of the Commission.
    c. Affidavits submitted to the Commission.
    d. Investigatory reports made for the Commission by various investigatory agencies of the Federal Government.
    e. Original documentary materials acquired from other persons as exhibits.
    f. Original photographic materials acquired from other persons.

Those exhibits in the nature of artifacts, such as items of clothing, weapons, and other physical material are still in the custody of the Federal Bureau of Investigation. No restriction on these materials or on the photographic exhibits is contemplated.

The most important of the documentary materials are the transcripts of testimony, the depositions and the affidavits (most of which were published in the 26 volume set, Hearings before the President's Commission on the Assassination of President Kennedy) and the reports of investigations made for the Commission by the FBI, the Secret Service, the CIA and other departments and agencies, many of which were not published in full.

These reports and allied papers are the raw data compiled by the investigators. Many of them reveal the techniques of investigation and the sources that the investigatory agencies rightly insist must not be disclosed. Many of them contain information concerning innocent third parties, information irrelevant to the investigation of President Kennedy's assassination, the release of which would embarrass or injure innocent persons.

Because investigative reports contain unevaluated data the investigatory agencies of the Government have always placed restrictions on their use. The National Archives at the request of these agencies has imposed a 75 year restriction on such materials. We believe that this restriction should be applied to similar materials in the Warren Commission records, and we recommend that the attached draft of a proposed reply to Mayor Johnson embodying this policy be used as a basis for the President's reply.

The attached draft has been concurred in by the following agencies: the U. S. Secret Service; the Department of Defense; the Department of State (in so far as the 75 year restriction is concerned); the Immigration and Naturalization Service; the Central Intelligence Agency; the Internal Revenue Service and the Federal Bureau of Investigation. Mr. Howard P. Willens of the Criminal Division, Department of Justice did not concur. We understand that he has indicated his position to you directly.

Enclosures

Lawson B. Knott, Jr.
Acting Administrator

cc:
Official file - N
A
Day file - N

RHBahmer:fg ND 1-15-65

ATTACHMENT C.

Tuesday, Dec. 22, 1964
The Washington Post

WARREN INQUIRY DATA SECURE FOR 75 YEARS

Evidence and investigating reports used by the Warren Commission have been stored in a special vault in the National Archives Building, where they will remain inaccessible to the public for 75 years.

Only under extraordinary circumstances will off-the-record parts of the historic material be made available either to scholars and writers.

Deputy Archivist Robert H. Bahmer said Thursday that each agency that furnished data may declassify its material, or parts of it, and grant permission for responsible persons to see it.

However, an outsider wishing to see all of the secret material would need the approval of all of the agencies involved in the investigation. These included the FBI, CIA, State Department and Immigration Service.

Public interest in the length of time required before the complete evidence became public was stirred by a remark by Chief Justice Earl Warren, the commission chairman.

Following testimony last February by Marina Oswald, widow of the presumed assassin, Warren told newsmen that some of the testimony might not be released "in your lifetime."

The next day the Chief Justice modified his statement, explaining that he was referring to matters involving the national security that conceivably could come up during the inquiry.

Bahmer said Thursday that, barring any grants of special permission, the National Archives will follow its policy of keeping the material classified for 75 years. This, he said, is the policy concerning all historic investigations.

He said that 75 years was chosen because it was considered to be the life span of an individual. The period is intended to serve as protection for innocent persons who could otherwise be damaged because of their relationship with participants in the case, such as Oswald's two infant daughters.

Bahmer said that the Kennedy assassination material will be stored in an inner vault equipped with highly sensitive electronic detection devices to guard against fire and theft. The vault will have temperature and humidity controls to prevent deterioration of the material.

The combination of the vault will be known by only two or three persons, he said.

The materials will include physical exhibits such as the rifle used to kill the president in Dallas Nov. 22, 1963.

20.
MEMORANDUM AND ORDER
[GRANTING DEFENDANT SUMMARY JUDGMENT ON
EXEMPTION 7 GROUNDS]

Plaintiff invokes the Freedom of Information Act, 5 U.S.C. § 552, in an effort to gain access to a transcript of the Warren Commission's January 27, 1964, executive session, presently in the custody of the National Archives. The defendant General Services Administration, which operates the Archives, has moved for summary judgment on the ground that the transcript at issue is shielded by the Act's first, fifth and seventh exemptions. 5 U.S.C. § 552 (b)(1, 5, 7). The issues have been thoroughly briefed by all parties and are ripe for adjudication.

Initially, the Court probed defendant's claim that the transcript had been classified "Top Secret" under Executive Order 10501, 3 C.F.R. 979 (Comp. 1949-53), since such classification would bar further judicial inquiry and justify total confidentiality. 5 U.S.C. § 552 (b)(1); E.P.A. v. Mink, 410 U.S. 73 (1973). However, defendant's papers and affidavits, supplemented at the Court's request, still fail to demonstrate that the disputed transcript has ever been classified by an individual authorized to make such a designation under the strict procedures set forth in Executive Order 10501, 3 C.F.R. 979 (Comp. 1949-53), as amended by Executive Order 10901, 3 C.F.R. 432 (Comp. 1959-63).

Filed: May 3, 1974.

Defendant's reliance on the seventh exemption, on the other hand, appears to be fully justified by the record. The Warren Commission was an investigatory body assigned to look into the assassination of President Kennedy and the subsequent murder of Lee Harvey Oswald. It can hardly be disputed that its findings would have led to criminal enforcement proceedings had it uncovered evidence of complicity in those events by any living person. The Archives' collection of Warren Commission transcripts therefore constitutes an "investigatory file . . . compiled for law enforcement purposes . . ." within the meaning of the seventh exemption. 5 U.S.C. § 552 (b)(7).

The instant case is squarely controlled by the decision of this Circuit in Weisberg v. Dept. of Justice, 489 F.2d 1195 (D.C. Cir. 1973), in which the same plaintiff sought access to certain materials collected by the Federal Bureau of Investigation during its investigation into the assassination of President Kennedy. The Court concluded that the Bureau's intensive inquiry, undertaken at the special request of President Johnson, was clearly conducted for law enforcement purposes even if no violations of federal laws were involved, so that the resulting investigatory files were protected. Id. at 1197-98. No less protection can be afforded to the files of the Warren Commission, which was also instituted by the President for the principle purpose of examining evidence of criminal conduct arising out of the assassination. See Executive Order No. 11130, 3 C.F.R. 795 (Comp. 1959-63).

It is therefore

ORDERED that defendant's motion for summary judgment is granted.

/s/_____
UNITED STATES DISTRICT JUDGE

May 3, 1974.

21.
MOTION FOR RECONSIDERATION

Pursuant to Rules 52(b) and 60(b) of the Federal Rules of Civil Procedure, plaintiff moves the Court to reconsider and vacate that part of the Court's May 3, 1974, Memorandum and Order which awarded the defendant summary judgment in this cause on the ground that the defendant's invocation of the investigatory files exemption to the Freedom of Information Act "appears to be fully justified by the record."

A Memorandum of Points and Authorities in support of this motion is attached hereto.

/s/_____
JAMES HIRAM LESAR
1231 Fourth Street, S. W.
Washington, D. C. 20024

Counsel for Plaintiff

Filed: May 13, 1974. MOTION FOR RECONSIDERATION denied by order
of Judge Gesell May 14, 1974.

MEMORANDUM OF POINTS AND AUTHORITIES IN SUPPORT OF
MOTION FOR RECONSIDERATION. MAY 13, 1974.

I.   NOTHING IN THE RECORD SUPPORTS THE DEFENDANT'S
      CLAIM THAT THE TRANSCRIPT SOUGHT IS ENTITLED TO
      EXEMPTION 7 IMMUNITY

In granting defendant's motion for summary judgment, the Court
stated that "Defendant's reliance on the seventh exemption . . . appears to be
fully justified." Contrary to this assertion, there is nothing in the record
which supports the defendant's claim of exemption 7 immunity except a
bald assertion that because it is part of the Warren Commission's files it is,
ipso facto, exempt from disclosure. For several reasons, this is totally inadequate to meet the defendant's burden of proof under the Freedom of Information Act and thus support a motion for summary judgment.

First, unlike Weisberg v. Department of Justice, 489 F. 2d 1195, which
will be discussed in more detail below, in the instant action no affidavit has
been submitted in support of the exemption 7 claim. As a consequence, the
defendant has made no evidentiary showing that the transcript sought is in
fact part of an investigatory file compiled for law enforcement purposes. Yet
such a showing is necessary for the defendant to meet its burden of proof. As
the Supreme Court said in Environmental Protection Agency v. Mink:

An agency should be given the opportunity, by means of detailed affidavits or oral testimony, to establish to the satisfaction of the District Court
that the documents sought fall clearly beyond the range of material . . . [sub-
ject to disclosure]. E.P.A. v. Mink, 410 U.S. 73, 93 (1973). [Emphasis added]

This Circuit has specifically adopted requirements that an agency must provide a detailed justification of its allegations of exempt status:

The problems of assuring that allegations of exempt status are adequately justified is the most obvious and the most easily remedied flaw in current procedures. It may be corrected by assuring government agencies that
courts will simply no longer accept conclusory and generalized allegations of
exemptions . . . but will require a relatively detailed analysis in manageable
segments. Vaughn v. Rosen, 484 F. 2d 820, 826.

Not only has the defendant failed to submit any affidavit in support of its
claim that the file is part of an investigatory file compiled for law enforcement purposes, but such evidence as there is in the record directly contradicts

the exemption 7 claim. Thus, when called on to state forthrightly <u>and under</u> <u>oath</u> that the January 27 transcript is being withheld as part of an investigatory file compiled for law enforcement purposes, the defendant declined to do so. [See answer to interrogatory six] This unwillingness to invoke exemption 7 under oath is not accidental; rather, as defendant's answers to other interrogatories establish, it arises from a well-grounded fear of committing perjury.

The answers to interrogatories 19 and 30 show that <u>no law enforcement officials ever saw the January 27 transcript until "1967-1968," three years after the Warren Commission had terminated its investigation.</u> The answer to interrogatory 15 establishes that no copy of this transcript was ever provided to the only law enforcement officials who did have jurisdiction to prosecute any persons involved in the assassination of President Kennedy. Given these facts it seems bizarre, if not ludicrous, to maintain that this transcript "relate(s) to anything that can be fairly characterized as an enforcement proceeding." [Bristol Myers Co. v. F.T.C., 424 F. 2d 935, 939] No doubt most citizens would find it curious and even a little unsettling to learn that investigatory files compiled for law enforcement purposes were not shown to law enforcement officials of any kind until more than three years after the investigation of the crime had ended.

The defendant has not claimed that all Warren Commission Executive Session transcripts are immune from disclosure under the investigatory files exemption. Indeed, Complaint Exhibit C shows that two of the four Executive Session transcripts which are still suppressed in toto are not claimed to be exempt from disclosure as investigatory files. This means that even the defendant invokes exemption 7 immunity only by reference to a particular transcript and not by deducing that status a priori from the fact that it is a Warren Commission file. This differs from the Court's decision, which is even more extreme than the defendant's, and which authorizes suppression of the entire Warren Commission files consisting of hundreds of thousands of pages. Conceivably George Orwell himself would be astonished to learn that, a full decade ahead of schedule, the Freedom of Information Act had become an instrument for suppressing all the records of an official commission established to make the truth about an assassination known to the public.

Bearing on this is the fact that many pages of the eighty-six page transcript sought by plaintiff have been sold for profit by a member of the Warren Commission (and before they were made available to law enforcement authorities). As this Circuit noted in Vaughn v. Rosen, "It is quite possible that part of a document should be kept secret while part should be disclosed." Vaughn, supra, 825. Counter to the directives of Vaughn, this Court has not required the defendant to index this transcript in manageable segments so that it can be determined if any of the eighty-six pages are properly withheld.

II.   THIS CASE IS NOT SQUARELY CONTROLLED BY WEIS-
        BERG V. DEPARTMENT OF JUSTICE

The Court has held that "the instant case is squarely controlled by the decision of this Circuit in Weisberg v. Department of Justice, 489 F. 2d 1195 (D.C. Cir. 1973)." However, plaintiff contends that this case differs in several important respects from that case.

Weisberg v. Department of Justice [hereafter referred to as Weisberg] involved a request for the results of certain spectrographic analyses which Weisberg asserts will show that the FBI deceived Warren Commission members and the American public as to whether their tests supported the official theory that Oswald and Oswald alone killed President Kennedy. Thus, Weisberg involves FBI files, whereas the present case involves only the transcript of a Warren Commission Executive Session. The Court of Appeals expressly confined its decision to FBI files: "We are not discussing any problem except that of compelled disclosure of Federal Bureau of Investigation investigatory files compiled for law enforcement purposes." Weisberg, supra, 1199-1200.

Secondly, the nature of the record before the court in Weisberg was totally different than it is in this case. In Weisberg the District Court had before it an affidavit by an FBI agent which stated that he had personally reviewed the spectrographic examinations sought and that:

3.   These spectrographic examinations were conducted for law enforcement purposes as a part of the FBI investigation into the assassination. The details of these examinations constitute a part of the investigative file, which was compiled for law enforcement purposes and is maintained by the Federal Bureau of Investigation concerning the investigation of the assassination of President John F. Kennedy.

4.   The investigative file referred to in paragraph "3" above was compiled solely for the official use of U.S. Government personnel. This file is not disclosed by the Federal Bureau of Investigation to persons other than U.S. Government employees on a "need-to-know" basis.

No such affidavit is on file with the Court in the present case. In addition, the answers to interrogatories dispute some of the assertions contained in this affidavit. For example, it is a matter of record that parts of the file have in fact been sold for publication, so it is not possible to pretend that the transcript was made available soley for the "official use of U.S. Government personnel" and is not disclosed "to persons other than U.S. Government employees on a 'need-to-know' basis."

Third, in the hearing before the District Court in Weisberg counsel for the defendant asserted that ". . . the Attorney General of the United States has determined that it is not in the national interest to divulge these spectrographic analyses." No such assertion has been made here. In the instant case plaintiff did call upon the defendant to repeat that claim under oath but the defendant wisely refused to do so. [See answer to interrogatory 4]

In fact, the record in the instant case demonstrates that an executive determination was made to make the Commission's files publicly available. Thus, Memorandum Exhibit H quotes former Chief Justice Earl Warren as saying: "Moreover, the Commission did not desire to restrict access to any of its working papers except those classified by other agencies." In addition, the attachment to Exhibit H, summarizes the views of the FBI on the disclosure of the records which it provided the Warren Commission as follows: "The Federal Bureau of Investigation recognizes that materials furnished by it for use by the President's Commission, except those which were classified for reasons of national security, are in the public domain." No such matter was in the record and before the District Court or the Court of Appeals in Weisberg. Thus, this Court must confront an entirely different record than was made in that case. The decision in Weisberg can in no way substitute for the finding of fact which must be made by this Court on the basis of the record before it in this case.

CONCLUSION

In view of the foregoing, plaintiff asks the Court to reconsider and vacate its order granting the defendant summary judgment on exemption 7 grounds. Plaintiff further requests that he be allowed to continue the discovery of facts relevant to the resolution of the exemption 7 claim. Finally, plaintiff suggests that the Court direct the defendant to support its exemption 7 claim by affidavit or other evidentiary means.

/s/ _____
JAMES HIRAM LESAR
1231 Fourth Street, S. W.
Washington, D. C. 20024

CERTIFICATE OF SERVICE.

I hereby certify that service of the foregoing Motion for Reconsideration and the Memorandum of Points and Authorities in support thereof has been made upon the defendant by mailing a copy thereof to its attorney, Mr. Michael J. Ryan, Assistant United States Attorney, United States Courthouse, Room 3421, Washington, D. C., on this 13th day of May, 1974.

/s/ _____
JAMES HIRAM LESAR

ORDER.

Having considered plaintiff's motion for reconsideration and the entire record in this case, it is by the Court this_____day of May, 1974,

ORDERED, that the Court's Order granting the defendant summary judgment is hereby vacated.

_____
UNITED STATES DISTRICT JUDGE

22.
DOCUMENTS GENERATED BY THE LEGAL PROCEEDINGS

Several documents generated by the legal proceedings are included in this section as germane to the issues involved and important for the historical record.

The testimony of Representative Gerald Ford given during the Senate hearing on his Vice Presidential nomination relates to his use of the January 27, 1964, transcript in his book. [Document A] Next is printed in full the Attorney General's attachment to his letter of April 19, 1965. The legal proceedings used only one page. [Document B]

Two letters from the Department of Justice relate to the White House efforts to make the Warren Commission records available to the public. [Documents C and D]

Two cover letters [Documents E and F] accompanying Chief Justice Earl Warren's letter of April 5, 1965, as well as the letter itself, [Document G] were generated by discovery. The Warren letter is highly important for our understanding of the Commission's view on the public availability of its records.

DOCUMENT A

Testimony of Representative Gerald Ford before the Senate Rules Committee. November 5, 1973.

SENATE RULES COMMITTEE
November 5, 1973
105 VCU-LINO

(On Friday, November 16, 1973, I went to the office of Mr. Joe O'Leary, Room 301, Old Senate Office Building, where I was allowed to read and transcribe, but not to xerox, the following testimony given by Representative Jerry Ford on November 5, 1973 — Jim Lesar)

THE CHAIRMAN—Now, Mr. Ford, it has been stated that as a member of the Warren Commission you voluntarily accepted constraints which all the members of the Commission accepted, providing that you would not publish or release any proceedings of the Commission.

You did, however, in association with another, publish a book and provide material for a Life magazine article on the proceedings of the Commission. Do you feel this was a violation of your agreement?

MR. FORD—To the best of my recollection, Mr. Chairman, there was no such agreement, but even if there was, the book that I published in conjunction with a member of my staff who worked with me at the time of the Warren Commission work—we wrote the book, but we did not use in that book any material other than material that was in the 26 volumes of testimony and sold to the public generally.

THE CHAIRMAN: The committee has been advised that you were paid $5,000 for the Life article, $10,000 by Simon and Schuster for the book, $3,000 by Ballantyne Books for a reprint, for a total of $18,000 plus royalties. Could you tell us if these figures are correct, and what the final total was, including royalties?

MR. FORD. Well, let's take the Life article first.

It was agreed that subsequent to the publication of the Commission Report, that I would write an article for Life magazine, giving my impression as a member of the Commission, and my feeling toward the report individually, as a member of the Commission. I did write that article, it was published after the Commission report was made public by President Johnson, I did receive the $5,000 for the article, in two checks. One a $4,000 check which I divided three ways, between former Congressman John Ray of New York, who came down here voluntarily, paid all his own expenses and worked with me for 9 months in helping me in my responsibilities as a member of the Commission.

Mr. Ray, who was a very distinguished Member of the House of Representatives, had been prior to his service in the House, a member of the—well, as I understand it, the general counsel for A.T. & T. He retired, and then when I was appointed to the Warren Commission, he volunteered his time at no expense to the Government.

Another member of my staff at that time was John R. Styles, of Grand Rapids. He came down and worked for me; I put him on my payroll at compensation just to pay his expenses while he was living in Washington and working with me on the Commission report.

I divided that $4,000 three ways: I gave Mr. Ray approximately $1,333, I gave Mr. Styles $1,333, and I kept the third share myself.

Now on the book which was published, the name of it was "The Portrait of An Assassin." This book came out almost a year after the Commission report was filed. I felt, and my coauthor felt, that the Commission report was a sound document. I supported it then and I support it today. But it was pretty heavy reading, Mr. Chairman. So Jack Styles and I thought we could make a better, more readable presentation of the Commission's conclusions by primarily using the testimony of the witnesses themselves—and that testimony was all a matter of public record.

We made a contract with Simon and Schuster in which they advanced us, as I recall, $10,000, which Mr. Styles and I divided between us. We checked the other day with Simon and Schuster to see how well it sold, and I am told that when they got all through with publication of the book and sales they came out about $3,000 in the red. So it wasn't a best-seller, by any means.

I am not familiar with the $3,000 from Bantam Books. I will check my records but—

THE CHAIRMAN. Ballantyne, Mr. Ford.

MR. FORD. Ballantyne? Excuse me. I know we did make an arrangement for a paperback publication, but if my recollection is accurate, we had
minimal benefits from that—far less than $3,000. I will check the records and
supply the Committee with whatever the facts are.

DOCUMENT B

Summary of Agency Views on Warren Commission Records being disclosed
to the public.

<u>Attachment</u>

Summary of Views of Interested Federal Agencies Concerning the Disclosure
to the Public of Materials Delivered to the National Archives by the President's Commission on the Assassination of President Kennedy.

In response to inquiry by the Department of Justice, the federal agencies which submitted reports or other materials to the President's Commission
expressed the following views regarding the disclosure of these materials to
the public.

1.   FEDERAL BUREAU OF INVESTIGATION. The Federal Bureau
of Investigation recognizes that materials furnished by it for use by the President's Commission, except those which were classified for reasons of national
security, are in the public domain. Most of the material furnished by the
Bureau was unclassified. Security classification was necessary in some instances to prevent the identification of confidential informants, to protect
the secrecy of confidential investigative techniques, to avoid disclosure of information showing the Bureau's coverage of the Soviet Embassy in Washington, D. C., and to maintain the classification imposed by other agencies on
information furnished by them to the Bureau. The Bureau believes that classified material should be disclosed only to persons having the necessary
security clearance.
        The Bureau believes that another problem is presented by unclassified
material, some of which contains reports of rumor, gossip, and similar data

involving innocent people. Some of this unclassified material contains the results of extensive investigations of Mrs. Marina Oswald and various associates of the Oswalds. Disclosure of such material, the Bureau believes, would be a source of unwarranted embarrassment to the people concerned. Some material contained in unclassified documents was furnished to the Bureau in confidence by sources such as banks and hotels. The records of these sources cannot be produced except pursuant to a court order. Public disclosure of this information might cause the Bureau to lose the cooperation of such sources in the future and might subject the sources to civil suit.

A separate problem is presented by records of the Bureau's investigation of Mr. Jack Ruby, whose conviction for the murder of Oswald is still under review in the Texas courts.

The Bureau, which has retained records of all material furnished to the President's Commission, is prepared to examine all classified documents in order to extract the classified information and make the remainder available to the public. In addition, the Bureau is prepared to review the classification of all classified documents at least once a year and at any time in response to a specific inquiry concerning the classification of a particular document.

While pointing out the problems noted above concerning undisclosed material, the Bureau makes no specific recommendations concerning such items.

2.   SECRET SERVICE. The Secret Service recommends that access to its investigative reports furnished to the President's Commission remain restricted for all reports in the following categories:

"(1) Reports affecting national security.

"(2) Reports which reveal the extent of Presidential protection or protective techniques.

"(3) Reports mentioning innocent persons having no connection with the subject of the investigation that would needlessly embarrass or damage the innocent parties.

"(4) Reports containing information given to us in confidence which, when investigated was found to:
       (a)   have no connection with the assassination;

(b)   be untrue, yet the reports would be embarrassing, both to the supplier of the information who may have acted in good faith in view of the importance of the subject matter of the investigation, or to the person concerning whom the information was furnished; e.g., derogatory remarks about President Kennedy attributed to persons before and after the assassination.

"(5) Reports containing information from confidential informants from which readers might draw in inference, erroneously or correctly, as to the identity of the confidential informant."

The Secret Service has indicated its willingness to examine the reports furnished by it to the President's Commission for the purpose of determining which items may be made available to the public now (including declassification, if necessary) and which may be made available at some future time less than 75 years hence. It has also recommended an annual review of the necessity for continuing restrictions on particular items.

3.   POST OFFICE DEPARTMENT. The Postal Inspection Service furnished documents and information to various investigative agencies including the Federal Bureau of Investigation and the Secret Service. It believes that the receiving agencies should determine whether or not such documents and information should be disclosed.

The Inspection Service submitted directly to the President's Commission a summary of its activities, which was not a classified document. The Service has no objection to the publication of this document, but believes that the approval of the Federal Bureau of Investigation and the Secret Service should be obtained. The Inspection Service furnished to the President's Commission "copies of the front and back of POD Form 2153-X, dated September 18, 1963, covering a publication 'OGONEK' addressed to Mr. Lee H. Oswald, Box 2915, Dallas, Texas." The Service believes that these copies should not be made generally available at this time.

The Service has indicated its willingness to examine any documents furnished by it to the President's Commission for the purpose of determining whether they can be released to the public.

4.   CENTRAL INTELLIGENCE AGENCY. The Central Intelligence Agency believes that items furnished by it to the President's Commission and

withheld from the public domain under security controls should not be excepted from the normal 75-year period of non-disclosure. The Agency cooperated fully with the President's Commission and made every effort to release material furnished to the Commission for the public record. Wherever it was possible without jeopardizing the national security of this country's posture abroad, security classifications were graded down. Because of this policy, very little of the material furnished by the Agency is now withheld from the public. The criteria which were applied in determining whether or not to release information were: (1) the evidential value of the information in question; (2) the protection of sensitive sources and methods of operation; and (3) the possibility of international ramifications in view of the fact that most of the material was acquired abroad, particularly in Mexico and the U.S.S.R. None of the withheld material has a direct bearing on the assassination of President Kennedy.

The Agency believes that the national security requires the continuance of restrictions on withheld documents and that this interest outweighs all other considerations. It recommends that at the end of the 75-year period another security appraisal be made before such documents are disclosed.

5. DEPARTMENT OF STATE. The Department of State made every effort to cooperate with the President's Commission in releasing to the public all significant information concerning the assassination of the President. In a small number of cases, the publication of documents was restricted in order to protect coding systems, in the interest of national security, to avoid personal embarrassment, or because a later revision of a draft document containing the substance of the draft had been released for publication. (Where coding was involved, the full substance of the document in question was made available for publication.) A few documents were classified and have been restricted accordingly.

Some of the material which has not yet been made available could probably be released if necessary. It will probably be possible to release other material within the next ten years. In cases where a document was furnished by the Department but originated with another agency, the approval of the originating agency should be obtained. The Department is prepared to examine material furnished by it to the President's Commission now and on an annual basis hereafter to reevaluate the necessity for non-disclosure.

6.   DEPARTMENT OF DEFENSE. The Department of Defense has examined material at the National Archives which has been identified as furnished to the President's Commission by the Department. Some of the material, consisting of investigative reports and other material relating to individuals, is of a kind normally not disclosed to the public. In view of the exceptional nature of the work of the President's Commission, however, the Department does not object to the disclosure of this material, all of which is unclassified. If further material is later identified as originating with the Department of Defense, the Department requests an opportunity to review such material before it is disclosed.

7.   INTERNAL REVENUE SERVICE. The Internal Revenue Service has no objection to unrestricted public examination of documents concerning matters included in the public record by the Report of the President's Commission.

Tax returns which have not been made a matter of public record are protected from disclosure by Sections 6103 and 7213 of the Internal Revenue Code and by 5 U.S.C. Section 22. The President has statutory authority to disclose such protected information, but the Service recommends that in accordance with the spirit of the statute, tax returns not made matters of public record not be made available for general inspection.

A determination concerning other items furnished to the President's Commission should be made on an individual basis. Many documents reflect protected tax return information. Others contain information which would indicate the identity of a confidential informant, which is scandalous and not relevant to the subject of the Commission's inquiry, which consists of unconfirmed allegations by third parties, or which discloses the Service's policies respecting collection, auditing, settling or prosecution. The Service has traditionally maintained a policy of nondisclosure of information of this sort and believes that the public recognizes the necessity for this policy. The Service believes that disclosure of material of the kind indicated would not add significantly to the comprehensive report of the President's Commission or to public information concerning the assassination of President Kennedy. Accordingly, the Service believes that no public interest would be served by disclosure. The Service believes that except in exceptional circumstances, documents of which portions must remain undisclosed be restricted in their entirety. If documents containing deletions are released they are likely to prompt curiosity about the deletions and may produce charges that significant information is being withheld.

As a means of assuring the public of the thoroughness of the Commission's investigation, the Service suggests that letters received by it from the President's Commission requesting documents, along with transmittal replies, be made available for inspection. Clearance to disclose such letters would have to be obtained from the President's Commission, the originating agency.

The Service has indicated its willingness to inspect material furnished by it to the President's Commission now and at periodic intervals to determine whether such material may be made available to the public. It suggests that material be withheld only if: (1) disclosure is prohibited by law or agency regulations; (2) disclosure would be detrimental to the administration of the laws administered by the agency concerned; (3) the material relates to scandalous information unrelated to the assassination; (4) the material consists of unsubstantiated information or allegations; or (5) the material could embarrass or damage innocent persons without serving the public interest in full disclosure of information pertaining to the assassination of President Kennedy.

8.   IMMIGRATION AND NATURALIZATION SERVICE. The Immigration and Naturalization Service has previously authorized the President's Commission to publish all documents furnished to it by the Service. Accordingly, the Service has no objection to the immediate disclosure of all such documents to the public.

DOCUMENT C

Letter to Dean Rusk, Secretary of State, from the Attorney General.

Honorable Dean Rusk   July 12, 1965
Secretary of State
Washington, D. C. 20520   20530

Dear Mr. Secretary:

In a letter of February 8, 1965, I requested an expression of the views of your Department with regard to public disclosure of unpublished documents that were furnished to the President's Commission on the Assassination of President Kennedy by your Department.

Following a review of the recommendations of your Department and of officials of other interested departments and agencies, I submitted a memorandum to McGeorge Bundy, Special Assistant to the President, proposing certain guidelines for determining which of those documents should be made available to the public. By a memorandum of April 19, 1965, Mr. Bundy approved those guidelines and asked me, in coordination with the National Archives, to instruct the appropriate agencies to conduct a review of pertinent documents in accordance with those guidelines and to complete that review by September 1, 1965.

In order to facilitate this review, the National Archives has prepared a list of the documents which are in the files of the President's Commission and which were submitted by, or originated in, your Department. This list includes only the documents that were not published by the Commission and those that could readily be determined to have been published only in part.

It is requested that you arrange for the prompt examination of the listed documents with a view to authorizing the removal of existing restrictions on public availability of as many of those documents as possible. The guidelines approved by Mr. Bundy, which are set forth in the attachment to this letter, should be applied in making the required determinations.

The document-by-document review that this procedure requires may be undertaken on the basis of file copies of documents which were retained in the files of your Department, or, since all records of the President's Commission have been transferred to the National Archives, the Archivist will arrange to give your representative access to the listed documents if that procedure would be more convenient. At the conclusion of your review, a copy of the enclosed list, marked so as to show which documents may be made public and which must remain closed for the time being, should be sent to Dr. Wayne C. Grover, Archivist of the United States. With respect to items that must be withheld from the public, please indicate the letter or number of the item in the attached guidelines that best describes your Department's reason for such withholding.

In addition, I am attaching lists, prepared by the National Archives, of documents which were acquired from the Governments of Mexico and West Germany, respectively. Would you arrange to have the Archivist advised as to whether those documents can be made available to the public.

It is essential that the Archivist of the United States receive your reply by August 15, 1965, since a report to the White House must be prepared and submitted by September 1 on the overall status of accessibility to the records of the Commission. If any questions or problems arise in the course of the review, your representative should contact Dr. James B. Rhoads, Assistant Archivist for Civil Archives, whose telephone number is code 13, extension 22442.

I am aware of the difficulties inherent in this undertaking, but the public interest in these documents, and the determination of the White House Office that they be disclosed to the fullest extent consistent with the national security, sound public administration, and the rights of individual privacy, require that this assignment be accomplished with care and dispatch.

Sincerely,

/s/

Attorney General

DOCUMENT D

Letter to Dr. Robert H. Bahmer from Frank M. Wozencraft.

DEPARTMENT OF JUSTICE
Washington

Dr. Robert H. Bahmer   August 17, 1965
Archivist of the United States
National Archives and Records Service
Washington, D. C. 20408

Dear Dr. Bahmer:

I have been asked to reply to the informal inquiries which you and the Deputy Administrator of General Services, Joe E. Moody, have made to this Department concerning the authority and procedures for releasing for public disclosure certain of the documentary material that was produced or acquired by the President's Commission on the Assassination of President Kennedy (the Warren Commission).

The Commission has, of course, completed its investigation, submitted its report, and transferred all of its records, papers, and other documentary material to the National Archives for preservation. Many scholars and other persons are anxious to study that material.

Last year, the Executive departments and agencies which had furnished documentary material to the Commission developed certain guidelines for determining which of the items they had furnished could be released to the public. As a result of the applications of those guidelines, approximately two thirds of that material has been made available to the public.

Since the Commission did not provide any guidance or impose any restrictions in this regard at the time that its files were transferred to your agency, since the Commission is now out of existence, and since your agency is now the receiver and custodian of the records of the Commission, this Department believes the Administrator of General Services, acting through you and your staff, is now in the same legal and administrative position with respect to the records, papers, and other documentary material transferred to your agency by the Commission, as the Commission was prior to that transfer.

Consequently, we believe that your agency has the authority and obligation to review that material and to determine which of it should be made available to, or withheld from, the public at this time, and to conduct subsequent reviews of such material at reasonable intervals until all of it is released. In this regard, we believe it would be appropriate for your reviews of that material to be made in conformity with the guidelines which were developed and applied by the various Executive departments and agencies with respect to the material they had contributed to the Commission. However, we do not consider those guidelines as imposing absolute standards for the release or disclosure of Commission-produced material in your custody. If in any specific case a sound legal basis exists for withholding or for releasing any such material notwithstanding provisions of the guidelines, your agency should, of course, disregard the guidelines. Similarly, if sound archival or other principles or reasons, not inconsistent with law, exist for disregarding the guidelines in some particular case, we believe that it would be appropriate for your agency to disregard the guidelines in that case. If any significant legal problem should arise in this regard, the Department of Justice will, of course, be happy to assist you in any way that we can.

Sincerely,

/s/

Frank M. Wozencraft
Assistant Attorney General
Office of Legal Counsel

DOCUMENT E

Letter of Henry E. Petersen to James Lesar.

UNITED STATES DEPARTMENT OF JUSTICE

WASHINGTON, D. C. 20530

Address Reply to the
Division Indicated
and Refer to Initials and Number
HEP: CWB: JRR: mac
      129-11

Sept. 6, 1974

Mr. James H. Lesar
Attorney at Law
1231 Fourth Street, S. W.
Washington, D. C.

Dear Mr. Lesar:

Although you requested a copy of a letter dated April 3, 1965, from then Chief Justice Earl Warren to the Attorney General, search of our files disclosed the only letter meeting your description was dated April 5, 1965. A certified copy of the April 5 letter is attached.

Sincerely,

HENRY E. PETERSEN
Assistant Attorney General
Criminal Division

By: /s/

CARL W. BELCHER
Chief, General Crimes Section

DOCUMENT F

Letter of Transmission.

United States of America

———

Department of Justice

August 28, 1974

I hereby certify that the annexed paper is a true copy of the original record which is in the official custody of the Department of Justice, to wit: Letter dated April 5, 1965, to Honorable Nicholas deB. Katzenbach, Attorney General of the United States, Justice Department, Washington, D. C., signed by Earl Warren, The Chief Justice, Supreme Court of the United States, re: consideration given by the President's Commission on the Assassination of President John F. Kennedy to the proper disposition of its records before it delivered them to the National Archives.

In witness whereof, I have hereunto set my hand, and caused the seal of the Department of Justice to be affixed, on the day and year first above written.

/s/ _____

Robert M. Yahn
Acting Chief, Records Section

DOCUMENT G

Letter of Chief Justice Earl Warren to Nicholas deB. Katzenbach.

Supreme Court of the United States
Washington, D. C. 20543

CHAMBER OF

THE CHIEF JUSTICE   April 5, 1965

Honorable Nicholas deB. Katzenbach,
Attorney General of the United States,
Justice Department,
Washington, D. C.

Dear Mr. Attorney General:

The President's Commission on the Assassination of President John F. Kennedy gave careful consideration to the proper disposition of its records before it delivered them to the National Archives. It wished them to be held there for the benefit of the American people. At that time, it decided that it was in the best interests of all concerned that the policy relating to the Commission's records provide for the fullest possible disclosure.

At the same time, the Commission recognized that its records contained investigative materials which were classified by the originating agencies to protect the security of the United States. Furthermore, among such materials were numerous items in which inhered serious potential for character assassination and other similar misuse to the injury of innocent persons.

The Commission, after full consideration, concluded that it did not have either the authority or the necessary information to determine the technical questions as to when the classified materials should be released without injury to the security of the country. It decided that the responsibility for that decision must of necessity be left with the originating agencies and the Attorney General, as the chief legal officer, in accordance with established law and policies of the Government. It also concluded that such agencies and the Attorney General could best determine what safeguards were necessary to protect innocent persons in the release of defamatory materials.

In arriving at the foregoing conclusions, however, the Commission assumed that all of the determinations by the agencies and the Attorney General would be made in recognition of the overriding consideration of the fullest possible disclosure, and that all other proper factors, including the disclosures that have been made, would be taken into account. The Commission had no desire to restrict public access to any of its working papers except those classified by other agencies. It was with these thoughts in mind that the Commission, on its dissolution, committed its papers to the National Archives subject to the laws and regulations concerning the release to the public of classified and restricted materials.

We hope that this report of the attitude and conclusions of the Commission concerning the full disclosure of its records will be helpful to you in the formulation of your proposal for making the materials of this Commission now in the National Archives available to the public.

Sincerely,

/s/

EARL WARREN

23.
THE JANUARY 27, 1964, WARREN COMMISSION
EXECUTIVE SESSION TRANSCRIPT

On May 3, 1974, Judge Gesell awarded the government summary judgment on the grounds that the January 27 transcript was protected from the public because it was part of a file compiled for "law enforcement purposes." He denied the claim that the transcript had been classified for national defense purposes. Then, on June 14, 1974, as Harold Weisberg and his attorney, James H. Lesar, were preparing to appeal the decision, Archivist James B. Rhoads mailed a copy of the transcript to Weisberg, saying in the cover letter that the Archives had just finished reviewing the classification of the document and had decided to release it. (Document A) Weisberg's letter in response asked why the release had occurred. (Document B) In Whitewash IV Weisberg discusses the issue further.

The transcript which follows is an exact copy of the original. The members present were Chief Justice Earl Warren, Senator John Sherman Cooper, former CIA director Allen W. Dulles, banker John J. McCloy, Senator Richard B. Russell, and Congressman Hale Boggs. Only Commissioner Congressman Gerald Ford was absent.

The page numbers of the original document are given in parentheses.

The National Archive's declassification stamp, dated 6/12/74, has been omitted from the title page.

DOCUMENT A.

Letter of Dr. James B. Rhoads to Harold Weisberg.

United States of America
General Services Administration
National Archives and Records Service
Washington, D. C. 20408

June 14, 1974

Mr. Harold Weisberg
Coq d'Or Press
Route 8
Frederick, Maryland 21701

Dear Mr. Weisberg:

Enclosed is a copy of the transcript of the executive session of the Warren Commission of January 27, 1964, to which you have sought access at various times. We treated your suit for access as a request for a mandatory review under the terms of Executive Order 11652. The declassification review of the transcript has been completed, and the transcript has been made available for research.

Our present charge for electrostatic copies is 15 cents per page. The cost of the copy of the transcript is $13.20. There is a balance in your deposit account of $7.90, leaving a balance due of $5.30.

Sincerely,

/s/

James B. Rhoads
Archivist of the United States

Enclosures

DOCUMENT B.

Letter of Harold Weisberg to Dr. James B. Rhoads.

                                                          Harold Weisberg
June 19, 1974   Frederick, Maryland 21701

Dr. James B. Rhoads
Archivist of the United States
National Archives and Records Services
Washington, D. C. 20408

Dear Dr. Rhoads:

Your letter baffles me and I solicit further explanation. You say, "We treated your suit for access as a request for a mandatory review."

Why did it require a suit when I made formal and proper application under the Freedom of Information law and your regulations? Why did you not then regard this, as I believe you should have, as a request for a review?

Why did you not regard my appeal from your personal refusal as a request for a review? Why was my appeal not forwarded, as required by your regulations, to the Assistant Administrator for Administration? And why, if indeed you did regard my suit as such a request, did you not review it then when I filed the suit instead of after decision by the District Court? Why did you have to clutter up the courts with a totally unnecessary suit, put me to this expense and deny me what I regard as my rights under the law and your regulations?

Or does this get to your appeals officer, Mr. Vawter's call to me begging me to file a suit as he did rather than give him appeals upon which to act?

I intend these questions seriously, not rhetorically. I believe I am entitled to an answer and I would think the judge is entitled to an explanation.

                                        Sincerely,

                                        /s/

                                        Harold Weisberg

Vol. 5

Copy 3 of 9

PRESIDENT'S COMMISSION

ON THE

ASSASSINATION OF PRESIDENT KENNEDY

Report of Proceedings

Held at

Washington, D. C.

Monday, January 27, 1964

PAGES 127 - 212

(Stenotype Tape, Master Sheets, Carbon and Waste
turned over to Commission for destruction.)

WARD & PAUL

OFFICIAL REPORTERS

917 G Street, N. W.

Washington, D. C. 20001

Area Code 202—628-4266

THE CHAIRMAN: Well, gentlemen, the meeting will come to order.

I am sorry that I was a little late but the Senator knows I wasn't out playing golf or anything.

Well, gentlemen, since we met last week, Mr. Rankin and I have explored this situation we discussed considerably. We talked to the Texas people, and we have given considerable thought to it since, and I am going to ask Mr. Rankin to start at the beginning and just tell you the story as we have got it.

MR. RANKIN: I received a call from Waggoner Carr, the Attorney General of Texas, and in that call he was quite excited. He was on his way to Texarkana from Austin.

MR. DULLES: This is after our meeting the other night?

MR. RANKIN: This was before.

MR. DULLES: Going back?

MR. RANKIN: Yes.

He said he thought he had some information that he thought should get to me immediately and it was to the effect that the F.B.I. had an undercover agent who was Oswald, and he said it came up this way, that the matter was developed at a meeting in chambers with the judge, Brown, of the court, and it was in relation to the production of evidence where Ruby's attorney asked that part of the evidence that the F.B.I. developed be furnished to them, and during that time the District Attorney had responded or opposed the motion for the evidence by saying (129) that the various usual grounds and that the F.I.B. never did this before, and in addition to that he thought he knew the reason why they were willing to do it this time, and it was that Oswald was an undercover agent for the F.B.I.

SEN. RUSSELL: Was this in open court, Mr. Rankin?

MR. RANKIN: That is what I understood.

MR. DULLES: In chambers?

MR. RANKIN: In chambers.

That he also knew the number that was assigned by the F.B.I. to Oswald which was No. 179, and he knew that he was on the payroll or employed, I think that is the way he put it, employed by the F.B.I. at $200 per month from September of 1962 up to the time of the assassination.

That was all that he knew about it. He didn't get the information from District Attorney Wade, but he had gotten it from someone else and he didn't tell me who that was, but he said it was a person in whom he had complete faith and could rely upon.

I called the Chief Justice immediately and went over and saw him and told him the story, and he thought it was material of such importance to the Commission that the entire Commission should be called and advised with regard to it.

We had a meeting, and told the information, and it was the consensus of the meeting that we should try to get those people up here, including the District Attorney, Wade, the (130) Attorney General, Special Counsel with the Attorney General, Leon Jaworski, and Bob Storey, and Mr. Alexander, the Assistant District Attorney at Dallas.

We asked them to all come up, and they did on Friday. At that time they were—they said that the rumors were constant there, that Oswald was an undercover agent, but they extended it also to the C.I.A., saying that they had a number for him assigned to him in connection with the C.I.A. and gave that to him, and none of them had any original information of their own.

They said that the source of their information was a man by the name of Hudkins who was a reporter for the Houston Post, and that it had been circulated by a greater portion of all the reporters in the Dallas area who had been working on this matter in various forms.

SEN. RUSSELL: Did he explain why it hadn't been published? This would have gone across the country like wild fire.

MR. RANKIN: Well, they said part of it had been published.

The fact that it was claimed that Oswald was an undercover agent, and I noticed The Nation, although I hadn't seen it before, refers to an article in January, the first of January by Hudkins from which he referred to the undercover agent's story.

But he does not give the number or the $200 a month at that time.

We then asked if they asked Hudkins of where he had got his story and they said they had not. We asked if there was (131) any other place, and they don't know of any other place that they could assign.

In fact, when we asked them at first, they did not reveal the name of Hudkins to us. They said the reporters generally were giving the story or discussing the story, and it was only after we urged them that they gave us Hudkins' name.

We did discover, amongst the papers that we received from the Secret Service, a report which the Chief Justice obtained from Mr. Moore, I believe it was Mr. Moore which referred to a Mr. Sweatt who was the Deputy Sheriff in Dallas County in which he said Oswald was an undercover agent and was being paid so much a month for some time back to September, and that it had a number which he gave and that report as No. 172. This report by the Secret Service agent was of a conference or inquiry that he made in the area to Sweatt back on December 17th. The report was dated January 3, and we didn't get it until January 23.

We wondered at the time when this matter first came to our attention, the Chief Justice asked Mr. Moore, Secret Service agent who was working here, if there was anything about this in their files that he would get it if there was and bring it to him directly personally, and this was the result.

We didn't know what to expect from this, because that was 20 days after the date of that report, and we wondered whether the Secret Service was withholding something from us, since they had this in their hands clear back on January 3, the date (132) of the report.

The explanation since has been that they were trying to check it out, that there was no purpose to withhold it from us even though it seemed like kind of a long period since they hadn't gotten any further report from Mr. Sweatt at all.

MR. DULLES: What was the origin, who was Sweatt?

MR. RANKIN: He was the Deputy Sheriff of Dallas County.

MR. DULLES: He was the one who gave it to the Secret Service?

MR. RANKIN: Yes.

MR. DULLES: He didn't say where he got it?

MR. RANKIN: No.

They have since then, the Secret Service, has investigated, we asked them to, and they have gone to Sweatt and Sweatt has said he got it from Hudkins. Back to the same source.

MR. DULLES: Back to the same source?

MR. RANKIN: And there is nothing that we have received from any investigative agency checking out Hudkins in regard to this report.

You probably saw the New York Times story, saying that the F.B.I., Sunday, that the F.B.I. denied that he was acting as an undercover—

SEN. RUSSELL: That is from Mr. Hoover somewhere in this material I read in which he denied this report. It apparently was current at some earlier date, that he wrote a letter (133) specifically stating that Oswald was never connected with the F.B.I. in any capacity, secret or otherwise.

MR. RANKIN: We asked them whether they had ever checked with any official or anybody who was connected with the county government or—we didn't reveal Sweatt's name to Wade, and the other Texas people, but we asked them in that form, whether they had ever checked out anything with anybody like Sweatt, and they said they hadn't.

We asked them if they had any jurisdiction over the county sheriff or deputy sheriff or anybody who is in office, in his office, and they said, no, they didn't. That they were all elected officials and were quite independent.

But they had never made any effort to go to Swett and see what his story was, although apparently it was common talk there, too, because there are some references to a public official saying that Oswald was acting as an undercover agent, and there is also some statements in the press that some police officers made such statements after the assassination.

But there is nothing to show that there was any effort to try to check that out.

Those stories we generally discount as possibly an effort to blame the F.B.I. for some of the matters involved.

SEN. RUSSELL: Has Hudkins claimed his journalistic immunity, have they gone back to him?

MR. RANKIN: They haven't even asked him, or at least [134] indicated they had ever taken his statement or anything like that.

Now, Mr. Wade, the District Attorney, was a former F.B.I. agent, and we thought possibly there was—he might have left under a cloud and there might be something of that kind and so we inquired into that.

He was an agent between 1939 and 1943, I think it was, and was claimed that he had no difficulties with them, that when he was ready to leave the F.I.B. they gave him three weeks and told him to go to New York and have a good vacation, and they would like to have him come back to see if he wouldn't be willing to continue, and he did come back and he said he wanted to go into the law practice and didn't want to stay with the F.B.I. But there was no ill feeling between them. He said he was stationed in South America for a year, and the other part of the time within the Continent of the United States.

He said he got a commission from the Navy, and when he was called up for that commission the F.B.I. indicated that they thought he was qualified for their work and he should take the commission and that he should come back to the F.B.I.

I think probably that would be some automatic—it would come up that way anyway.

He said they did make that request and he was able to get around it and told them he didn't want to go to the F.B.I., and wanted to go to the Navy, but he told about that to indicate there (135) was no ill feeling, no reason why they should be unhappy with him or he with them, if they even wanted him again at that time.

He did say he has had considerable experience with the F.B.I., and knew their practices, that he handled as much as $2,000 a month during the war period in which he paid off informers, and undercover agents in South America, and he knew that it wasn't revealed on any records he ever handled who he was paying it to and he never got any receipts, and it wasn't the practice to get receipts; that he would have a list of numbers in his office, that was one of the most closely guarded records that he had, and he would put down the amount he paid off, including such people as the head of the government in Ecuador, or the police in Ecuador, and he said that he was paying him more than his salary each month, so that they got better service than the local government did. And so he indicated that he knew how these things were handled at that time.

He was frank, however, about stating that he didn't know whether that practice continued, he didn't know how they were doing it, that was a long time ago and how the F.B.I. would handle any such transaction now.

He didn't know. He thought that the postal box was an ideal way to handle such transactions, and was a way that he had used at various times in the past, too.

He didn't indicate that he was sure that this was the case at (136) all. He just indicated that it was a possibility, and some of the things that had happened he thought were curious.

My impression of Wade was that he was a very canny, able prosecutor, that he would do a good job on this Ruby case, and that defense counsel had a man to deal with that knew his business.

SEN. RUSSELL: He has that reputation out there as being a very effective prosecutor.

MR. RANKIN: I was well impressed with him that way.

SEN. RUSSELL: What steps, if any, have we taken to clear up this matter, Mr. Rankin, if it can be cleared up, to determine whether there is anything to this or not?

MR. RANKIN: Well, we have discussed various possibilities, that is the Chief Justice and myself have, and I want to tell you about them, and I think you will have to instruct us what you want us to do.

We thought, first, about approaching the Department with a request that the Attorney General inform us as to the situation, not only as to what he would say about whether Oswald was or was not an undercover agent, but also with the supporting data that the commission could rely upon, and there is some difficulty about doing that. As the head of the department, the F.B.I., of course, is under the Attorney General, but I think we must frankly recognize amongst ourselves that there is a daily relationship there involved in the handling of the problems of the (137) Department and the work of the F.B.I. for the Department, and that we wouldn't want to make that more difficult.

We were informed by Mr. Willens, the liaison with the Department, who has worked with us and has done very fine work here, that it is the feeling of the Department, not the Attorney General because he is not here, but Mr. Katzenbach, and Mr. Miller, Assistant Attorney General in charge of the Criminal Division, that such a request might be embarrassing, and at least would be difficult for the Attorney General, and might, if urged, while we would get the information we desired, make very much more difficult for him to carry on the work of the Department for the balance of his term.

SEN. RUSSELL: If he would transmit to us what they told him, the F.B.I. has a very large measure of autonomy in their operations.

MR. RANKIN: In light of that, I suggested the possibility for the Commission to consider that I should go over and see Edgar Hoover myself, and tell him this problem and that he should have as much interest as the Commission in trying to put an end to any such speculations, not only by his statement, which I would be frank to tell him I would think would not be sufficient, but also if it was possible to demonstrate by whatever records and materials they have that it just couldn't be true, and see if we couldn't get his cooperation to present that with the understanding that the Commission, and stated understanding, at the (138) time, the Commission would have to feel free to make such other investigation and take testimony if it found it necessary, in order to satisfy the American people that this question of an undercover agent was out of the picture.

REP. BOGGS: What other alternatives are there?

MR. RANKIN: Well, the other alternatives would be to examine Hud-kins, the reporter, to examine Sweatt, who says now that he—

MR. DULLES: Where is Hudkins now, do you know, down in Dallas?

MR. RANKIN: In Houston, yes, I assume.

MR. DULLES: What paper is he with?

MR. RANKIN: The Houston Post.

MR. DULLES: That would be the Hobby paper, isn't it?

REP. BOGGS: No, I think that is Scripps-Howard.

(139) MR. RANKIN: To examine Hosty, the FBI Agent who was working in that area, and to examine the Special Agent in Charge of the area, and to examine Mr. Hoover, under oath, right up the line.

I felt, however, as I told the Chief Justice, that I thought this Commission was entitled to have the full cooperation of another Government Agency, and that we don't have what I would consider any substantial proof of this rumor.

We do have a dirty rumor that is very bad for the Commission, the problem and it is very damaging to the agencies that are involved in it and it must be wiped out insofar as it is possible to do so by this Commission.

So it seemed to me in light of that the way I would treat it if I were in their position would be to have someone approach me, tell me the problem and see what I frankly could do to clear my skirts if there was a way to do it and as long as the Commission didn't agree not to go further, if they felt that would not satisfy them, I don't see how the Commission would be prejudiced.

REP. BOGGS: Mr. Wade, what significance did Wade attach to this?

MR. RANKIN: I don't think he—you could say he believed. I don't think you could say he disbelieved it. He had just thought there was too much there to disregard but he just thought, he seemed to indicate, in his statements, that he couldn't believe that it would be possible.

But he didn't indicate by any statement that he didn't (140) believe it couldn't happen. He just couldn't believe that the FBI would ever let that happen to get to that position.

THE CHAIRMAN: Well, Lee and I both agreed that we shouldn't leave this thing in this present posture, that we should go ahead and try to clear the matter up as best we can. We did argue a little about the approach, whether we should go first to the FBI and ask them for an explanation or whether we should first go and try to see if there is any substance to the claim by interrogating the newspaperman who claims that he has the knowledge of the situation, or whether we should first go to the Bureau.

Now, my own suggestion was to Lee that we find out first from these people as far as we can if there is any substance to it or whether it is just plain rumor.

We were told that Sweatt says he got his information from one fellow, Alexander claims he got it from Sweatt, and somebody else claims he got it from the newspaper man.

Now I thought that if it were necessary we could get these three people in one room at the same time, and find out if anybody claims or has claimed in the past to have had actual knowledge of it, and if they don't claim to have it, we will find out why they spread the rumor.

It may be that Houston will, or whatever his name is, Hudkins would claim privilege. If he did, I thought that after we tried to get him to see that it was in the interest of his country to state the facts that we might go to the publisher of his paper (141) and see if we couldn't get—enlist him to have this man tell us where he got his information.

I think it is one thing for a newspaper man to claim a privilege after he has written a story and published it, and it is another thing for him to claim a privilege when he is peddling gossip around the community.

SEN. RUSSELL: I think you are right about that as a matter of law. If he hadn't published the story, I doubt if he can claim it.

THE CHAIRMAN: I think so, too. In those circumstances, if he wants to deal fairly with the Government, he would tell, and if he didn't, I think his publisher ought to feel the responsibility of telling him.

I said to Lee that if I were in the position of the FBI, and I was asked to respond to a rumor, just a plain rumor of this kind, that I would be inclined to ask for what facts, what the facts were and what they were based on before I was obliged to make a statement.

I think that would—you don't like to talk into an empty barrel. You want to attach your writing to something substantial.

Lee, on the other hand, felt it would be the better part of cooperation to go over and see Mr. Hoover and tell him frankly what the rumor was, state that it is pure rumor, we haven't evaluated the facts, but ask him, first, if it is true, and secondly if he can supply us with information to establish that (142) these facts are not true, and they are inconsistent with what would be the way of operation of their Bureau.

Now I don't know, whatever you agree to would be all right with me. Lee thought that if he went down and asked those people to come up here and testify that they might use the fact that we had asked them to testify as the springboard for an article which would blow this thing out into the public domain, and that we might do a disservice in that way.

But I am not so sure of that. I rather dislike going to the FBI and just ask them to establish to us that a rumor can't be true until we have at least looked into it.

SEN. RUSSELL: There are two reasons for that, Mr. Chairman. One would be if you went down there in the first instance to the FBI and got a statement and when you start pursuing it you would look like you are impeaching.

THE CHAIRMAN: That is my point.

REP. BOGGS: Exactly.

SEN. RUSSELL: I think the best way to handle it would be to try to exhaust it at the other hand before you go to the FBI. That would be my judgment.

REP. BOGGS: Well, the point you make is the thing that has been running through my mind all through this discussion. If you get a statement from responsible officials in that agency and then you say, "Well, we are not going to take this statement on face value, we are going to go behind it", this could become a (143) matter of grave embarrassment to everybody.

MR. DULLES: Hasn't it gone maybe a little further in the press. Here is the New York Times of Sunday, January 26, that is yesterday. Here are 12 questions, this is an article from Dallas by Jack Langguth of the Times. Here are 12 questions sometimes asked and the most authoritative answers now available.

The first question, "Did Oswald serve at some period as a paid informer for the Federal Bureau of Investigation?

"A spokesman for that agency denied today that Oswald was at any time employed by the Bureau in any capacity.

"Newspapers and magazine articles have speculated that Oswald was in the service of the FBI infiltrating leftist organizations at its request.

"The Bureau's denial is categorical."

So we have—

MR. McCLOY: We don't know who the spokesman is.

SEN. RUSSELL: If Oswald never had assassinated the President or at least been charged with assassinating the President and had been in the employ of the FBI and somebody had gone to the FBI they would have denied he was an agent.

MR. DULLES: Oh, yes.

SEN. RUSSELL: They would be the first to deny it. Your agents would have done exactly the same thing.

MR. DULLES: Exactly.

SEN. RUSSELL: Say I never heard about the man who may have (144) been on the payroll for five years.

SEN. COOPER: Yes.

MR. DULLES: But it is out in the domain, it is in the public domain.

SEN. COOPER: If you know, if you have these people up and examine them, of course the FBI will know that.

MR. RANKIN: They already know about this apparently.

SEN. COOPER: That these people came up?

MR. RANKIN: Yes.

REP. BOGGS: You mean the other people?

MR. RANKIN: Yes, that is right. I had thought that the probabilities are that when we get these people under oath that they will say that they have heard this rumor, that someone told them but they can't remember now, and that is about as far as we go with it.

I just don't think that they are going to come out and say they fabricated this, if it is a fabrication. It is too serious for that.

REP. BOGGS: Of course, we get ourselves into a real box. You have got to do everything on earth to establish the facts one way or the other. And without doing that, why everything concerned, including everyone of us is doing a very grave disservice.

SEN. COOPER: There is a point I want to raise. If it is possible the FBI knows now, we should have these people up here (145) before.

MR. RANKIN: Yes.

SEN. COOPER: Of course, if we bring a reporter, they will know that, and they will know we are looking into matters that concern them.

I was thinking about another alternative and that is that you advise them about these rumors and that you have to look into them before you ask them, to prevent any evidence to the contrary.

But I think I would maintain a kind of relationship with them where they would not feel you were around investigating the FBI. Is that possible?

MR. RANKIN: Well, I think that is possible. I would think that if it is definitely untrue, if it were my agency, I would be all over saying "let me prove it. Let me show you anything you can to satisfy you that it isn't true."

SEN. COOPER: We have a duty which is outside the FBI's position, which is if you believe there is something which should be looked into it, and we wouldn't believe that if we weren't talking about it.

My only point is whether or not it would be reasonable to inform the FBI that you have had these statements, therefore you have to ask these people where they got their information.

Before you asked Mr. Hoover you present us with all the proof to the contrary, because as you say, if he presents all (146) this proof to the contrary, then the situation changes a little bit. It would appear to him that you are trying to impeach his testimony.

In the other way, it seems to me we are just telling him that it was brought to us and we ought to inquire into it.

MR. McCLOY: Do we have a statement from Mr. Hoover that this man was not an agent? Was that communicated in the record?

MR. RANKIN: Yes.

THE CHAIRMAN: It was? A letter.

SEN. RUSSELL: I know there was a letter, I don't know who it was written to, a very short letter.

THE CHAIRMAN: It was in one of those letters we responded to last week, it was in that letter—

REP. BOGGS: I think that was a letter that had to do with a request directed to us on what degree of cooperation we should give the defense counsel in the Ruby trial, isn't that right?

MR. RANKIN: Yes.

THE CHAIRMAN: That is right. It was one of those letters, there were three of them. It was in one of those letters, and I remember in the letter of counsel for Ruby, it was also stated that that accusation had been made but that in their opinion it was preposterous, and I wondered why at the time that the defense counsel for Ruby would put such a statement in the letter to us. It seemed as though it were dragged in by the heirs.

REP. BOGGS: Deliberately.

(147) SEN. COOPER: That was in the letter from Tonahill.

THE CHAIRMAN: Tonahill, yes.

MR. McCLOY: I would like to examine again this relationship between the Department of Justice and the FBI. Just why would it be embarrassing for the Attorney General of the United States to inquire of one of his agencies whether or not this man who was alleged to have killed the President of the United States, was an agent.

Does the embarrassment supersede the importance of getting the best evidence in such a situation as this?

MR. RANKIN: Well, I think it is a question of whether we have to put him into that position in order to get the job done, because there is, in my opinion, not any question but what there will be more friction, more difficulty with his carrying out his responsibilities, and I think we have a very real problem in this Commission in that if we have meetings all the time and they know what it is about that they know these people are up here, and they know this has come out in the paper now, it is in The Nation article, and we are meeting rather rapidly here in the last few days, and they can guess probably what it is about, certainly after the meeting with the Texas people.

REP. BOGGS: Who was The Nation, do you have it?

MR. RANKIN: The Nation article deals with it and tries to show all the various other materials that would contribute to this kind of conclusion that there is something to the rumor.

(148) REP. BOGGS: This is exactly the kind of thing that you can anticipate being written.

SEN. COOPER: I would like to suggest something else. In view of all the rumors and statements that have been made not only here but abroad, I think to ask the President's brother, the dead President, to do this, it wouldn't have any backing in it. It would have no substance in his purpose but some crazy people would translate it from his official position to a personal position. It may sound far fetched but he would be implying as a person that something was wrong. You can't overlook any implications.

MR. McCLOY: I think that would perhaps be an element in the thing, but it still wouldn't divert me from asking this man who happens to be the Attorney General whose sworn duty it is to enforce justice, to ask him just what is within his knowledge in regard to such a serious thing as this. It is awkward affair. But as you said the other day, truth is our only client.

REP. BOGGS: Yes.

MR. McCLOY: I think we may have to make this first step, that the Senator speaks about, but I don't think that we could recognize that any door is closed to us, unless the President closes it to us, and in the search for the truth.

MR. RANKIN: I was asking the question and talking with the Chief Justice, and say we ran this out with Hudkins and these other people, and found that they said they would not give us the source (149) of their information, they wouldn't say it was a fabrication, but they wouldn't—so it isn't washed out, and then are we going to be able to leave it there or don't we always have to go back to our own Federal agency and try to establish the truth.

THE CHAIRMAN. We do.

MR. RANKIN: I don't see how the country is ever going to be willing to accept it if we don't satisfy them on this particular issue, not only with them but the CIA and every other agency.

REP. BOGGS: Apparently this fellow Hudkins, according to this piece, has already published the information in the Houston Post.

MR. RANKIN: January 1st.

REP. BOGGS: January 1st. Hudkins of the Houston Post published a story under the headline, "Oswald rumored as informant for U. S.", and it goes on in detail what he said.

MR. McCLOY: I haven't read it yet.

REP. BOGGS: It is just an article.

MR. DULLES: It is quoted there. I haven't read that either.

MR. McCLOY: Mr. Chief Justice is there a privilege between the reporter and his source, isn't this something which is just alleged. But there is not a common law privilege. I just read rather recently there was a contempt case in Great Britain.

MR. DULLES: They sent two people to jail.

MR. McCLOY: Sent them to jail because there was no privilege. (150) And I don't know. I know that doctor-patient.

MR. DULLES: They have an Official Secrets Act which we haven't.

MR. McCLOY: It is not recognized in law generally this privilege.

MR. DULLES: You remember this one reporter for the Herald Tribune who went to jail rather than disclose her source up in New York. The court didn't recognize any privilege.

MR. McCLOY: This is a matter of tradition, perhaps of—

MR. DULLES: But they don't generally prosecute.

MR. McCLOY: They don't generally prosecute but I don't think we can draw back from a non-legal privilege in the course of our inquiry, if it leads us to this relationship. I don't believe in any State that I know of that there is a statute which permits it.

Do you, Senator?

SEN. RUSSELL: I am frank to say, I haven't studied it very closely. I was going by Congressional Committees. They generally recognize it.

MR. McCLOY: It is a sort of law, it is a sort of custom but I don't think it is a legal privilege.

SEN. RUSSELL: I never had a case in this area when I was practicing law and I never had occasion to brief it but over in the Congress, I have never seen it pursued any further, if a reporter claimed that it was a matter of privilege not to disclose (151) it.

MR. McCLOY: I think we will have to cross it.

THE CHAIRMAN: I think there are some States that by statute.

MR. McCLOY: It is not in New York State, at least not to my knowledge.

MR. DULLES: I don't know of any.

MR. McCLOY: I don't know in New York State. This law may have been changed since I was more familiar with it.

THE CHAIRMAN: Whether he has privilege or not, I think he should be made to claim it.

SEN. RUSSELL: We can't afford not to ask him, whatever the law in Texas is we can't afford not to ask him a question.

THE CHAIRMAN: That is right.

MR. McCLOY: You know in reading over this testimony again, this morass of testimony or evidence we have got here, I notice that Mrs. Oswald, the mother, said perhaps he was an agent, perhaps he might have been an agent, in trying to explain why he went to the Soviet Union.

THE CHAIRMAN: She has made statements on that.

MR. RANKIN: I think the assertion is in that article in The Nation.

MR. McCLOY: To that effect.

MR. RANKIN: Yes.

MR. DULLES: Since this has been so much out in the public, (152) what harm would there be in talking to Hoover without waiving any right to make any investigation in the public?

MR. McCLOY: This is going to build up. In New York I am already beginning to hear about it. I got a call from Time-Life about it. Maybe it is prompted by this letter with these 12 perplexing questions—no, it wasn't because it came before that. "What is there to this story?"

MR. DULLES: There is a terribly hard thing to disprove, you know. How do you disprove a fellow was not your agent. How do you disprove it.

REP. BOGGS: You could disprove it, couldn't you?

MR. DULLES: No.

REP. BOGGS: I know, ask questions about something—

MR. DULLES: I never knew how to disprove it.

REP. BOGGS: So I will ask you. Did you have agents about whom you had no record whatsoever?

MR. DULLES: The record might not be on paper. But on paper would have hieroglyphics that only two people knew what they meant, and nobody outside of the agency would know and you could say this meant the agent and somebody else could say it meant another agent.

REP. BOGGS: Let's take a specific case, that fellow Powers was one of your men.

MR. DULLES: Oh, yes, he was not an agent. He was an employee.

(153) REP. BOGGS: There was no problem in proving he was employed by the CIA.

MR. DULLES: No. We had a signed contract.

REP. BOGGS: Let's say Powers did not have a signed contract but he was recruited by someone in CIA. The man who recruited him would know, wouldn't he?

MR. DULLES: Yes, but he wouldn't tell.

THE CHAIRMAN: Wouldn't tell it under oath?

MR. DULLES: I wouldn't think he would tell it under oath, no.

THE CHAIRMAN: Why?

MR. DULLES: He ought not tell it under oath. Maybe not tell it to his own government but wouldn't tell it any other way.

MR. McCLOY: Wouldn't he tell it to his own chief?

MR. DULLES: He might or might not. If he was a bad one then he wouldn't.

REP. BOGGS: What you do is you make out a problem if this be true, make our problem utterly impossible because you say this rumor can't be dissipated under any circumstances.

MR. DULLES: I don't think it can unless you believe Mr. Hoover, and so forth and so on, which probably most of the people will.

MR. McCLOU: Allen, suppose somebody when you were head of the CIA came to you, another government agency and said specifically, "If you will tell us", suppose the President of the United (154) States comes to you and says, "Will you tell me, Mr. Dulles?"

MR. DULLES: I would tell the President of the United States anything, yes, I am under his control. He is my boss, wouldn't necessarily tell anybody else, unless the President authorized me to do it. We had that come up at times.

MR. McCLOY: You wouldn't tell the Secretary of Defense?

MR. DULLES: Well, it depends a little bit on the circumstances. If it was within the jurisdiction of the Secretary of Defense, but otherwise I would go to the President, and I do on some cases.

MR. RANKIN: If that is all that is necessary, I think we could get the President to direct anybody working for the government to answer this question. If we have to we would get that direction.

MR. DULLES: What I was getting at, I think under any circumstances, I think Mr. Hoover would say certainly he didn't have anything to do with this fellow.

MR. McCLOY: Mr. Hoover didn't have anything to do with him but his agent. Did you directly or indirectly employ him.

MR. DULLES: But if he says no, I I didn't have anything to do with it. You can't prove what the facts are. There are no external evidences. I would believe Mr. Hoover. Some people might not. I don't think there is any external evidence other than the person's word that he did or did not employ a particular man as a secret agent. No matter what.

(155) MR. McCLOY: If we get a statement from the Department that the Attorney General and perhaps from Mr. Hoover or from Mr. Hoover which said, "I am telling you that this man was not in any way employed by the FBI", or in the case of John McCloy or the CIA, I think that probably stops us, unless we run into something—

MR. DULLES: That would be all right with me. Whether it meets with the others—

MR. McCLOY: Now there is put in our hand a document that shows he was paid a certain amount of money. Maybe we would have to go further than that but I think it would be almost incumbent upon us to ask the head of the agencies whether or not this man was an employee.

REP. BOGGS: Just to examine a little further your statement, I would believe that could establish whether or not this fellow got $200 a month, almost certainly establish it.

MR. DULLES: How could you? He is dead and you haven't got his bank account or anything of that kind.

SEN. RUSSELL: The only trouble is those undercover agents they don't keep one line of writing, not one word anywhere.

MR. DULLES: Sometimes you very often, in the Soviet, they did it all the time, they wanted to compromise a person and they would deliberately see that there was a record, they would keep it, and they would force money on people, and force money, people to give receipts, sometimes they would want to do that. But that (156) is when you are, I don't know whether too much of this should be on the record as far as the Soviet is concerned. If you want to incriminate someone and tie them to you, you would give them money and give them a receipt. But that doesn't by any means overlap. But on occasion.

SEN. RUSSELL: Is that when you would want to blacmail him?

MR. DULLES: That is correct. Klaus Fuchs, take Hiss with the rug, they wanted to have some evidence, he couldn't run away then, he was caught, he was trapped.

SEN. COOPER: I was reading some place that it has been said in the Soviet papers that this man was in the employ of the FBI.

MR. RANKIN: Yes, the Information Service has given us that.

SEN. COOPER: The fact that these officials have come here give us something official in the way that we did not have beford, I would think.

MR. RANKIN: Allen, how would you feel about it, if you were head of the CIA now, and the same claim was made and this Commission was worried about the claim being believed by the public, and they would ask you, would you want the Commission to come to you directly?

MR. DULLES: Oh, yes, certainly I would.

MR. RANKIN: Or would you want us to go out and examine witnesses first?

MR. DULLES: I think I would want you to come so I could (157) give you leads as to how you could examine witnesses if you wanted to.

MR. RANKIN: If you had us out examining witnesses about whether you had the man in your employ, would you feel that we were not very fair to you?

MR. DULLES: No, I don't think I would.

MR. RANKIN: That wouldn't bother you.

MR. DULLES: No.

MR. McCLOY: Do you think it might be quite appropriate for us?

MR. DULLES: It would depend whether there were international complications or foreign government involved, then I might say we would do it this way or that way to keep from being in trouble with the foreign country. But as far as the U. S.—

MR. McCLOY: But wouldn't we be putting your agency in great trouble if we went out finding out who your agents were and put out the report and make it public knowledge, wouldn't you think it strange if we didn't come to you with our problem.

MR. DULLES: Yes, I think it would be.

MR. McCLOY: That is what I think.

MR. RANKIN: Then you would leave doubt you were out investigating around before you had any real leads.

MR. McCLOY: We might get a lead and then we have it and then we have to publish.

(158) SEN. RUSSELL: There is no man in the employ of the Federal Government who stands higher in the opinion of the American people than J. Edgar Hoover.

MR. DULLES: That is right.

SEN. RUSSELL: Of course, we can get an affidavit from Mr. Hoover and put it in this record and go on and act on that but if we didn't go any further than that, and we don't pursue it down to Hudkins or whoever it is, there still would be thousands of doubting Thomases who would believe this man was an FBI agent and you just didn't try to clear it up and you just took Hoover's word.

Personally, I would believe J. Edgar Hoover, I have a great deal of confidence in him.

MR. DULLES: I do, too.

SEN. RUSSELL: But the other people—I would believe, a simple statement as Holy Writ, this one statement without being under oath, but you can't try cases that way, and you can't base the conclusions of this Commission on that kind of material.

SEN. COOPER: I would like to have your idea bout what I suggested.

MR. McCLOY: State it again.

SEN. COOPER: We know these people have been here, so this speculation or rumor is just some official, we will not say approval, but they don't disapprove it.

MR. McCLOY: They have cognizance of it.

(159) SEN. COOPER: That being true, since we are under a duty to see what Hudkins and Sweatt say about it, where you got that information, my suggestion was we do that, but apprise Mr. Hoover about the facts, where this information comes, we have to inquire into it, we will inquire into it, and then talk to him further about it and see if there are any facts which he ought to know about, and it would be a matter of justice to him instead of having him disprove it from the beginning.

MR. McCLOY: What is your objection, John, to going to it, I don't know whether it is Hoover or the Department of Justice, and the CIA, John McCone, or under-Secretary of Defense, he has an intelligence unit too, this man, it has come up, we would like to know, can you give us any information which would prove or disprove this rumor.

SEN. RUSSELL: I haven't got objection to it but even if, if we are dealing with the FBI now, if Mr. Hoover makes his statement, I think still by reason of the fact you have heard these people and they have said that Hudkins does have some information about the truth of it, whether it is or not, you still are under a duty to examine them.

MR. McCLOY: I think it would be wrong for us, this is off the top of my head, listening to this thing, I think it would be wrong for us to start an independent examination of who the agents of this, of the various law enforcement agencies of the country were without notifying the head of that agency that we (160) were doing it and why we were doing it.

SEN. COOPER: That is what I think.

MR. McCLOY: In other words, you would communicate with the head of the agency, whether it be the Attorney General or Mr. Hoover or John McCone, whoever it might be, at the same time you would be taking a look at Hudkins.

SEN. COOPER: Yes.

MR. McCLOY: The sources.

SEN. COOPER: I think if there was suspicion we ought to clear it up.

MR. DULLES: They are on notice on it and they have not denied it. These are not official denials here but the other letter was.

MR. McCLOY: They are not on notice of these last developments in the Commission, the last information.

SEN. COOPER: They probably have notice that these people have been here, and therefore suspect already that we are looking into it because knowing exactly what we are doing.

MR. McCLOY: Have you talked to Catzenbach, Lee?

MR. RANKIN: No.

MR. McCLOY: Willens has indicated that Katzenbach says they will be embarrassed.

MR. RANKIN: Greatly embarrassed.

MR. McCLOY: Greatly embarrassed.

SEN. RUSSELL: If what?

(161) MR. RANKIN: If the Attorney General were asked to check this out and then report to us.

THE CHAIRMAN: But they seemed to think there would be no embarrassment for us to check it out ourselves. They think that is all right, they think it is all right for us to do that.

Now, my own thought is this: I am not going to be thin-skinned about what Mr. Hoover might think, but I am sure if we indicated to Mr. Hoover that we were investigating him he would be just as angry at us as he was, or would be at the Attorney General for investigating him.

Now, I thought that the better way to do it would be to try to establish in our own minds whether or not there is any truth to this thing or whether it is—as to whether it is based on any one who assumes to have positive knowledge or whether it is just a rumor that has developed through a lot of gossip from the press rooms, or not, and if we decide that there is nothing to it except rumor, as far as we can find, I would still ask Mr. Hoover to report to us on it, tell him that this rumor has persisted, that Oswald was on the payroll of the FBI, and that the date of his employment was stated, his number was stated, his wages were stated, and that we would like anything he has in his records or through his investigation to disprove that thing.

Now, I don't see how a man in a public position whose own reputation is at stake in the thing, could object to such procedure. I don't think that is unfriendly in any way, shape or form. But (162) I do believe, I am inclined to believe, if we just go and indicate to Mr. Hoover that we are now investigating his probity without having tried to determine whether it is fact or fiction, that he might have reason to believe that we were doing it.

SEN. RUSSELL: Back to the way I felt about it.

MR. DULLES: We ought to go to him.

THE CHAIRMAN: That is the difference between my approach and his approach. We must go into this thing from both ends, from the end of the rumormongers and from the end of the FBI, and if we come into a cul de sac why we are there but we can report on it.

Now that is the way it would appeal to me. These are things where people can reasonably disagree. Whatever you want to do I am willing to approach it in that manner.

MR. DULLES: I agree with that, Mr. Chairman. May I point out, I don't think there is necessarily a question of probity. It might look so to the country. It is Mr. Hoover's job to watch the Fair Play for Cuba Committee and to try to penetrate it in any way he could. The reason I don't believe it is this fellow was so incompetent that he was not the kind of fellow that Hoover would hire. If this fellow was hired, I wouldn't discredit this might be a normal thing to do but he was so stupid. Hoover didn't hire this kind of a stupid fellow but for him to want to penetrate the Fair Play for Cuba Committee and find out what it is doing in this country is just as much of his duty as it is to penetrate (163) the Communist Party in this country and he has been doing that right along.

So I don't think really you have a question of probity.

MR. McCLOY: I wouldn't put much confidence in the intelligence of all the agents I have run into. I have run into some awfully stupid agents.

MR. DULLES: Not this irresponsible.

MR. McCLOY: Well, I can't say that I have run into a fellow comparable to Oswald but I have run into some very limited mentalities both in the CIA and the FBI.

(Laughter)

THE CHAIRMAN: Under agents, the regular agents, I think that would be right, but they and all other agencies do employ undercover men who are of terrible character.

MR. DULLES: Terribly bad characters.

SEN. RUSSELL: Limited intelligence, even the city police departments do it.

THE CHAIRMAN: It takes almost that kind of a man to do a lot of this undercover work.

MR. DULLES: They ought to be fairly smart. They may not be of high moral character but they ought to be fairly smart.

MR. McCLOY: Most of them certainly are. But you couldn't base an argument on the fact that the man, because he is not intelligence hasn't been retained.

MR. RANKIN: Would it be acceptable to go to Mr. Hoover and (164) tell him about the situation and that we would like to go ahead and find out what we could about these—

MR. McCLOY: Hudkins' sources.

MR. RANKIN: Then if he reacts and says, "I want to show you that it couldn't be", or something like that, beforehand, what about that kind of an approach?

THE CHAIRMAN: Well, Lee, I wouldn't be in favor of going to any agency and saying, "We would like to do this". I think we ought to know what we are going to do, and do it, and take our chances one way or the other.

I don't believe we should apologize or make it look that we are in any way reticent about making any investigation that comes to the Commission.

But on the other hand, I don't want to be unfriendly or unfair to him.

My own judgment was that the most fair thing to do would be to try to find out if this is fact or fiction.

MR. RANKIN: What I was fearful of was the mere process will cause him to think, in light of these people being here and all, and the meetings of the Commission, that we are really investigating him.

THE CHAIRMAN: If you tell him we are going down there to do it, we are investigating him, aren't we?

MR. RANKIN: I think it is inherent.

THE CHAIRMAN: If we are investigating him, we are investigating (165) the rumor against him, we are investigating him, that is true.

I don't want to belabor the thing at all.

REP. BOGGS: Does anyone have—I mean, Mr. Dulles, when you headed up the CIA, the notion that you would know the countless informers and people employed by the agencies was fantastic. You couldn't know about all of that.

MR. DULLES: No, but after a thing like this happens and it is in the paper two or three times I would get hold of the proper person and say, "Have we hired anybody in that particular area?" By this time I would have known whether we did hire him or not because otherwise certainly not. I had to authorize it. I had to trust that to the other agents.

MR. McCLOY: You would know in this case who, if there was anybody, who would have hired Oswald, who it would be.

MR. DULLES: Certainly within an area, certainly no one had authority to do it. Now someone might have done it without authority. The CIA has no charter to hire anybody for this kind of work in the United States. It has abroad, that is the distinction.

But in the war time, in the early days when Wade was working for the CIA during the war, the CIA had jurisdiction over Latin America, so they did run agents in Latin America in his day.

MR. McCLOY: You mean FBI?

MR. DULLES: FBI ran agents in Latin America during the war.

(166) MR. McCLOY: I remember that.

MR. DULLES: That jurisdiction was transferred to the CIA after CIA was organized in '47. But the CIA has no charter. I don't say it couldn't possibly have done it but it has no charter of authority to run this kind of agent in the United States; that would be other departments of government, particularly the FBI. We wouldn't investigate the Fair Play for Cuba Committee in the United States, in the CIA. But there is no reason why an inquiry shouldn't go. I think it should, if the charge has been made, in my opinion.

MR. McCLOY: This is going to loom up in all probablility to be one of the major issues in our investigation, I think. That and whether there is a relationship between Ruby and Oswald. It explains a good bit, this starts off, The Nation article, starts off, "Well, why wasn't the Secret Service notified that there was this defector in this building?"

If he was on the payroll of the FBI they would think he was all right, they would not think of his being a defector.

There are other things that you can put two and two together and make five out of but it is going to, I think, foment a good bit of comment, and we are going to have to have a very solid record on it.

THE CHAIRMAN: Lee, what was that we were told today about, what was it today, about this FBI agent in Dallas who had gone to the police shortly after the assassination and had (167) said he knew Oswald because, and then he made some statement about having, he having been connected up with two known subversives a short time before, do you remember that conversation? Will you tell us, please.

MR. RANKIN: At the police station, just after the assassination, Hosty, the agent for the FBI in the Dallas area, said that he knew that Oswald had been—had visited two known subversives.

MR. DULLES: Said to whom?

MR. RANKIN: To the police, the Dallas police, two known subversives within two weeks of the day of assassination.

SEN. RUSSELL: He didn't relate who they were?

MR. RANKIN: No.

SEN. COOPER: Do they know the name of the FBI people?

MR. RANKIN: This was Hosty.

MR. DULLES: Has Hosty been talked to later to get the names?

MR. RANKIN: Nobody has asked him.

THE CHAIRMAN: They never talked to Hosty, he is an FBI agent, and we asked, Hosty had been around there for, a year or two, something like that, and we asked—and was there on the day of the assassination—we asked the District Attorney, and his assistant if he had seen him around there since and he said no he had never seen him since.

MR. RANKIN: I checked on that and that is inaccurate. He is still in that area, although I don't know whether he is around (168) visiting the police.

THE CHAIRMAN: They did tell us that.

MR. RANKIN: Yes.

SEN. COOPER: May I ask a question?

MR. DULLES: Do we know who those two people are? It might be important.

SEN. COOPER: Now this man Hudkins published an article in January. But if he were brought before us and put under oath and testified then he could publish whatever he wanted to, about his testimony.

MR. RANKIN: That is correct.

SEN. COOPER: And be relieved in some way from the possibility of libel.

MR. RANKIN: Well, he would certainly be free to tell what he had testified to himself. If he lied about it here, I don't think his testimony before this Commission would protect him against his own lie.

SEN. COOPER: No, that would be perjury.

THE CHAIRMAN: He can write the same thing now with whatever privilege he would have after testifying, I would think.

MR. McCLOY: I wonder whether—this brings up to my mind again, the desirability of our talking to the chief investigator of the FBI. We here, we don't know whether somebody checked up on Hosty again or whether he didn't. Why don't we get him in and just talk with him. I don't know whether we want to examine (169) him under oath but talk to him about the extent of the FBI investigation. We hear they are continuing to investigate. What have they done. There is this loophole about it, "What have you done about this? What have you done about that? What do you have in mind for future investigations", and he will say "We have in mind this". Have you thought about that avenue. I would think the time is almost overdue for us being as dependent as we are on FBI investigations, the time is almost overdue for us to have a better perspective of the FBI investigation than we now have.

MR. RANKIN: Well, the difficulty with doing that, we had hoped to do that about two and a half weeks ago and we were going to come back to them with a great many obvious questions, and holes in what we have been given. But then we got a supplemental report, and it filled in some of the holes but not all of them, two-thirds of them or more, that were not, and we didn't want to ask them questions that they would say, well haven't you read our supplemental report, it is all there. Our relations would breakdown very rapidly if we did business that way, so we had to go and analyze all this new material and, not only supplemental report but all their additional raw materials they gave us at that time, and now we are in the process of trying to give them the demands.

There may be a thousand different requests for additional investigation that we will come up with in all this area.

(170) Now the difficulty with trying to get the man in charge and asking him those questions is how much do you know about what he is giving. If we get him here before the Commission, I think you could ask him a good many things but he would probably say two-thirds or more of the time, "I told you this and I told you this and my reports", and so forth.

So I don't think we have equipped you as Commissioners so that you could do that.

He would soon find you didn't know anything like what he did about the matter.

As far as we are concerned, the men are getting advised of the areas as rapidly as possible, and they are coming back with these further inquiries, but there are vast areas that are unanswered at the present time.

We have some differences between the Secret Service and the FBI, we have location of their cars and where the shots were and things where they differed as much as 17 feet, and we are trying to find out how they could have that much difference between them, and there is an explanation. It isn't as bad as that, because some of it is part of calculations.

MR. McCLOY: Calculating their speed, I suppose.

MR. RANKIN: That is right. And whether or not the first shot occurred behind the sign or just as he came out from behind the sign and matters of that kind.

MR. McCLOY: I can see the difficulty with that. But on the (171) other hand, I have a feeling we are so dependent upon them for our facts that it might be a useful thing to have him before us, or maybe just you talk to him, to give us the scope of his investigation, and as of that date, some of the things that are still troubling us, and we will be able to ask him, for example, to follow up on Hosty.

MR. RANKIN: Part of our difficulty in regard to it is that they have no problem. They have decided that it is Oswald who committed the assassination, they have decided that no one else was involved, they have decided—

SEN. RUSSELL: They have tried the case and reached a verdict on every aspect.

REP. BOGGS: You have put your finger on it.

MR. McCLOY: They are a little less certain in the supplementals than they were in the first.

MR. RANKIN: Yes, but they are still there. They have decided the case, and we are going to have maybe a thousand further inquiries that we say the Commission has to know all these things before it can pass on this.

And I think their reaction probably would be, "Why do you want all that. It is clear."

SEN. RUSSELL: "You have our statement, what else do you need?"

MR. McCLOY: Yes, "We know who killed cock robin". That is the point. It isn't only who killed cock robin. Under the terms (172) of reference we have to go beyond that.

REP. BOGGS: The most difficult aspect of this is the Ruby aspect.

MR. RANKIN: That is one very difficult area. Then you have some clear proof of some kind of a Cuban connection there, and there is a difference in regard to the testimony of what it is. You run into clear proof that his brother had some kind of a Cuban connection.

MR. McCLOY: Ruby's brother?

MR. RANKIN: Yes, in Detroit but that sort of dries up when we try to get at the detail of what it is. But I don't see how you can pass on these questions without really knowing about those things as far as it is possible to know, because it might just blossom out and give you the answer to a good many things here.

THE CHAIRMAN: Well, Lee, as I understand your approach would be this: You would go to Mr. Hoover and say, "Now, Mr. Hoover, as you know, there are rumors that persist in and around Dallas and it is getting into the national press, to the effect that Oswald was an undercover FBI agent. The rumor has gone to the extent of stating the date on which he was employed, the number under which he was employed, and the amount of money that he received for his services, and that continued up until the time of the assassination.

"Now we are going to have to try to run that rumor down to (173) see if anyone claims positive knowledge or whether it is plain rumor.

Can you, and will you, give us all the information that you have which will enable us to ferret that thing out, to the very limit"?

MR. RANKIN: That is what I would like to do. Reserving at the same time the right to go to these other people and take their testimony.

THE CHAIRMAN: That would be implicit in it.

(174) REP. BOGGS: What about the point that Senator Russell makes. Assuming that you had these people who are involved here, that you had not

talked to them, and you get a statement from the Justice Department, or from Mr. Hoover, or from whoever it may be which is categoric in its denial. Where does that place us where you decide to go talk to these other people?

MR. RANKIN: Well, I had in mind going to Mr. Hoover and asking him as the Chief Justice said, for more than his expression of the truth or falsity of it. Asking him for what he knows his organization presumably, what can he do to help us in regard to the proof of the facts in regard to this particular matter.

Now, it is like the questions you asked, Congressman, of Mr. Dulles, and if you would ask, I am sure Mr. Hoover knows many of those, he may not know about particular individuals, just like Mr. Dulles wouldn't, but he knows who to ask, and ring a button and say, for the record how could we establish this? I never had that kind of a problem when I was with the Department of Justice. But I am sure within the F.B.I. Mr. Hoover knows where to find out who was hired on any particular date and the basis of it, and I thought if it was my situation, and I was being reflected on that I had had somebody like this under my employ I would like to be approached, first, and I wouldn't feel that it was a reflection on me, or at least I would feel the reflection was already involved in these kinds of articles and claims, and I would rather you would come to me than to go to someone else and (175) ask him about the rumors, and let me see if I couldn't establish it. I don't think the country is going to be satisfied with the mere statement from, not to use Mr. Hoover's name, but just examine about any intelligence agency that Oswald wasn't hired in light of this kind of an accusation, a rumor.

I think that the country is going to expect this Commission to try to find out the facts, as to how those things are handled to such an extent that this Commission can fairly say, "In our opinion, he was or was not an employee of any intelligence agency of the United States."

SEN. RUSSELL: Did you ask Wade if he had taken any statements of these people?

MR. RANKIN: Yes, I did, and he had not.

SEN. RUSSELL: He had not. Did he propose to?

MR. RANKIN: He didn't indicate he was going to.

THE CHAIRMAN: He said it didn't make any difference in his Ruby case.

MR. DULLES: Could I add one thing, on the suggestion that I would make, I would suggest that you ask Mr. Hoover for the right to see any reports that agents made who did contact—we know he was contacted by the F.B.I. at various times.

I think they say the last date was August, was it, but we know he was contacted at various times for various reasons.

Now, normally, an agent makes a report to headquarters when he has a contact of that kind. There ought to be some reports.

(176) MR. RANKIN: And we have those.

MR. DULLES: You have those reports?

MR. RANKIN: But we don't have any assurance that those are the only reports, you see.

MR. DULLES: I see.

MR. RANKIN: There could be a report for this purpose and there could be more reports and all that kind of thing.

MR. DULLES: You should ask him that, if there are reports.

MR. RANKIN: He had a report from, in October, from Mrs. Payne and from Marina Oswald, if you remember, but he didn't go directly to Oswald himself. That is a curious factor in itself, that he made no approach—

SEN. RUSSELL: That has always been a queer thing to me before this rumor came up. I couldn't understand why they went to Mrs. Payne and Mrs. Oswald, but didn't go to him.

MR. RANKIN: That is correct. We have the August conversation when he returned to this country and the first time they approached him, Marina Oswald, the wife, said that the two F.B.I. agents talked to him for two hours, and when he returned to the house from talking to him out in the car or out in the yard he was very much disturbed—that is her expression of it.

We don't have any report that would cover anything like a two hour conversation.

It is a relatively short report.

Now, what occupied the rest of the time—well, it could have (177) been something not related to his at all, but it seems to me if someone else is going to take this material after we get through and make a report they are going to say, how can you spend two hours on a thing like that? What happened to the rest of the time, and they will try to draw the inference.

SEN. RUSSELL: It seems to me we have two alternatives. One is we can just accept the F.B.I.'s report and go on and write the report based on their findings and supported by the raw materials they have given us, or else we can go and try to run down some of these collateral rumors that have just not been dealt with directly in this raw material that we have.

REP. BOGGS: I think we must do the latter.

SEN. RUSSELL: So do I.

THE CHAIRMAN: I think there is no question about it.

SEN. RUSSELL: Of course the other is much easier.

MR. McCLOY: We certainly wouldn't be doing the F.B.I. a service and doing the Commission a service.

SEN. RUSSELL: The F.B.I. would like to see us very much do it.

MR. DULLES: I think it is the question of the procedure, I don't think there is any difference among us as to what is to be done.

MR. McCLOY: You see, here is this sheet, this is designed to be an attack on the F.B.I.

REP. BOGGS: Sure.

MR. McCLOY: And there are a lot of people who would like to (178) attack the F.B.I., and we don't want to be in the position of attacking the F.B.I.

REP. BOGGS: Of course not.

SEN. RUSSELL: I don't propose to attack the F.B.I. unless there is some startling revelation that they have evaded their responsibility.

MR. McCLOY: I think the F.B.I. is an agency which has the security of this country, and a very important agency, as has this Commission.

REP. BOGGS: What we have to do is tell our counsel what to do.

THE CHAIRMAN: Yes.

What do the rest of you think of the approach of Mr. Rankin, the way we have just laid it out here in the last few minutes?

MR. DULLES: Doesn't that combine your idea, too, Mr. Chairman? It seems to me it is a marriage of the two.

THE CHAIRMAN: It is just a question of whether you have the cart or the horse first. We disagreed a little on which approach to take, but if you think his approach is reasonable, is a reasonable approach to it, it is perfectly all right with me. I would be glad to go along with it.

MR. McCLOY: I think it is fundamentally the same as yours. It may be a little—it is almost a collateral approach.

THE CHAIRMAN: Yes, there isn't any great difference.

SEN. RUSSELL: Do you propose to let Mr. Hoover send out some (179) F.B.I. agents to interview this fellow Hudkins to kind of find out where he got this information?

MR. RANKIN: No.

SEN. RUSSELL: What are you going to do after telling him all this?

THE CHAIRMAN: That is a good question.

MR. RANKIN: I thought from what I know about him that he would say, "We will do anything we can to help you. We will make anything available from our records", and then I would say to him, "You know your records and I don't. What will prove that this rumor is false?"

And there may be some—

THE CHAIRMAN: From his standpoint, he couldn't possibly have any proof other than his statement.

MR. RANKIN: Well, he may have a lot of proof.

THE CHAIRMAN: You mean that he was not an F.B.I. agent, under-cover man?

MR. RANKIN: Well, he may be able to prove who were, that is that there were certain ways of checking that out.

MR. DULLES: If you could get all the conversations of the agents with him and they were correct, then you might get some bearing on the situation. Because if they had five meetings and talked to him five times or the number of times this was, and this was never mentioned, it didn't come up at all, he didn't volunteer, or they didn't ask him anything, that depends, of course, (180) upon getting the conversations as they took place.

SEN. RUSSELL: Do you have any contacts with any United States district attorneys in Texas in whom you have confidence? Is any one of them that you think you could get to interview this man?

MR. RANKIN: Well, I had in mind that the Commission should go directly with some member of its staff to interview him and interview each of these people, but as we proceed with that I thought we would have Mr. Hoover understand we were doing that and that he recognized that we had to do it and that was—

SEN. RUSSELL: I have no objection to that.

Of course I think he is going to offer to interview them, if he hasn't already done it.

MR. RANKIN: I think the Commission needs to have its own record on that, and I think it might be very desirable to have them here under oath for the Commission to see them and be present when they give their story.

This is, in my opinion, one of the major points that is constantly raised to try to explain this situation. If we can put it to rest in any way, it is of major importance.

SEN. COOPER: That is the point I have felt, we have to interview these people. But I thought, also, that you have to let the F.B.I. know that you are interviewing them because all the other, the great bulk of the testimony we have got we have received from them.

(181) I think we would have to—they are apprising us of what they say they are doing, I think we have a duty of apprising them of what we are doing, and in truth, in investigating the credibility of what they are doing, because if this should turn out that they knew it, and never reported it, it would be—a blow.

MR. DULLES: Did these people point out that this all stems back to Hudkins?

MR. RANKIN: Yes, that is the only explanation, except I think where you have a statement of a secret service man by a deputy sheriff that you can't disregard it even though he tells someone again.

MR. DULLES: Right.

MR. RANKIN: It seems to me you probably would want all of these people who participated in that and get it out on the paper.

REP. BOGGS: What role did this man Alexander play in this?

MR. RANKIN: Well, it appeared to have started earlier than—he was as active, but it is possible, I don't know—

THE CHAIRMAN: I think he is the fellow who blew the whistle so far as this Commission is concerned. I think that is where Carr got his information, don't you think?

REP. BOGGS: From Alexander?

THE CHAIRMAN: From Alexander, yes. And Alexander was up here and sat in that chair, and said that it wasn't exactly the way Carr had presented it, that there were two different things.

One, that was involved in Carr's story to Lee. One of them had (182) to do with hearing in chambers on some papers they wanted from the defense, and then after that was over he went out into the corridor and then down to the pressroom and he said they were all talking about it then, he said all the press were, it is a matter of common knowledge among the press, this rumor, and he just shrugged the whole thing off, and Carr was sitting here where the Senator is and he didn't object to anything that Alexander said, although it varied radically from what he told you a day or so before.

SEN. RUSSELL: Well, Mr. Chairman, I was not primarily responsible for Mr. Rankin's employment by this Commission but he is our counsel and if that is the way he wants to do it, I will make a motion that he proceed as he thinks is best in respect to this matter.

THE CHAIRMAN: Is there a second?

MR. McCLOY: I think that is all right.

MR. DULLES: Along the lines he discussed here.

THE CHAIRMAN: Those in favor say aye.

(Chorus of aye)

THE CHAIRMAN: Contrary, no.

(No response)

THE CHAIRMAN: Unanimously adopted.

MR. RANKIN: We were going to outline our approach to the ideas about the whole procedure of the staff in trying to develop this material for you. But in light of the time, I do not know (183) how much time you yet have and whether you want to see the members of the staff, and it takes some time for me to try to tell you about each of these areas, our approach.

What is your pleasure?

REP. BOGGS: I think we had better do it as quickly as we can.

THE CHAIRMAN: All right, go ahead.

MR. McCLOY: The appointment I have at the White House has been cancelled.

THE CHAIRMAN: Go right ahead.

MR. RANKIN: The first area is the day of the assassination, and all of the various elements that are involved in that, and includes the plans for the trip, the program at the Trade Mart, the checking out of that area to be sure that it was secure, all of the steps that were made by the Secret Service in that regard, the collaboration between the police, and the Secret Service, and any other agencies such as the county sheriff in connection with the parade and the route that was designated or planned.

The decision as to when that material would be released to the public, and the date of the release. The fact that the intention of the President to go to Dallas was not indicated in the press until in October, but the fact that he was going to Texas as distinguished from Dallas was indicated September 26. September 26 is the date that Oswald went down to Mexico City, and (184) the article about the President coming to Texas was in the paper on that day before he went to Mexico City as far as we can determine.

Now, we have difficulty determining the exact time that he went to Mexico City, because the exit record on the border is such that it extends from the period 8 in the morning until 7 at night, and he was shown to have passed through but the exact time is not shown by the materials we have yet.

However, we do have a record that he was supposed to have gone one way by car and one way by bus, and they haven't gotten the exact time on the bus for us, and they haven't got the story of what—who he went with in the car.

So that it is important to keep in mind in connection with that the fact that he could have known that the President was probably coming to Dallas, because we think that, and we have checked this out somewhat, that if the President was going to Dallas on what was a political trip, and this was a political as distinct from a governmental.

MR. McCLOY: You said Texas, not Dallas.

MR. RANKIN: Presumably, he would not go to Houston or San Antonio without going to the Dallas area. That it has been in the nature of politics that Presidents in going to Texas make it a point to try to get to the middle area as well as the Houston area if they are going to go there on political trips.

So we believe that it is reasonable to assume that the moment (185) it appeared in the papers on September 26th that the President decided to go to Texas, even though he didn't specify Dallas or Fort Worth, that it was probable that he was going to go there.

We also checked with the Secret Service people, and there was, as you may recall, another building that would have served well as the purpose of the meeting despite the Trade Mart and that was the Woman's building. It was located in a different area of the city. But the Secret Service people say that a President would be expected to go down the Main Street and having his parade, and so forth, and if either way it would be expected that he would go down Houston Street, which enters into Elm, one way if he was from the Woman's Building he could come down from the other section of the city and come to Houston which would be right by the window on the sixth floor of the Depository Building where, as you recall the pictures, he would have an excellent shot right down Houston Street in order to go over to Main or if you go the other way around, in order to go the Trade Mart, Building he would come down Main, go down Houston and Elm like he did.

So that to anticipate that this particular location would be a prime location for anything like this depending upon either of the probable places where he would have such a banquet or a dinner is reasonable in light of our conversations with the Secret Service, and how they would expect a parade route to be laid out.

(186) MR. DULLES: If he was making a speech in the evening would he have gone there, I rather thought not from something I read, probably would go to a big banquet room in a hotel. That might be worth looking into.

MR. RANKIN: That might be difficult, we didn't canvass it except for the luncheon, as I recall he was going on down as soon as the plans were announced to another locality.

MR. DULLES: As soon as the plans were announced, the plans were fixed. But at this stage I don't think they could tell whether it would be luncheon or dinner, whatever it would be, midday.

MR. RANKIN: That is right.

So it is possible he could have made as part of his plans from the time he left to go to Mexico City to try to locate in this building and go ahead with the assassination.

Now, that would assume that it is possible that he talked to people about such plans, and had collaborators concerning them in Mexico City. We do not have enough information about that to know what happened there except we do have information that he tried to get a visa at the Cuban Embassy, and he tried to get a visa at the Soviet Embassy, and we know the hotel he stayed at, and we have a very limited report from the hotel keeper about most of it to the effect that they knew nothing about him, didn't even know that he came or went, although there were seven days between the time he went down on the 26th, and the third when he came back.

(187) It also indicated that he had a limited visa from the United States, and, therefore, could not expect to get another one in connection with his travels down in Mexico.

MR. DULLES: We don't give visas to Mexico.

MR. RANKIN: It was a border crossing.

MR. DULLES: I thought these travel things in Mexico were limited.

THE CHAIRMAN: A travel permit for two weeks.

MR. RANKIN: Fifteen days.

MR. DULLES: I think that is Mexico and not the United States.

SEN. COOPER: Trying to get them to speed up their actions.

MR. RANKIN: Yes.

So that we have a wide range of inquiry yet in Mexico City as to the seven days and his activities there.

SEN. RUSSELL: Who has been doing the investigating in Mexico?

MR. RANKIN: The C.I.A. has been working with us in regard to that area, and the F.B.I. has an attache there who has done some work but most of it has been by the C.I.A., and we have a question there of how much of our information we have gotten from the F.B.I. in an exhibit to the C.I.A. and prior to that, and we need some instruction with regard to that.

Now, we are going to have a meeting with the agencies and see if it is acceptable to them in such a meeting to supply the (188) information themselves rather than having the Commission supply the information it has received from any of the agencies to these—the C.I.A. and other people that we will need help from.

SEN. RUSSELL: Mr. Rankin, have you given any thoughts to the fact that Oswald was not familiar with Dallas. He had this road map to go around to inquire for jobs and yet you are assuming that he knew all about these routes and everything else, when he posted himself up there to shoot the President, if he did in fact shoot him, and of course the evidence seems to be overwhelming that he did. That has caused me to believe that he had to have someone somewhere to advise him about that.

MR. RANKIN: Well, that Nation article is very interesting, Senator, in regard to your question, because—

SEN. RUSSELL: I haven't read that article, but that occurred to me at the outset. Everybody said he posted himself there and got this employment and all, but he was not familiar with Dallas. Apparently he hadn't lived there—

MR. McCLOY: It was published in the Dallas paper with an arrow showing what the direct line was to be two days before the President came, I mean the Dallas paper had a diagram showing him coming down the street and going—

SEN. RUSSELL: But he has already been in Mexico City before that, some time before that.

MR. McCLOY: Yes, that is true.

MR. RANKIN: This article sets out in some detail there a (189) quotation of some of his letters when he was in Russia.

REP. BOGGS: Yes.

MR. RANKIN: And it is very difficult to understand how anyone could write the letters he did from Russia and then write the other letters he wrote in regard to the Fair Play for Cuba.

REP. BOGGS: Right. The spelling has changed.

MR. RANKIN: It is a world of difference. It is hardly believable that anyone could have acquired such information during that period of time.

REP. BOGGS: One of the big gaps in the reports that I have read involves this shot, it was one shot, wasn't it, that he took at General Walker, with both motive and all sorts of things.

MR. RANKIN: Yes.

Well, his story about that, of course, as you recall, he left this memorandum which was found in the cookbook, and Marina Oswald, the wife, didn't ever give any explanation of that or mention until they found that and then she finally said that that was her cookbook and she remembered it, and he went there to the Walker affair around 9 o'clock, was the time it was reported that the shooting occurred, and he said to her afterwards that he buried his rifle and then he dug it up at some vacant lot near there and he fired and he didn't know whether he had been successful or not.

Then he doesn't come home until midnight, according to the (190) story, her story, and that is three hours difference, and there isn't anything to explain that long period of time, and when he got home he was very much disturbed and excited, and at that point he turned on the radio later to find out what happened, and he told her that he had shot at General Walker. He didn't know yet whether he had been killed or not. In fact, he seemed to be thinking that he might have, and he later told her that a lot of people thought that in order to do anything like that they had to have a getaway car, an automobile or something like that, and he just used a bus, that was the most effective way, and apparently he had taken his gun on the bus, and then buried it, dug it up, and had it shot, buried the gun again, and from the reports that we have and the news accounts it looks like if Walker had not backed away from the desk at the time he did he might have gotten him.

SEN. RUSSELL: The article I read Walker fortuitously moved just as the shot, otherwise it would have hit him in the head.

MR. RANKIN: He apparently turned out the light then so there was not an opportunity for another one.

She, on the other hand, threatened him if he ever did—she asked him why he would do that, and he said he was such a terrible person because he was the head of the Fascists in this country and she said if he ever did that again she was going to report it to the police, and that was her explanation for the reason she kept this memorandum that she put away in the cookbook.

(191) Now, that could have been an accurate story. It is possible, it is believable, because it may explain some of his efforts to conceal some of his additional actions and later he proceeded to try to separate her and to keep her over at Mrs. Payne's although that was a rather fortuitous arrangement anyway because he didn't pay her anything to keep her there, it didn't cost him anything, and then he lived in town at one time, as you recall, he lived under the assumed name, and she found a telephone number that he had not given her, but some of his papers and she called up and she tries to locate him, and they say he isn't there but it is somebody else, and he does come to the telephone and he is very angry with her for trying to track him down, and so it may be in explanation for some of the action that he took in the assassination of the President, and her failure to know about some of those things because of this threat that she made to him she was going to report anything that he did of this kind, if he ever did it again.

On the other hand, she claims in her testimony, all the way through that she doesn't know that he went to Mexico at all. She doesn't know anything about the fact that he was going to the Cuban Embassy about a visa, she doesn't know that he planned to go to Cuba. That whole episode is entirely unknown to her, and yet he has some note in this little notebook that he had in which he has a silver bracelet that has a name Marina on it that apparently is Mexican, characteristically Mexican bracelet, and he (192) went to, apparently, a bull fight and Jai alai and other things down there, according to his little notebook, and it is difficult to believe that he could be gone that long from her and come back and she would never ask him where he had been, and if he gave her this bracelet which she never says that she ever received, but we are going to have to ask her about all of that, how she could have not known something that was going on about that.

In addition to that, there is this Spanish dictionary, and the books about Spanish where he was trying to learn Spanish, although he had known some Spanish before he went to Russia, and we are trying to run that down to find out what he studied at the Monterey School of the Army in the way of languages because she used to make fun of him, according to some of their Russian friends, about his pronunciation of Spanish words, and he was very clumsy at it, and was embarrassed by her making jokes about that.

THE CHAIRMAN: How would she know that, that he was mispronouncing Spanish words? She couldn't speak Spanish. She couldn't even speak English, she spoke Russian. How would she know that, I wonder.

MR. RANKIN: There is no explanation of her friends saying, and it is possible she got that from her other Russian friends, but there is no indication that they were Spanish-speaking so far as anything we have.

(193) THE CHAIRMAN: Of course there are so many Spanish-speaking people down in Texas.

MR. RANKIN: In the area.

THE CHAIRMAN: That she might have gotten it from someone else.

MR. RANKIN: Then there is a great range of material in regard to the wounds, and the autopsy and this point of exit or entrance of the bullet in the front of the neck, and that all has to be developed much more than we have at the present time.

We have an explanation there in the autopsy that probably a fragment came out the front of the neck, but with the elevation the shot must have come from, and the angle, it seems quite apparent now, since we have the picture of where the bullet entered in the back, that the bullet entered below the shoulder blade to the right of the backbone, which is below the place where the picture shows the bullet came out in the neckband of the shirt in front, and the bullet, according to the autopsy didn't strike any bone at all, that particular bullet, and go through.

So that how it could turn and—

REP. BOGGS: I thought I read that bullet just went in a finger's length.

MR. RANKIN: That is what they first said. They reached in and they could feel where it came, it didn't go any further than that, about part of the finger or something, part of the autopsy, and then they proceeded to reconstruct where they thought (194) the bullet went, the path of it, and, which is, we have to go into considerable items and try to find out how they could reconstruct that when they first said that they couldn't even feel the path beyond the part of a finger.

And then how it could become elevated; even so it raised rather than coming out at a sharp angle that it entered, all of that, we have to go into, too, and we are asking for help from the ballistic experts on that.

We will have to probably get help from the doctors about it, and find out, we have asked for the original notes of the autopsy on that question, too.

Now, the bullet fragments are now, part of them are now, with the Atomic Energy Commission, who are trying to determine by a new method, a process that they have, of whether they can relate them to various guns and the different parts, the fragments, whether they are a part of one of the bullets that was broken and came out in part through the neck, and just what particular assembly of bullet they were part of.

They have had it for the better part of two and a-half weeks and we ought to get an answer.

So the basic problem, what kind of a wound it is in the front of the neck is of great importance to the investigation.

We believe it must be related in some way to the three sheets from the rear.

SEN. COOPER: You mean in the back?

(195) MR. RANKIN: One, or something from a shot at the top of the head.

MR. McCLOY: It is possible that the third shot could have had a fragmentation.

SEN. COOPER: One doctor, as I remember, projected manual massage, to resuscitate him, that would cause the bullet to come back out of the back. Do you remember that?

SEN. RUSSELL: Have you collected these charges against the raw material in here?

MR. RANKIN: I haven't, we may.

MR. McCLOY: Are we going to have at the examination of Marina the exhibits, for example, the bracelet and the rifle itself, because she has testified first that the rifle was not the rifle. Later she changed her testimony in that respect.

MR. RANKIN: Yes.

MR. McCLOY: Will we get the rifle and the bracelets so she will be confronted with them?

MR. RANKIN: Yes.

Her testimony about the rifle, you know she only admitted to that after pictures were found and she had destroyed the pictures that were in the photo album after the mother had suggested that to her, and they found this in one of his sacks that they found other material, other clothing.

They have better than 400 different objects of physical evidence. Some of them are not related at all. They just happened (196) to find them.

We think that the wound in the neck has to be related to one of these others, but the problem is difficult to determine because we have a statement from the hospital that the bullet that was more whole than the other was found on the stretcher which they brought the President in to the hospital on, and then we have other testimony later that goes back over the same ground in which the person in charge of the stretcher and the attendant said that this bullet was found under the blanket on the stretcher Governor Connally was on, and it is a complete—

SEN. RUSSELL: I thought it was found on the stretcher of the President.

MR. RANKIN: That was the first story. And that is what we have to deal with, a story of that kind to try to reconcile it with people who actually handled the stretcher that Governor Connally was on and picked the bullet from under the blanket.

Now, that evidence is quite superior to the other man's, but we have to check it out some more to determine that.

SEN. RUSSELL: This isn't going to be something that would run you stark mad.

MR. RANKIN: I don't know what we will run into, but—

Let me ask you about it because I have never seen anything about it. Whatever happened with that fellow who bought the front page ad and called the President a Communist?

(197) MR. RANKIN: We haven't anything on that at all.

THE CHAIRMAN: We ought to find that out.

REP. BOGGS: We ought to find it out. A most mysterious thing.

THE CHAIRMAN: And I will tell you, we also ought to find out who published and circulated that little, not pamphlet but the little handbill that they put out about the President that morning. "Wanted for Treason".

REP. BOGGS: That is right.

THE CHAIRMAN: That has got to be run down. There is no question about that.

REP. BOGGS: That is right.

SEN. RUSSELL: You know the F.B.I. must have looked into that.

MR. McCLOY: Yes.

(198) MR. RANKIN: We have considerable material and we are going to go into some extent and I wanted to get the Commission's instructions about this, into the atmosphere, this hate material that was very common in that area in many regards. It was in the newspapers, it was in circulars of various kinds, it was in letters to the editor in the newspaper. It was also involved in sermons from the pulpit in some of those, in at least one of the leading churches of the city was involved in financing various forms of hate literature in very large amounts from that particular area, and it may well be that it was a contributing factor in not just as was suggested by some as far as the extreme right is concerned but also in stirring up various elements of the community who were expressing themselves in very extreme forms against anybody in power from the President on down from time to time.

And it may well be—

SEN. RUSSELL: Who printed this now?

MR. RANKIN: Well, the newspapers had some of it, the pamphlets were commonly circulated there, and I presume you are familiar with some of the H. L. Hunt's financing of various—

SEN. RUSSELL: Yes, we got that about every two weeks, I don't read it but I get it.

MR. RANKIN: And all kinds of things coming from out there in substantial amounts and it apparently was not only exacerbating the community in a number of ways, not only of the extreme reight and the extreme left but also the elements of the people more (199) moderately inclined who didn't assert themselves in regard to that, and from some of the information we have, it is really the communities can be like people, and if you let those forces work long enough it will have an effect upon their approach to many problems, and it may be something that the country should well be aware of.

SEN. RUSSELL: Do you think there is evidence of any connection between Oswald and any of those groups? The FBI is supposed to check that out pretty closely.

MR. RANKIN: We have no evidence that is clear that Oswald was connected with anybody but we also have very great problems—

SEN. RUSSELL: We know he was connected with the Fair Play for Cuba Committee.

MR. RANKIN: Yes.

REP. BOGGS: They denied he was a member, didn't they?

MR. RANKIN: They denied he was a member, and also he wrote to them and tried to establish as one of his letter indicates, a new branch there in New Orleans, the Fair Play for Cuba.

REP. BOGGS: That letter has caused me a lot of trouble. It is a much more literate and polished communication than any of his other writings.

MR. RANKIN: That is right. And he also proceeded to set it up by himself without anybody else as a member or anything, and I don't know as he ever got a member.

REP. BOGGS: They tried to get a list, you know, of his membership. He never produced a single person.

(200) SEN. RUSSELL: He produced a card saying—he had one or two cards with his name.

SEN. COOPER: He had it printed and set up an office.

REP. BOGGS: That was a fictitious name that he used.

SEN. COOPER: I have one suggestion about what we have been talking about, I would think if we find out who put these advertisements in the paper and all that is very important. The other can come in as it is developed, but I think we might talk about this hate element too much because, I will tell you why, because people will begin to get the idea as some have already expressed of going away from evidence and trying to build up some situation which is apart from the evidence.

MR. RANKIN: Yes.

REP. BOGGS: I think these factors such as that add, and these circulars should certainly be looked into.

MR. RANKIN: Then in the period that they lived in Russia there are manifold problems about the fact that the way he lived, the additional income he received under the name of the Red Cross, you will remember, the question of when that income terminated. She said he had never been to Leningrad. He said he had, she went to Kharkov, and there is no explanation of any communications between the two of them during that period of time. There is a period when they were there that she indicated she was fearful of her marriage, and whether it was—it may not be maintained, there is no explanation of that in anything she has given in any of her (201) interviews.

The fact that he was paid proportionately so much more than she was when he was a workman in the factory and she was at least a semi-skilled person with her pharmacy knowledge, and all, is another problem that isn't covered by any of her testimony.

The fact that they moved to another apartment during the period that they were trying to arrange to come to the United States, which according to what their testimony—what she testified to, was going to be of relatively short time, that she would get an answer and it doesn't seem like there was any good reason for them to move to another apartment.

That is unexplained, and the members of her family are a curious thing. She was apparently a child with a father unknown at the time she was born, and yet she acquired a name of a father in some of the registrations under the Soviet system. Well, according to information we have it is very rare that they would insert anything like that or would allow it, because their controls are so carefully made to try to identify people all their life and particularly where they were born so they can trace down through for the rest of the period, and that is an unexplained feature.

Then the fact of her uncle and what his status was apprently a part of the Interior government and not a part of the Intelligence, but nevertheless he had a telephone, and the style in which they lived, and the partment and all were very unusual comparatively.

(202) SEN. RUSSELL: You mean while they were in Russia?

MR. RANKIN: Yes, I mean not only Oswald but this uncle, too, and it would appear that he was much more than just a person of the Interior government like she had said from what we have been able to get from the CIA and others about it.

Then the fact she was allowed to leave the country the way she was is not adequately explained by her testimony, her statements or anything.

Why they did it so relatively promptly when that is a very difficult operation with most people, and what he did in Moscow when he want there, and was there for better than a month, and was there, and there's no explanation of what he did there.

MR. DULLES: The beginning of his trip, you mean?

MR. RANKIN: Yes.

MR. DULLES: When he tried to commit suicide?

MR. RANKIN: Yes. And then this period that he belonged to the gun club, and there is no explanation by her of that or what he did in that. He might have had all kinds of training during that period, that is entirely unexplained.

The fact that they went to, when they came back, they went to Amsterdam and were there for, I think, it was two days before they went to Rotterdam to take a boat, and it is unexplained why they happened to go there and stay, and get a place to live, some little apartment, and what they were doing in the interim, that entire period is just full of possibilities for training, for (203) working with the Soviet, and its agents, and unusual compared with the experience of most Americans.

Now, you recognize it is going to be very difficult to get all of that out of her no matter how well informed we are about her, what she has testified to, what she has given statements about, and she has given a good many of them, and what her written statement in Russian is, all of those things will be—we have, and we examined them in great detail and are prepared on them, but whenever she gets to these areas that might be enlightening for us she is unable—

SEN. RUSSELL: "Don't understand what you are talking about"?

MR. RANKIN: That is correct. Give us anything on it and just seems to come up to a blank.

We are trying to get sufficient material to try to get to persuade her to explain how these things were possible, and it is difficult to anticipate what she will do except she may just say she can't understand or she doesn't know, and that will be all we can get out of her.

MR. DULLES: Has the letter gone forward to the State Department for the Russians?

MR. RANKIN: It hasn't, it isn't going forward yet because we have to ask them about that, and the CIA is going to help us develop the questions, and they have been working.

MR. DULLES: I think we ought to get that off as soon as we can.

(204) MR. RANKIN: Yes.

MR. DULLES: If she has any chance to tell the Russian embassy, I don't know whether she will do it or not, she might after this interview, she might ask, get in touch in some way with the Russian embassy, they would be very anxious to get in touch with her. I guess the guard is such that they couldn't do that.

MR. RANKIN: Well, the Secret Service has been with her constantly and all. I don't know how much longer after we would take her testimony you would want that to continue.

SEN. RUSSELL: What interpreter have you arranged to have?

MR. RANKIN: We have asked the State Department to furnish one and they have said they would do so. And we also are going to have a man from the Secret Service here who has been talking to her and translated every-thing so we could be sure about anything she said we wouldn't have to rely on just one person.

SEN. RUSSELL: There is a fellow here named Reuben Efrom who is one of the best that I ever saw.

MR. RANKIN: Is he with the State Department?

SEN. RUSSELL: Do you know him, Mr. Dulles?

MR. DULLES: I don't think I do.

THE CHAIRMAN: Senator, is he with the State Department?

SEN. RUSSELL: No, sir.

MR. McCLOY: There is another fellow named Akelovsky who is a star. He may be over in Geneva. It is awfully important that you get a bi-lingual man.

(205) MR. RANKIN: We have a vast area about Ruby.

MR. DULLES: This completes the other, the Oswald one?

MR. RANKIN: Just in a general way.

SEN. RUSSELL: Has it every been determined whether he could drive an automobile or not? There has been a conflict in that in nearly everything I have read.

MR. RANKIN: They claim he never could drive an automobile. He didn't know how. That he took a lesson, I think about Mr. Paine's car and he got along all right but it was just a very preliminary.

SEN. RUSSELL: Who drive him down to Mexico?

MR. RANKIN: That we haven't gotten.

REP. BOGGS: He went on a bus, didn't he?

MR. RANKIN: He went one way on a bus.

THE CHAIRMAN: One way on a bus.

SEN. RUSSELL: I thought he want down on bus and came back in a car.

MR. RANKIN: That is right.

SEN. COOPER: That would be very important, with whom he stayed down there. That is one of the curious things about it.

REP. BOGGS: I read that in some report.

SEN. RUSSELL: That is right, I remember I did, too.

SEN. COOPER: What about the Paine's, is anything developing about them?

MR. RANKIN: Well, we asked for a full background report on the (206) Paine's, and it is a very curious situation. She is a member of the Friends Society, and they are separated, and he is a member of an old New England family, and apparently quite well educated. She was teaching Russian in a school there where she lived, and she said that she was very much interested in having Marina stay with her so she could become more proficient in speaking Russian.

MR. DULLES: Paine's father was a member of the Trotskyite Society of, I think, 11 members.

MR. RANKIN: Yes, sir, and there was no indication—

SEN. RUSSELL: Whose father?

MR. DULLES: Paine's father, the man's father. And the grandmother is around and she is quite an extraordinary character, I understand, Mrs. Young, she might have a good idea on this family.

MR. RANKIN: She has said that she didn't ever receive anything from them for food or lodging or anything, and apparently that is true from Mrs. Oswald, from what she says, and she has had just to learn what she could about Russian.

SEN. RUSSELL: Oswald said the same thing along that line, I read something along the line.

MR. RANKIN: She seemed to be fond of Oswald's little girl June, they wrote a number of letters in which she wrote back and wanted to send her love to the little girl. She went down to New Orleans and brought Marina back.

SEN. RUSSELL: Is she living alone in this place?

(207) MR. RANKIN: Yes.

SEN. RUSSELL: That accounts for a good deal of the explanation.

MR. RANKIN: And she seemed to remember some of the things about the Oswalds and their difficulties and quarrels they had about him. She thought he was quite a disagreeable person, she said. But on the detail, when he went to Dallas, and whether he took the gun or whether the gun was in the garage, on that part, not much help there, and yet it is difficult to believe that two women would have this gun in a blanket in the corner of a garage and especially after that Walker affair and never even peak in there to see if that gun was there or what kind of a gun it was or whether he took it out sometimes and brought it back, and, of course, there are a good many stories about his practicing with a gun, you know, around various rifle ranges and so forth.

We have checked those out, and none of them stand up at all. We have gone over all of that to try to find out where he could ever gain the proficiency that he apparently had in this shooting that was done.

THE CHAIRMAN: He was a sharpshooter in the Marines.

MR. McCLOY: In the Marine Corps?

MR. RANKIN: Yes.

MR. McCLOY: That is above the ordinary.

MR. RANKIN: But that is quite always below expert.

THE CHAIRMAN: Marksman is average, but sharpshooter is above.

(208) SEN. RUSSELL: Pretty near all of them are sharpshooter if they work at it.

THE CHAIRMAN: Thank you, Senator, for coming.

Lee, you probably couldn't get into the Ruby affair anyway tonight, could you?

MR. RANKIN: There is a tremendous bulk of material on it.

REP. BOGGS: Could you give us just a quick synopsis of it?

MR. RANKIN: Apparently Ruby was born in Chicago, and after some years he went to the West Coast, Los Angeles, and then he came back to Chicago, and he changed his name, and then he went to Dalls, and then he came back from Dallas to Chicago, and then he goes back to Dalls, that is a brief history about what he did.

He has apparently all kinds of connections with the underworld, and he had a number of petty arrests, but the convictions were very unimportant. There weren't any—I can't even remember one that amounted to anything.

MR. DULLES: He never got to jail, did he?

MR. RANKIN: No, he paid a small fine on one or two. There are stories about his being a homosexual, and those don't pan out as far as any real proof, but it seems to be very current. There are also all kinds of stories about his girls and striptease girls and that they—he spent time with them all the time, and there are some stories that he is a bisexual.

There isn't any question but what he planned to go down to Cuba, and he did, and the story was that it was in regard to arma-(209)ments—

MR. DULLES: Cuba?

MR. RANKIN: Yes.

REP. BOGGS: This was after Castro?

MR. RANKIN: Yes.

REP. BOGGS: You are sure about that?

MR. RANKIN: No, I am not. I had better check on that. But my recollection is that it was one of the stories was that he was to try to sell guns and ammunition to Castro, that is the way—

THE CHAIRMAN: And jeeps.

MR. McCLOY: Yes, and jeeps.

MR. RANKIN: That is all denied, and that he was going down there to make the money on other kinds of sales but not anything that was munitions or armaments. There is no explanation of where he was there, what he did, or who his connections were. He had all kinds of connections with the minor underworld, I think you would call it, in Dallas and Chicago, but I don't—it isn't apparent that any of the important people in the underworld would have given him any consideration at all as far as being a part of it.

Now, it would seem that he might have—he might be the kind of person they might try to use. He was a habitue apparently of the Police Department, and was able to go to any part of it at any time, and they knew him. I was surprised at the conference we had with the District Attorney, that they said that when they had the lineup, he was in the same room. That is the first time I had (210) ever run across that, and he was in the back of the room, and then they had the screen where they lined up Oswald and several others for the lineups, to see if they could be recognized and the reporter said they couldn't take a decent picture through the screen, wouldn't they take Oswald to the side away from the screen so they could take some good pictures and so they did that, and they got him over to the side and they took the pictures and then Ruby came up, and he said, "Hello, Henry," and seemed to know Wade about as well as he knew all the police people, too, and he said, "Hello" to him.

And then they took Oswald out, and took him down the corridor, and then Ruby went out, and Wade talked to the press for two or three minutes, and then as he was going out, went out, started down the corridor, Ruby called to him from one of the inner offices of the police, and said that the TV station wanted to talk to him on the telephone.

Apparently he had called the TV station and told them that Wade was there, and they said call him to the telephone and we will get an interview with him.

So, apparently that is another thing that Wade thought was particularly important, you will be interested in it from the standpoint of premeditated action on his part, because this was—this is a day and a half beforehand, and he was there, and showed no animosity at all at that time, but around—but Wade doesn't know whether he had his gun that day or not, but he had a consider-(211)able opportunity, even if you consider the various possibilities, at that time.

MR. DULLES: That will be brought out at the trial, won't it?

MR. RANKIN: Yes.

SEN. COOPER: There hasn't anything been developed to show that they knew each other.

MR. RANKIN: There is no showing of connection, there is no showing that Oswald was the kind of person that would hang around the joints that Ruby had, either. It is possible that he could have in earlier days before he ever went to Russia, and that he might have just with some young people stopped in but that would have been a long time before.

REP. BOGGS: Oswald apparently didn't to to night clubs.

MR. RANKIN: He didn't have the income to do it very often.

MR. McCLOY: He seemed to have gathered up a considerable amount of income from that article from time to time. He had $435. We know he had $150, plus $435. We know he had carfare to Mexico, which is not—

REP. BOGGS: I must go, too, Mr. Chief Justice.

MR. DULLES: When do you want another meeting, Mr. Chairman. Do you have any idea?

THE CHAIRMAN: We haven't at the present time, Allen. This is all we have to present to you today. We will keep at it and we will let you know as soon as we pick up something that should challenge our attention.

(212) REP. BOGGS: It is a very fine presentation.

MR. McCLOY: February 5th I go out of the country for a week. The plot thickens, doesn't it?

MR. RANKIN: Would you have time tomorrow?

MR. DULLES: Yes.

MR. RANKIN: About the meeting with the CIA and the FBI and the State Department, would you have time tomorrow if I can set that meeting up?

THE CHAIRMAN: Yes, I will do it.

All right, gentlemen, thank you.

The meeting is adjourned.

(Whereupon, at 5:50 o'clock p.m., the President's Commission adjourned subject to call of the Chair.)

- - - - - - -

24.
THE JANUARY 22, 1964, WARREN COMMISSION
EXECUTIVE SESSION TRANSCRIPT

Early in the course of his investigation of Warren Commission records Harold Weisberg discovered the existence of a secret Warren Commission executive session of January 22, 1964. No public records of any kind acknowledged the executive session had taken place, but he had pieced together isolated documents from the housekeeping files to show that a stenographic tape listed on an inventory sheet pertained to the session. Ostensibly the tape had never been transcribed. The National Archives refused to transcribe the tape or permit a copy of it to be made because it bore a Top Secret classification.

In 1974 it became possible for Mr. Weisberg's attorney, James Lesar, to pursue this through correspondence with the National Archives and then appeals under the Freedom of Information Act to seek declassification and obtain its transcription. Just before he was to file a Freedom of Information Act lawsuit to attempt to force the document into the public domain, the Archives declassified it. Instead of having the official court reporter make the transcription, they used a Pentagon stenotypist. They then forwarded a copy. Lesar and Weisberg believe the precedent established in C.A. 2052-73 had enabled them to prevail, without resorting to the courts, over an attempt to forbid access on grounds of national security.

There is an historical importance in having the two transcripts printed in the order they appeared for public scrutiny. The subject matter of the

January 22 session illumines that of the January 27 session and provides some explanation for the fierce resistance by the government in C. A. 2052-73.

In the transcript of the executive session reproduced here it is obvious the stenotypist was unfamiliar with the names and places associated with the subject matter, and many inaccuracies, misspellings, and awkward phrases occur. Many of these require no comment. Some are not so clear and additional material has had to be added in brackets within the text as well as by way of footnotes. This has been sparingly done.

The following editorial changes were made:

[   ] means a blank was left in the text by the military stenotypist who was apparently unable to decipher a word or phrase.

A bracketed letter or word means the editor has added that material to the text of the original typescript, as for example: [supplemental] .

On page two of the typescript original the editor added the paragraphing.

The name of J. Lee Rankin, chief counsel of the Warren Commission, was misspelled as Rawkin every time it appeared in the text, and this has been changed to the correct spelling.

The word "more" occurred at the bottom of every page save the last one of the original, and these were omitted.

"A:" and "Q:" were used by the stenotypist, and it is often difficult to ascertain to which person they refer. "A:" apparently refers to either Rankin or Warren. "Q:" might refer to the last person other than Rankin or Warren who spoke. Where internal evidence suggests the speaker, the name has been added, properly bracketed.

There was no title page.

The page numbers of the original document are given in parentheses.

The National Archive's declassification stamp, dated 3/27/75, has been omitted from transcript page 1.

[MR. WARREN] : Gentlemen:

I called this meeting of the Commission because of something that developed today that I thought every member of the Commission should have knowledge of, something that you shouldn't hear from the public before you had an opportunity to think about it. I will just have Mr. Rankin tell you the story from the beginning.

MR. RANKIN: Mr. Wagner [Waggoner] Carr, [1] the Attorney General of Texas, called me at 11:10 this morning and said that the word had come out, he wanted to get it to me at the first moment, that Oswald was acting as an FBI Undercover Agent, and that they had the information of his badge which was given as Number 179, and that he was being paid two hundred a month from September of 1962 up through the time of the assassination. I asked what the source of this was, and he said that he understood the information had been made available so that Defense Counsel for Ruby had that information, that he knew that the press had the information, and he didn't know exactly where [Henry] Wade had gotten the information, but he was a former FBI Agent.

That they, that is, Wade before, had said that he had sufficient so that he was willing to make the statement.

FORD: Wade is?

[MR. RANKIN] A: The District Attorney [of Dallas] .

FORD: Carr is the Attorney General.

BOGGS: Right, of Texas.

RANKIN: I brought that to the attention of the Chief Justice immediately, and he said that I should try to get in touch with Carr and ask him to bring Wade up here, and he would be willing to meet with him any time today or tonight to find out what was the basis of this story. I tried to get Carr (2) and he was out campaigning in Texarkana and so forth, and so it took us quite a while to get back to him and talk to him. I just got through talking to him and he told me the source of the information was a member of the press who had claimed he knew of such an agency, that he was an undercover agent, but he now is coming with the information as to his particular number

---

[1] Waggoner Carr, Attorney General of Texas, head of the special Texas Court of Inquiry into the assassination. Members of the court: Henry Wade, District Attorney of Dallas; Counsel Leon Jaworski, member of a respected and prestigious Houston law firm and later Special Watergate Prosecutor; Robert Storey, Dean emeritus of Southern Methodist University Law School.

and the amount he was getting and the detail as to the time when the payments started.

Wade said he as well as him did not know the name of the informant but he could guess who it was, that it was given to his assistant, and he was sure that he knew, and he said he was trying to check it out to get more definite information.

Carr said that he could bring Wade in some time the first of the week, but in light of the fact that it was this man of the press and that they did not think it would be broken by the press immediately, although there had been all kinds of stories down there but Carr said there were some 25 to 40 different stories about this being the case admonishing the press themselves, but this was the first time that he got something definite as to how they were handling it or how it could be handled by himself.

But I was concerned of an undercover agent. He thought that the press would not bring the story without some further proof, and they are working on that now, he said. So he thought that if he brought Wade back on Monday or Tuesday, that that would still take care of any major problem.

When he first told us, he said the press had it and he was fearful because he hadn't even gotten this from Wade. He got it from another man that the press would bring it before we could know about it and the Commission would be asked all kinds of questions without having information about it. Now he said Wade told him that the FBI never keeps any records of names.

MR. BOGGS: Wade is the District Attorney for Dallas County?

RANKIN: That is right.

(3) Q: And the other man, Carr, is the Attorney General?

[MR. RANKIN] A: That is right.

Q: And the other people who have knowledge of this story?

[MR. RANKIN] A: He indicated that the press down there had knowledge of this story, and that the information came from some informant who was a press representative, and he, that is, Wade, could guess who it was but his assistant knew and he never asked him. They were trying to get more explicit information.

[MR. WARREN] A: Lee, would you tell them?

MR. DULLES: Who were you talking with when you got this information, Wade himself?

[MR. RANKIN] A: I was talking with Carr.

BOGGS: There is a denial of this in one of these FBI records, as you know.

A: Yes.

COOPER: In this file we had yesterday, one of the lawyers for this fellow who claims to represent—

BOGGS: Thornhill, I think. [Joseph Tonahill]

COOPER: Oswald or one of them, Ruby, told about this, do you recall it, he said it was being rumored around.

RANKIN: Yes, it was being rumored that he was an undercover agent. Now it is something that would be very difficult to prove out. There are events in connection with this that are curious, in that they might make it possible to check some of it out in time. I assume that the FBI records would never show it, and if it is true, and of course we don't know, but we thought you should have the information.

[MR. WARREN]   A: Lee, would you tell the gentlemen the circumstances under which this story was told?

[MR. RANKIN]   A: Yes, When it was first brought to my attention this morning—

(4) BOGGS: What time was this, Lee?

[MR. RANKIN]   A: 11. 10.

BOGGS: That is after the Ruby episode of yesterday?

[MR. RANKIN]   A: That is right.

Q: Yes.

[MR. RANKIN]   A: And Mr. Carr said that they had used this saying before the Court that they thought they knew why the FBI was so willing to give some of these records to the Defense Counsel, and they were [   ] ing to the Defense Counsel being able to get the records and asking the Court to rule that they couldn't get them.

Q: That is, the District Attorney was?

[MR. RANKIN]   A: That is right, and he said a number of these records were furnished by the Texas authorities, and that they should not be given up to the Defense Counsel, and that the reason he thought that they were so eager to help Ruby was because they had the undercover, that Oswald was the undercover agent and had the number of his badge and so much, he was getting two hundred a month and so forth, and that was the way it was explained as his justification to the Court as a basis for determining the records and that that was the excuse the FBI, the reason the FBI had for being so eager to give the records up. That is the way it was developed. Now Mr. [Leon] Jaworski, who is associated with the Attorney General working on this matter was reported to you before, and [   ], story [Robert Storey], I don't talk to Stor[e]y about it but I did talk to Jaworski and he said he didn't think Wade would say anything like this unless he had some substantial information back of it, and thought he could prove it, because he thought it would ruin many in politics, in Texas, to be making such a claim, and then have it shown that there was nothing to it.

(5) BOGGS: No doubt about it, it would ruin many.

[MR. RANKIN] A: And Jaworski is an able lawyer, mature and very competent. We have complete confidence in him as a person. Now that is the evaluation of the situation.

FORD: He hasn't made any investigations himself?

[MR. RANKIN] A: No, he has not.

FORD: Was Wade or anyone connected with Wade?

[MR. RANKIN] A: No.

DULLES: Talking about Stor[e]y, just a few minutes ago just telling him I wasn't going to be down in Texas, I had told him I was going to be down at the time, he didn't indicate that he had anything of any importance on his mind. Maybe he won't offer it to him obviously.

RANKIN: I don't know that it was even brought to his attention.

DULLES: I don't believe it was, now. Of course, he is not in the hierarchy.

[MR. RANKIN] A: Well, I think they were planning on telling the Attorney General and Jaworski.

FORD: How long ago did they get a feeling that there was some substance to the rumors that apparently had been—I just assumed, and I didn't ask them that, that Carr called me and seemed to be in a matter of great urgency at 11:10 this morning, and that he was fearful that they would bring in the papers before we would even get to know about it, and that is the way he was talking and acting about it.

COOPER: He felt there was . . . He didn't know the name of the informant?

[MR. RANKIN] A: No, he did not.

Q: What then would lead him to think it had substance?

[MR. RANKIN] A: Well, he said that the reason he thought it might have substance was because Wade had heard these rumors constantly, and his assistant had gotten (6) this information from the informant as to a definite bad[g]e number, and the amount and the date.

COOPER: How would you test this kind of thing?

[MR. RANKIN]   A: It is going to be very difficult for us to be able to establish the fact in it. I am confident that the FBI would never admit it, and I presume their records will never show it,[2] or if their records do show anything, I would think their records would show some kind of a number that could be assigned to a dozen different people according to how they wanted to describe them. So that it seemed to me if it truly happened, he did use postal boxes practically every place that he went, and that would be an ideal way to get money to anyone that you wanted as an undercover agent, or anybody else that you wanted to do business that way with without having any particular transaction.

FORD: There might be people who would see what was going on with that particular box, because the postal authorities do watch, they have means of watching in many places that no one could see. They can watch the clerks as to what they are doing in these boxes, and they can watch individuals that are going in and out. They do that only when they have an occasion to be suspicious, but they might, in watching for somebody particularly, they might also see other things that they just have to note. That is a possibility.

DULLES: What was the ostensible mission? I mean when they hire somebody they hire somebody for a purpose. It is either . . . Was it to penetrate the Fair Play for Cuba Committee?[3] That is the only thing I can think of where they might have used this man. It would be quite ordinary for me because they are very careful about the agents they use. You wouldn't pick up a fellow like this to do an agent's job. You have got to watch out for your (7) agents. You have really got to know. Sometimes you make a mistake.

FORD: He was playing ball, writing letters to both the elements of the Communist parties. I mean he was playing ball with the Trotskyites and with the others. This was a strange circumstance to me.

_____

[2]The Warren Report, p. 327, states: "Director Hoover has sworn that he caused a search to be made of the records of the Bureau, and that the search discloses that Oswald 'was never an informant of the FBI, and never assigned a symbol number in that capacity, and was never paid any amount of money by the FBI in any regard.' This testimony is corroborated by the Commission's independent review of the Bureau files dealing with the Oswald investigation."

[3]Lee Harvey Oswald established a chapter of the Fair Play for Cuba Committee in New Orleans. He was the sole member. The organization was pro-Castro but used the return address of a right-wing, anti-Castro organization located in a building housing a Central Intelligence Agency office.

DULLES: But the FBI get people right inside you know. They don't need a person like this on the outside. The only place where he did any at all was with the Fair Play for Cuba Committee.

BOGGS: Of course it is conceivable that he may have been brought back from Russia you know.

A: If he was in the employ from 1962, September 1962, up to the time of the assassination, it had to start over in Russia, didn't it, because didn't he get back in February? When did he get back here from Russia?

A: I think it was February; February of this year.

Q: Of '62, Was it of '62?

A: Oh yes, that is right, it was '62.

DULLES: They have no facilities, they haven't any people in Russia. They may have some people in Russia but they haven't any organizations of their own in Russia.

A: Yes.

DULLES: They might have their agents there. They have some people, sometimes American Communists who go to Russia under their guidance and so forth and so on under their control.

COOPER: Of course there are rumors all around Dallas, of course the FBI is acquanited with rumors too.

[MR. WARREN] A: One of the strange things that happened, and it may have no bearing on this at all, is the fact that this man who is a defector, and who was under observation at least by the FBI, they say they saw him frequently, could (8) walk about the Immigration Office in [New] Orleans one day and come out the next day with a passport that permitted him to go to Russia. From my observations of the case[s] that have come to us, such passports are not passed out with that ease.

DULLES: Mr., I think you are wrong on that.

[MR. WARREN] A: I could be.

DULLES: Because the passports are issued valid for anywhere except specified countries. There is a stamp as I recall that says not good for Communist China, North Vietnam, and so forth. For a long time they had on the stamp not good for Hungary. But any American, practically any American, can get a passport that is good for anywhere. An American can travel and Russia is one of the countries that you can now travel to.

[MR. WARREN] A: Well, maybe you can.

DULLES: You can get them quick.

[MR. WARREN] A: I think our General Counsel and I both have some experience in cases that have come before our Court which would indicate that that isn't exactly the fact.

DULLES: I think in the State Department . . .

[MR. WARREN] A: They have great difficulty, some of them, in getting a passport to go to Russia.

BOGGS: Particularly for someone who has any Communist . . .

[MR. WARREN] A: Oh, yes.

DULLES: Is there any evidence that State Department has that record in the files? I don't think that record has ever turned up.

COOPER: They admitted there wasn't any.

[MR. WARREN] A: What record, that he was a defector?

(9) DULLES: Yes, I don't think the State Department or in the Passport Bureau, there was no record. It didn't get down to the Passport offices. That is one of the things we ought to look into.

[MR. WARREN] A: The State Department knew he was a defector. They arranged for him to come back.

DULLES: But it don't get [   ] passport files or the passport records. They are issuing hundreds and thousands of passports. They have their own particular system.

[MR. WARREN] A: Yes.

DULLES: They don't run around from time a man comes in. If they don't find any clue, and they don't according or our record here they don't find any warning clue in his file—they should have a warning clue in his file but as I recall they don't.

COOPER: That is what they admitted, that they had not supplied the warning.

DULLES: And the Passport Office don't on its own ussually go around and inquire. They wait until it is assigned there. Then they follow it up.

COOPER: This may be off the point a bit, but as I re-read the report, the chronology of the FBI checks on Oswald, they knew that he had gone to Texas. They learned from Mrs. Payne [Mrs. Ruth Paine] : they knew where Mrs. Oswald was living. They talked with her. They knew where he was working.

BOGGS: Sure. That is all in the file.

COOPER: I know that. I say they knew where he was working.

BOGGS; I am sure you went over that material that we received a few days ago. You will find the report from the FBI dated back last summer, and months before that and then months after that, why some agent would make a report on it.

(10) COOPER: Sure.

A: I think it was in October.

RANKIN: They had a report on many, they had an agent go and see him when he was in prison.

BOGGS: In New Orleans?

A: In New Orleans.

Q: Right.

A: And he lied to them before the police. He said his wife was a Texas girl, and he married her in Texas, and a whole string of stuff, and in Dallas they had a report prior to that that was definitely contrary to it.

BOGGS: The fellow [Edward Scannell] Butler, who works for the [non-?] profit organizations that Dr. Oxnard heads to disseminate and tie Communist propaganda to Latin America, is the one who confronted him on the streets in New Orleans.[4] I know Butler. He is a very fine young man. It was . . . Butler says that this was the first time that they established that he had been in Russia and that he had defected at one time and then returned. You have that undoubtedly in your files, that film,[5] that tape that was made and borrowed in New Orleans?[6]

---

[4]The transcription of the tape is not clear. Butler was executive vice president of The Information Council of the Americas, also known as INCA, an organization that distributed extremist right-wing information in Latin America. The organization and its members' links with the Oswald story in New Orleans is related in Harold Weisberg, Oswald in New Orleans. Case for Conspiracy with the CIA (New York: Canyon Books, 1967).

[5]Presumably the film is the 16 mm reel of WDSU-TV (New Orleans) footage involving Oswald taken in August, 1963, and now deposited in the National Archives. The footage has been edited; the editing is not indicated.

[6]Presumably the tape is "Conversations Carte Blanche," aired by New Orleans radio station WDSU in August, 1963, where Butler, Oswald, and others engaged in a conversation. An inaccurate transcript of the show is printed in the Warren Commission's Hearings before the President's Commission . . . (Washington: Government Printing Office, 1964), volume XXI, pp. 633-641.

The most glaring error in the transcript occurs when Oswald is said to respond: "I worked in Russia. I was not under the protection of the—that is to say I was not under the protection of the American Government."

The tape says: "I worked in Russia er, I was er under the protection er, of er, that is to say I was not under protection of the American government . . . " See, Weisberg, Oswald in New Orleans, p. 132.

A: Yes.

BOGGS: Of course on that tape—I listened to that tape—he gives the normal Communist line, reaction to everything.

A: That is right.

Q: The same old stereotyped answer?

A: Yes.

COOPER: How do you propose to meet this situation?

BOGGS: This is a serious thing.

(11) [MR. RANKIN] A: I thought first you should know about it. Secondly, there is this factor too that a [   ] consideration, that is somewhat an issue in this case, and I suppose you are all aware of it. That is that the FBI is very explicit that Oswald is the assassin or was the assassin, and they are very explicit that there was no conspiracy, and they are also saying in the same place that they are continuing their investigation. Now in my experience of almost nine years, in the first place it is hard to get them to say when you think you have got a case tight enough to convict somebody, that that is the person that committed the crime. In my experience with the FBI they don't do that. They claim that they don't evaluate, and it is uniform prior experience they don't do that. Secondly, they have not run out all kinds of leads in Mexico or in Russia and so forth which they could probably—It is not our business, it is the very— [7]

DULLES: What is that?

[MR. RANKIN] A: They haven't run out all the leads on the information and they could probably say—that isn't our business.

Q: Yes.

[MR. RANKIN] A: But they are concluding that there can't be a conspiracy without those being run out. Now that is not [   ] from my experience with the FBI.

Q: It is not. You are quite right. I have seen a great many reports.

A: Why are they so eager to make both of those conclusions, both

---

[7]The Warren Report, p. xiii, states: "Because of the diligence, cooperation, and facilities of Federal investigative agencies, it was unnecessary for the Commission to employ investigators other than the members of the Commission's legal staff."

in the original report and their experimental [supplemental] report,[8] which is such a departure. Now that is just circumstantial evidence, and it don't prove anything about this, but it raises questions. [   ] We have to try to find out what they have to say that would give any support to the story, and report it to you.

(12) FORD: Who would know if anybody would in the Bureau have such an arrangement?

[MR. RANKIN] A: I think that there are several. Probably Mr. Belmont would know every undercover agent.

Q: Belmont?

[MR. RANKIN] A: Yes.

Q: An informer also would you say?

[MR. RANKIN] A: Yes, I would think so. He is the special security, of the division.

DULLES: Yes, I know.

[MR. RANKIN] A: And he is an able man. But when the Chief Justice and I were just briefly reflecting on this we said that if that was true and it ever came out and could be established, then you would have people think that there was a conspiracy to accomplish this assassination that nothing the Commission did or anybody could dissipate.

BOGGS: You are so right.

DULLES: Oh, terrible.

BOGGS: Its implications of this are fantastic, don't you think so?

[MR. WARREN] A: Terrific.

RANKIN: To have anybody admit to it, even if it was the fact, I am sure that there wouldn't at this point be anything to prove it.

---

[8]Reports prepared by the FBI that became Warren Commission documents. Commission Document Number 1: Investigation of Assassination of President John F. Kennedy, November 22, 1963, Washington, D. C.: Federal Bureau of Investigation, 1963. Five volumes. These contained less than 450 words on the murder and omitted one wound on the President's throat and the missed shot that wounded citizen James Tague. Commission Document Number 107: Investigation of Assassination of President John F. Kennedy, November 22, 1963, Supplemental Report. Washington, D. C.: Federal Bureau of Investigation, 1964. One volume.

DULLES: Lee, if this were true, why would it be particularly in their interest—I could see it would be in their interest to get rid of this man but why would it be in their interest to say he is clearly the only guilty one? I mean I don't see that argument that you raise particularly shows an interest.

BOGGS: I can immediately—

[MR. RANKIN] A: They would like to have us fold up and quit.

(13) BOGGS: This closes the case, you see. Don't you see?

DULLES: Yes, I see that.

RANKIN: They found the man. There is nothing more to do. The Commission supports their conclusions, and we can go on home and that is the end of it.

DULLES: But that puts the men right on them. If he was not the killer and they employed him, they are already it, you see. So your argument is correct if they are sure that this is going to close the case, but if it don't close the case, they are worse off than ever by doing this.

BOGGS: Yes, I would think so. And of course, we are all even gaining in the realm of speculation. I don't even like to see this being taken down.

DULLES: Yes. I think this record ought to be destroyed. Do you think we need a record of this.

[MR. WARREN] A: I don't except that we said we would have records of meetings and so we called the reporter in the formal way. If you think what we have said here should not be upon the record, we can have it done that way. Of course it might . . .

DULLES: I am just thinking of sending around copies and so forth. The only copies of this record should be kept right here.

BOGGS: I would hope that none of these records are circulated to anybody.

[MR. WARREN] A: I would hope so too.

RANKIN: We also give them to you Commissioners. Now if you don't want them, those are the only ones who get them but sides [besides] himself: off the record.

END

EMENDATIONS

Section 2;   p. 12, in paragraphs numbered 15, 19, and 20, "Janaury" to "January".

Section 5;   p. 20, in paragraph two "examption" to "exemption"; a superfluous "and" is omitted following 10501 in the last paragraph.

Section 10;   p. 39, in paragraph four "if fails" to "it fails".

Section 11;   p. 44, in paragraph two, "nation" to "national", "pri" to "private", and "Top" to "Top Secret"; p. 45, in paragraph one "idetity" to "identity"; p. 47, in the penultimate sentence "lenghty" to "lengthy"; p. 52, in paragraph one "commerciall" to "commercial"; p. 53, "Hirma" to "Hiram" and "Frederic" to "Frederick"; p. 55, in paragraph number 12 "March 4, 1963" to "March 4, 1964"; p. 56, in paragraph number 16 "stampt" to "stamp".

Section 15;   p. 86, in paragraph two "classificaction" to "classification".

Section 16;   p. 89, the prefatory "State of New York, County of New York, City of New York, ss.:" is omitted.

Section 18;   p. 97, in paragraph four "Executive 10501" to "Executive Order 10501"; p. 100, in paragraph one "shall no" to "shall not"; in paragraph four "deletitions" to "deletions"; p. 105, in paragraph number 10 "sesion" to "session"; p. 106, in paragraph number 13 "Executice" to "Executive"; p. 107, in paragraph number 18 an isolated "t" is omitted; p. 108, in paragraph number 21 "Rhoades" to "Rhoads"; p. 118, "Sen. Ford" to "Rep. Ford" and "FBI I though" to "FBI I thought"; pp. 121-123, classification stamps appeared on all pages of Exhibit C, but were omitted.

Section 21;   p. 152, in the second paragraph the quotation was originally cited on pages 199-1200.

Section 22;   p. 166, "Aug. 17, 1966", to "Aug. 17, 1965".

Section 23;   numerous misspellings are reprinted as in the original;
p. 176, "F.I.B."; p. 179, "Swett" in the first Rankin
statement; p. 190, "McClou" as the speaker; p. 191,
the third Dulles statement contains "I I"; p. 192, in the
Russell statement "blacmail" lacks a "k", and the
second Cooper statement contains "beford"; p. 213,
"sheets" in the last sentence of Rankin's first statement; p. 215, "reight" in the last Rankin statement;
p. 217, "partment" in paragraph four; p. 219, "every"
in the fourth Russell statement; p. 220, "peak" in the
fifth Rankin statement; p. 221, "Dalls" appears twice;
p. 223, "to" in the first Boggs statement and "Cheif"
in the second.

Section 24;   except where noted on pp. 224-225, the text is copied
exactly from the original.

BIBLIOGRAPHY

Bibliographical Aid

Wrone, David R. The Assassination of John Fitzgerald Kennedy. An Annotated Bibliography. Madison: State Historical Society of Wisconsin, 1973.

Articles and Books

Feldman, Harold. "Oswald and the FBI." Nation, 198 (January 27, 1964), 86-89.

Ford, Gerald R. "Piecing Together the Evidence." Life, 57 (October 2, 1964), 42, 47-50.

_____ and Stiles, John R. Portrait of the Assassin. New York: Simon & Schuster, 1965. New York: Ballantine, 1966.

Meagher, Sylvia. Accessories After the Fact: The Warren Commission, the Authorities, and the Report. With an introduction by Leo Sauvage. New York: Bobbs-Merrill, 1967. New York: Vintage, 1976.

_____. "The Curious Testimony of Mr. Givens." The Texas Observer (August 13, 1971), 11-12.

_____. "Post-assassination Credibility Chasm." The Minority of One, IX (March, 1967), 21-22.

_____. "Wheels with Deals: How the Kennedy 'Investigation' was Organized." The Minority of One, X (July-August, 1968), 23-27.

Roffman, Howard. "Freedom of Information: Judicial Review of Executive Security Classifications." University of Florida Law Review, XXVIII (1976), 551-568.

_____. Presumed Guilty. Lee Harvey Oswald in the Assassination of President Kennedy. Cranbury, New Jersey: Farleigh Dickinson University Press, 1975. New York: A. S. Barnes, 1976.

Weisberg, Harold. Oswald in New Orleans. Case for Conspiracy with the CIA. Foreward by Jim Garrison. New York: Canyon Books, 1967.

_____. Photographic Whitewash: Suppressed Kennedy Assassination Pictures. Hyattstown, Maryland: By the author, 1967.

_____. Photographic Whitewash: Suppressed Kennedy Assassination Pictures. New edition with epilogue. Frederick, Maryland: By the author, 1976.

——————————. Post Mortem. JFK Coverup Smashed! Frederick, Maryland: By the author, 1975.

——————————. Whitewash: The Report on the Warren Report. Hyattstown, Maryland: By the author, 1965. New York: Dell, 1966.

——————————. Whitewash II: The FBI-Secret Service Cover-up. Hyattstown, Maryland: By the author, 1966. New York: Dell, 1967.

——————————. Whitewash IV. JFK Assassination Transcript. Legal Analysis by Jim Lesar. Frederick, Maryland: By the author, 1974.

Wrone, David R. "The Gratuitous Mystery." Madison, Wisconsin, Capital Times, December 1, 2, 3, 4, 1975.

Government Documents and Publications

Code of Federal Regulations. Washington: Government Printing Office, 1949-1973.

U. S. Congress. House. Committee on Government Operations. National Archives—Security Classification Problem Involving Warren Commission Files and Other Records. Hearing before the Government Information and Individual Rights Subcommittee. Committee Print. 94th Cong., 1st sess. 1975.

——————————. Committee on Government Operations. U. S. Government Information Policies and Practices—Security Classification Problems Involving Subsection (b) (1) of the Freedom of Information Act. Hearings before the Foreign Operations and Government Information Subcommittee. 92nd Cong., 2nd sess. 1972. Part 7.

[U. S. Warren Commission]. Investigation of the Assassination of President John F. Kennedy: Hearings Before the President's Commission on the Assassination of President Kennedy. Washington: Government Printing Office, 1964. 26 volumes.

——————————. Report of the President's Commission on the Assassination of President John F. Kennedy. Washington: Government Printing Office, 1964.

TABLE OF CASES

Secretary of Defense, 190, 191
Secret Service, 46, 56, 72, 118, 119, 136, 140, 143, 159, 178, 198, 200, 206, 207, 218, 219
Senate Joint Resolution 137: 106, 122
Silbert, Earl J., 14, 18, 25, 78, 83, 88, 95
Society of Friends, 219
Soviet Embassy, 133, 158, 209, 218
Spectrography, 152, 153
State Department, 66, 118, 135, 140, 144, 145, 161, 218, 232
Steele, Charles Hall, Jr., 61
Steele, Charles Hall, Sr., 61
Stiles, John R., 46, 47, 56, 65, 157
Storey, Robert, 137, 177, 228, 229
Sweatt, Allan, 178, 179, 181, 183, 193

Tague, James, 235n
Texarkana, 226
Texas, 12, 49, 119, 176, 179, 205, 207, 208, 228, 229, 232, 233
Texas School Book Depository, 68, 69, 208, 209
Time-Life, 189
Times Herald (Dallas), 70
Tippit, J. D., 67, 70
Tonahill, Joseph, 186, 228
Trade Mart, 207
Trotskyites, 220, 230

United States Code: Title 18, section 798, 81
United States Customs Bureau, 67
United States District Court for the Eastern District of Virginia-Alexandria Division, 100
United States Foreign Operations and Government Information Subcommittee, 102-103, 108
United States General Services Administration, 1, 12, 13, 18, 27, 28, 42, 77, 85, 106
United States Marine Corps, 220, 221
United States Marine Corps Intelligence, 138
United States Senate, Committee on Rules and Administration, 1, 12, 46, 155-158
U-2, 71

Vawter, Richard Q., 3, 8-10, 13, 26, 29
Voebel, Edward, 61, 63

Wade, Henry, 12, 66, 67, 68, 71, 72, 137, 176, 177, 179, 180, 182, 197, 202, 222, 226 and n, 227, 229
Walker, Edwin A., 69
"Wanted for Treason" handbill, 214
Ward, Jesse L., Jr., 60, 61, 62, 91-93
Ward & Paul, 44, 54, 55, 56, 62, 89, 91-94, 100, 105-106, 108, 109, 139, 175
Warren Commission, 1, 6, 7, 19, 25, 28, 44, 49, 51, 54, 55, 57, 58, 60, 66-75, 76, 87, 89, 91-93, 94, 97, 99, 106, 109, 113, 119, 120, 127, 134, 182-186, 199-200. See also, Executive Sessions